In the Wake of the Frontier

In the Wake of the Frontier

A true account of living in Alaskan isolation

Ruth E. Vincent

Ruth E. Vincent

iUniverse, Inc.
New York Lincoln Shanghai

In the Wake of the Frontier
A true account of living in Alaskan isolation

Copyright © 2005 by Ruth E. Vincent

All rights reserved. No part of this book may be used or reproduced by any means, graphic, electronic, or mechanical, including photocopying, recording, taping or by any information storage retrieval system without the written permission of the publisher except in the case of brief quotations embodied in critical articles and reviews.

iUniverse books may be ordered through booksellers or by contacting:

iUniverse
2021 Pine Lake Road, Suite 100
Lincoln, NE 68512
www.iuniverse.com
1-800-Authors (1-800-288-4677)

ISBN-13: 978-0-595-37256-0 (pbk)
ISBN-13: 978-0-595-67477-0 (cloth)
ISBN-13: 978-0-595-81653-8 (ebk)
ISBN-10: 0-595-37256-2 (pbk)
ISBN-10: 0-595-67477-1 (cloth)
ISBN-10: 0-595-81653-3 (ebk)

Printed in the United States of America

*Because others have faith in us,
we accomplish unplanned goals.
This book was written at the urging of my dear mother,*

Annie Irene Marr Anderson,

and from the encouragement of my sweetheart husband,

Robert Earl Vincent.

*It is dedicated in memory of these two,
who made my life complete.*

Acknowledgments

Not only do I value those within this book who enriched my Alaskan years—even making the adventure possible—but I am deeply indebted to others. I greatly appreciate helpful editing from my two daughters, Carol Teegarden and Jan Galbreath. Also, the careful editing from my warm friend, Andrea Seavers, was of great benefit. My gratitude and thanks are expressed to son-in-law Darrell Teegarden for his patient computer aid and generous time commitment. Then, at just the right time, Leslie Leland Fields critiqued and cut this manuscript to make the story march forward more forcefully. Especially, I give thanks to Paul W. Barkley, a neighbor and long-standing friend who suggested, encouraged, and edited with an expert eye. Also, I thank Jeanne Popovich, another neighbor and friend, who patiently proofread each word. Help from these supportive friends and others who have graciously shared their time has been of immense value, and their questionings have added clarity.

Most of all, I am grateful to my late husband, Robert E. Vincent. His insights broadened my observations during those Alaskan years, and these chapters were improved because of his useful suggestions and emotional support.

The solitary scene on the cover was a photograph I captured of my husband walking across frozen Jennifer Lake, just east of our peaceful haven of Kitoi Bay in Alaska. All of the pictures in this book are ones my husband and I personally took as we sought to permanently capture our unique experiences.

Contents

List of Maps and Photographs	xi
Prologue	1
Wilderness Wife	3
Settling In	15
Neighbors in the Wild	19
Mail Days	27
Trip to Surf Lake	33
Winter Society	45
Enjoying Rather Than Wishing	53
Emergencies	65
Bush Pilot in Distress	79
Change of Scenery	87
Loss and Gain	95
Big City	103
The Noisy Season	119
Anniversary Adventures	141
Digging into the Past	153
A Changing Culture	161
Transitions	171
Afterword	181
Appendix A: Bear Hunt	187
Appendix B: Menu Planning	191
Index	203

List of Maps and Photographs

Figure 1. Afognak Island lies just north of Kodiak Island 7
Figure 2. Kitoi Bay Research Station (later Kitoi Bay Hatchery) in October 1954 with Vince Daly's Grumman Goose. 9
Figure 3. A serene view of Pacific waters from our station. 19
Figure 4. Willie the Weasel with food. 20
Figure 5. Silver fox. 21
Figure 6. Frosty and Dinky fighting. 23
Figure 7. Clams dug at low tides were one source of fresh meat. We also ate crab, snowshoe hare, duck, and fish. 28
Figure 8. Icicles frame the frozen ocean saltwater. 32
Figure 9. Timed during low tides, our water source was Big Kitoi Creek. 34
Figure 10. Kitoi Bay and surrounding area of Afognak Island 37
Figure 11. Evolution of a bear trail: tracks (left), ruts (center), and trail (right). 39
Figure 12. Even in the winter, Bob took water samples to determine the water's temperature and oxygen content. 40
Figure 13. Dinky curiously peers through our window. 50
Figure 14. Fox-watching. 51
Figure 15. Winter mail delivery on Big Kitoi Lake. 56
Figure 16. Christmas mail brought news and excitement. 58
Figure 17. Dinky eyes the ice cream freezer. 62
Figure 18. Bob running the skiff. 65
Figure 19. Walter, Veneta, and Dave Vincent. 79
Figure 20. Shelikof Strait area of southern Alaska. 80
Figure 21. Bob at the short-wave radio. 86
Figure 22. A change-of-scenery outing. 89
Figure 23. Otter trail. 92
Figure 24. Razor clams sizzling. 94
Figure 25. Our fox friends were like pets. 96

Figure 26. Soon I stopped envisioning an Alaskan king crab as a monstrous spider. 97
Figure 27. A Grumman Widgeon landing in Kitoi Bay. 104
Figure 28. Departing for Kodiak. 104
Figure 29. A Kodiak street. 111
Figure 30. Aerial view of Kodiak, Dog Bay, and Near Island. 115
Figure 31. Completed wooden pipeline. 120
Figure 32. Preparing dinner in the kitchen/laboratory. 122
Figure 33. Little Kitoi weir. 124
Figure 34. Pinkie at the barbershop. 130
Figure 35. A mealtime snapshot (Leo at end of table; Molly at far right). 132
Figure 36. Our "shack on the hill." 135
Figure 37. Our shack became the "mansion on Kitoi Bay Heights." 137
Figure 38. Baby seagull in the cleft of a rock. 142
Figure 39. Kitoi and Izhut Bays showing Ruth Lake and Jennifer Lakes. © Alaska Department of Fish and Game. Used by permission. 144
Figure 40. Our sixth wedding anniversary at a typical flat-slate beach. 145
Figure 41. Charlie, a Kodiak brown bear cub, appears at our back porch. 147
Figure 42. Twelve-year-old Pinkie carefully cleans his catch of rainbow trout. 149
Figure 43. Stone oil lamp found by Quent Edson. 153
Figure 44. Izhut Bay artifacts. 157
Figure 45. Aleut oven. 158
Figure 46. A whale rib made a good bench. 169
Figure 47. A humpy swimming upstream to spawn. 171
Figure 48. Construction of hatchery addition expanded Kitoi Bay Research Station. 175
Figure 49. Artificial spawning. 176
Figure 50. Bill Harvey beside his new 1957 Super Cub. 178
Figure 51. Ruth Lake cabin. 178
Figure 52. Ruth and her seal. 179
Figure 53. Kodiak brown bear. 188

Prologue

In 1954, I was a sheltered twenty-five-year-old woman teaching elementary school in Oregon. I had never lived outside the Willamette Valley and had certainly never dreamed of moving out-of-state, much less out-of-country to the Territory of Alaska. (Alaskan statehood did not come until 1959.) The vast Alaskan region was a rugged, isolated land, especially Afognak Island, part of the Kodiak Archipelago on the southwestern fringe of the Territory.

My husband, Bob, and I were headed to live on this island for an indefinite time while Bob was to do fishery research on the freshwater life history of the red salmon, which would be a help in salmon rehabilitation. He was also to help in getting the facilities in operation and organizing the research program. Most Alaskan natives depended on salmon fishing or its related industry for their livelihood. Since salmon runs had been steadily declining, the red salmon fish runs needed to be reversed, and new runs of returning adult red salmon needed to be established. Returning salmon runs to their former abundance would bring greater economic stability to the area.

Family and friends were amazed at our plans—perhaps even our sanity—and wondered how anyone, especially a woman, could live in such primitive isolation. Months without seeing another female might seem like unending torture to many, but because I had always thrived on new experiences, this was one I was eager to embrace.

At that time, short-wave radio and letters were our only means of communication. Since no time could be spent shopping, socializing, commuting to work, or helping others, there was time to construct a thorough, descriptive accounting of our activities. Most of this was done through lengthy letters to our families at home in Oregon. To my surprise, my mother, Irene Anderson, carefully saved all of these detailed letters and subsequently urged me to compile them into a book. So out came my old portable, manual typewriter with a poor ribbon, and during the third and last year on Afognak, a land where time is determined by tides more than by clocks, I created a book-length manuscript of our Alaskan life.

Not until this year, 2005, did I resurrect that old, faded manuscript and transfer it onto modern word-processing equipment so we could give copies to our children and grandchildren. Reading it again has brought back many enjoyable memories of our three years in the bush. This manuscript is much as I wrote it fifty years ago, so it reflects the culture, the monetary values, and our own perceptions and expressions of that time.

Let's step away from our present fast-paced, noisy world, away from roads and cars, away from people and stores and into the stillness of the Alaskan Territory, a land of green spruce trees, of animals, of water, boats, and bays…

Ruth E. Vincent
September, 2005

Wilderness Wife

Taking a backward glance at the small town of Kodiak, our last contact with civilization, we stood next to the water waiting to crawl through the magazine-sized door of the twin-engine amphibian airplane that was to take us from Kodiak to Kitoi Bay on Afognak Island. Afognak Island lies directly north of Kodiak Island. On this second day of August, 1954, we expected to experience the realistic remnants of a frontier that for most people had faded into nothing more than a collection of phantom stories.

My husband, Bob, and I felt nothing but anticipation for this adventure—a pioneer lifestyle on an isolated Alaskan island. Knowing that we were on the last leg of our two-day air journey, we felt a surge of optimism. Yet with typical feminine instincts, questions filled my mind: "Will there be running water in our new home? If we have a wood-burning cookstove, will I remember to keep wood in it? How cold will it get in the winter?"

This moment was in sharp contrast to my stable childhood in northwestern Oregon. My home had been quiet. Some of this calm stillness was because we had no neighbors living within sight and because I had only one sibling, Donna, who was six years younger. It also existed because work was the family focus. Both parents taught and exemplified honesty and hard work without complaints. My authoritarian father, Loyd L. Anderson, was a mechanically inclined farmer who strove for economic security. During the Great Depression, I watched him carve farmland out of hillsides by clearing 42 acres of stumps with horse, dynamite, chain, and grub hoe. Mother was self-sacrificing, exceedingly generous, and had an exceptional love of people. She spent hardly any money. Of course, family vacations were never considered. Neither entertainment nor church was part of my early childhood. The one highlight of the week was driving seven miles in our farm truck each Saturday into Forest Grove to purchase groceries and to visit my maternal grandparents. A few times these grandparents invited me to accompany them and Marjorie, my aunt who was only five years older than I, to stay at the Oregon Coast for a week. We would stay in a rented unit, sometimes at the very edge of the beach where we could see and hear the ocean waves. I worked jigsaw puzzles with Grandma. Marjorie and I walked narrow railroad rails, strolled the beaches, and during WWII waved to the service men flying blimps low overhead.

Other than the few breaks my grandparents provided, my summers were spent harvesting fruit in the orchards on my parents', relatives', or neighbors' farms. In regular succession came gooseberries, strawberries, cherries, blueberries, various cane berries, peaches, pears, and prunes. No sooner had one harvest ended, than another began. After-school and Saturday work included harvesting filberts and walnuts. Walnuts were picked from the ground by crawling on knees, usually in the mud since often the nuts did not drop until after Oregon's heavy autumn rains began. Although I had not participated in sports, my agricultural summers had made me comfortable with the outdoors, a good preparation for the Alaskan frontier.

Work came naturally, but I enjoyed reading and new activities. My parents valued education, so unlike my father in his elementary school years, I was never kept out of school to do any type of work. School gave me a sense of adventure and increased my desire for additional experiences. During most of the grades-one-through-eight years, the library at my one-room country school consisted of two short shelves of old books with extremely fine print. Even so, reading *Little Women* and *Little Men* by Louisa May Alcott opened a new world of imagination to me. The real excitement in this tiny library came in 1937 when a salesman entered our house with a set of *Compton Encyclopedias* to show to my father, who was the school board chairman. The salesman asked me to read aloud from them to illustrate how readable they were. It amazed me that even my father, who was very reluctant to spend money, agreed that the school board should purchase these books for the school's library. Years later when I became teacher in that little country school, the same encyclopedias were still there but in a larger library.

My thoughts traveled back to Bob's background as well, and I pondered his preparation for the challenges that awaited. His childhood had been lively, and he was rather used to change since his family had lived in several small mill towns of western Oregon. The Vincent family was jovial with lots of laughter, as well as being a family of avid readers. Alice, Walt, Mae, Bob, and later brother Dave created imaginative games and engaged in many outdoor activities. The children made a park by the creek and constructed a log cabin from alder trees that they had cut down. A primary pleasure was camping at the coast as a family, which included cutting ferns to make beds and cooking over the campfire.

The boys fished and hunted with their father. Each spring the men spent week-day evenings spading the garden plot in order to save Saturday entirely for fishing and Sunday for church. After a long day of fishing, they would come home to the aroma of the traditional Saturday-night meal of boiled ham bone and beans plus homemade bread. The day's catch of rainbow or cutthroat trout would be cooked for Sunday morning breakfast.

When he was seventeen and just out of high school, Bob enlisted because he wanted to spend his WWII time in the Army and not the Navy as might have happened had he waited to be drafted. This added a fourth star to the banner in the Vincent family front room window: a recognition of having four children in the Armed Forces. Bob completed his basic training in California and was immediately sent to the Pacific Theater. During much of his service time, this young boy, who did not want to be in the Navy, spent many months as a seaman: running a twenty-eight-ton LCM (a fifty-six-foot-long landing craft) and later leading a squad of twenty men in six boats. Bob was better prepared than I for this new life that we were about to begin.

After his discharge, Bob enrolled at Oregon State College and, reflective of his childhood background, chose Wildlife Management for his major. He commuted to college while living at home with his family. It was at this time that we met because I was living in a college dormitory in his small hometown of Monmouth. During our courtship, it worried me when Bob's mother told me that fishing ranked number one with the Vincent men. I had hoped to soon rank number one.

Six months after we had met, Bob's mother became seriously ill. Thus, the meals I often had enjoyed in the Vincent household began to be cooked by Bob. The family depended on him because his father worked long hours as superintendent of a planing mill and only his younger brother still lived at home. Not only did Bob perfect his cooking skills, he also developed brotherly parenting skills. Although I had sometimes secretly wished that eleven-year-old Dave were not accompanying us on so many of our dates, I admired Bob's patience and kindness to him.

Later, after the death of Bob's mother and after our marriage, Dave, Bob, and Dad even included me on those Saturday fishing trips. Walking and fishing along the Upper South Fork of the Alsea River after a week of teaching fifth graders were refreshing. Even in those years, Bob continued patiently untangling Dave's fishing line, and with the same gentle perseverance, he taught me how to cast.

Soon after marriage, Bob took me on my first camping experience. Having no camping equipment, we had to take wedding presents. Shiny Revere Ware copper-bottom pans and new blankets from our own bed went with us to the woods. Bob showed me how to cook over a campfire. We slept under the stars, and my new husband was surprised that I slept nary a wink.

But now, with undergraduate work finished for both of us and with Bob newly employed by the territorial Alaska Department of Fisheries, we were standing on the gravel beach of Kodiak Airways waiting to step into a Grumman Widgeon. With this step my life would change and bring greater excitement than a first camping experience and even more isolation than my childhood. Of course, Bob would be in his element: the outdoors, pioneering, and scientific research.

I was slightly apprehensive, but each of us looked forward to this new adventure. Both of our stable backgrounds, my quiet childhood (but desire for new experiences), and Bob's cheerful personality combined with his outdoor abilities and army life should fit a frontier lifestyle, I reasoned. Even a few years previously with friends, Jerry and Marge, we had brainstormed about adventuring to Alaska as two couples to take advantage of the Homestead Act. Our vision was to build log cabins and to be independent. We made lists of items to take—necessities nature would not provide. That dream did not materialize as we had imagined, but now Bob and I were going to a pioneer-like situation in Alaska with the added incentive of what for us was an enormous yearly salary, $4200. Our backgrounds and dreams had prepared us for this moment.

At the time Bob had accepted this fishery biologist position to study the life history of the red salmon, Clarence L. Anderson, Director of the Alaska Territorial Department of Fisheries, strongly suggested that I wait a few months before coming to Kitoi Bay Research Station so that living conditions would be more suitable. We chose not to follow this advice. Because of this, I was absolutely determined not to let even a mere twitch of a facial expression show discouragement or disapproval of existing conditions.

Ducking as I entered the plane door snapped me out of my thoughts. The bush pilot insisted I ride in the cockpit with him, even though I was being brought in as "freight" to save money. (It cost $36 per round trip for a person but only seven cents per pound for freight.) Bob squeezed his long legs into the side bench just behind me. In the cargo section along with Bob was Robert Parker, a senior biologist and Bob's immediate boss, plus numerous boxes of supplies and groceries. I could not help but notice that between the pilot's operations of warming the engines and his pre-flight check, he looked at me with a quizzical, dubious expression as if to say, "My dear lady, you will have no need of those teetering high heels where you are going! In the next thirty miles you shall have exchanged concrete sidewalks for muddy bear trails and jostling, elbowing people for prickly devil's club stalks." As I apprehensively looked behind into the cargo section, Bob gave me a warm, reassuring smile. Although my husband had been in the Pacific Theater of WWII, neither of us had ever been in an airplane before boarding a Constellation the previous day when we flew from Portland, Oregon, to Anchorage, Alaska. Other passengers had also dressed up for this elegant experience. We had taken Dramamine to prevent air sickness, were served steak on china dishes with real silverware by doting stewardesses, and had even been offered a visit to the cockpit. After a stop in Juneau where Robert Parker joined us, we landed in Anchorage to spend the night. Even flying at 10,000 feet, we had to look upward at majestic Mount Fairweather and later at the sparkling white peaks of the St. Elias Range; in contrast, we noticed Anchorage's flatness and blooming flowers. The town seemed new with mainly one-story buildings. Alex McRae, sports fisheries biologist of Alaska Department of Fisheries, and his wife, Margaret, invited the three of us for dinner. The next morning we flew in a DC-3 to Kenai, then to Homer, and finally to Kodiak, where we now were in this little amphibious Widgeon.

Taxiing down the steep gravel beach, the seaplane rolled into salt water. Immediately, all former thoughts disappeared with the exhilaration of the plane doing battle with the swells of the Pacific Ocean. The propellers splashed salt water spray against the window like bullets, completely obscuring outside vision. The roar of the two engines increased and the plane picked up speed; suddenly we were tossing weightlessly in the air.

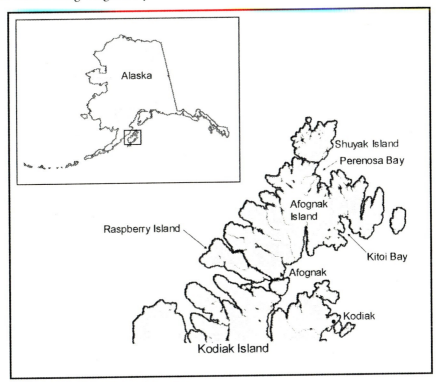

Figure 1. Afognak Island lies just north of Kodiak Island.

We circled over the small town of Kodiak, winging northward toward a tiny bay called Kitoi on the island of Afognak. Kitoi Bay is a thumb off the much larger Izhut Bay *(see Figure 39)* that indents into Afognak, the second largest island of the Kodiak Archipelago. Kodiak Island, covering 3,700 sq. miles, is the largest, but even Afognak Island covers an area of approximately 1700 sq. miles. The sea pushes fingers far into the mostly mountainous terrain, giving the island only 700 sq. miles of actual land surface. These fjord indentations give it miles and miles of coastline. The pilot mentioned that Afognak Island was not entirely uninhabited because an Aleut native village (also named Afognak) was located on the far southern edge. Since this village was inaccessible without a sizable fishing vessel, the humans there would be unreachable to us. Our nearest neighbors would be in Kodiak, the small, historical town we had just left.

The Grumman bounced and tipped sideways at sharp angles in an attempt to stay level against the gusty wind. Was the pilot doing this purposely in order to frighten me? No, surely not. Knowing that Kitoi Bay was located only thirty direct ocean miles away—only twenty-five minutes by air—from Kodiak neighbors led us to feel our new home would not be extremely isolated. Now, however, we looked down to see mile-upon-secluded-mile of jagged cliffs and rolling, spruce-laden hills against a dusty blue backdrop of distant Duck Mountain. Not a single building broke the beauty of this wild expanse. Suddenly, we more fully comprehended that life on this isle of spruce would be an abrupt change. We had just come from living in Corvallis, Oregon, in a small, furnished apartment closely surrounded by a noisy fraternity and two sorority houses adjacent to the Oregon State College campus. Here, our plane was a mere speck in the vastness; the land below would be endless silence.

"I have to make a stop at Port Bailey for Robert Parker to pick up a package," the pilot explained as he winged the plane downward to the left. He was busy with the controls while I—not wanting to miss a moment of the thrill of my first water landing—concentrated on his actions and the plane's responding maneuverings. As we neared the water, the pilot appeared to raise the nose of the plane slightly and gun the engines to even greater speed. Slap! Slap! Slap! Were it not for the splash and spray, we would have thought we were hitting a series of rock piles. The safety belts anchored us to our seats to prevent our being injured. I was shocked by the violent landing, with waves of water spraying over the windows, but decided such blinded sight and jolting must be a necessary and usual part of landing on water. The pilot cast a glance in my direction between the now lessening slaps. I did not want him to know this had been my first amphibious landing so I simulated complete composure, even feigning a relaxed expression to help cover my inner terror. Later, Robert Parker said, "That landing was nearly the worst possible. Certainly it was the roughest flying and landing that I have experienced." Likely, the cause was a gusty southwest wind coming off the hill behind Port Bailey.

Soon the pilot had accelerated the engines in a take-off. Dark, blue-green spruce and gray water were again my view. Sitting in the cockpit had the viewing advantage over the windowless cargo bench where Bob sat. Quickly, we were over the fiord-like coastline of Afognak, amidst heavy updrafts of air that are usually experienced only when crossing points of land but which were exaggerated on this particular windy flight.

Figure 2. Kitoi Bay Research Station (later Kitoi Bay Hatchery) in October 1954 with Vince Daly's Grumman Goose.

"Take a look down to the right and you'll see Kitoi Bay," yelled the pilot above the din of the engines as he banked and swept down at a sharp angle to facilitate our viewing. Bright sunshine beamed down on my first glimpse of the tiny research station that would be our home. It looked enormously lonely dwarfed by the tall Sitka spruce and the waters of the bay. I felt a surge of joy as I noticed that the small building with an aluminum roof was stained a rich brown, and...yes, as we dipped lower, I saw it was trimmed with green. What had I expected—a shack made of driftwood, a cedar-thatched hut, a log cabin? Surely, I had not envisioned a tidy, well-constructed dwelling. A skiff tugged gently on an anchor buoy in the sheltered bay, replacing the more conventional car and garage. Charming, I concluded. Perhaps our facilities were going to be modern enough after all.

A fishery biologist and a construction worker were supposedly already at the station, but no further time was left to ponder our new associates or living conditions because we were already swooping down for a landing. In this bay protected from the southwest wind, the landing was smooth. Our pilot quickly taxied the plane to the water's edge, lowered the wheels, ran up on the tiny, black-graveled beach, and spun around. We had reached our destination.

The tranquil beauty far surpassed our expectations. We were surrounded by a dense mature stand of spruce up to three feet in diameter with an under-story of devil's club, its evil thorns contrasting with cherry-bright red berries. Salmonberry and ferns grew out of a soft, moss carpet covering the ground, the logs, and even coating many of the tree branches. Our surroundings were a virtual fairyland. The beach was not composed of smelly, mud flats as we had feared, but instead was black slate rock and gravel.

Quentin Edson, the fishery biologist, and Claude, the shaggy-haired construction worker, came out of the station to greet us. It was evident they had recently shaved and had no doubt put on clean clothes in honor of our arrival. Their friendliness and warm hospitality immediately made us feel welcome.

In contrast to the outside beauty, we were now ushered into the brown-stained and green-trimmed house that had looked so tidy from the air. My heart sank! Junk! Junk! Topless heaps of junk! The five of us could hardly find standing room among the strange mixture/medley of indeterminable objects. The floor was laden with construction materials and biology tools: plywood, saws, packboards, wrenches, water samplers, outboard motors, file cabinet, bathroom fixtures, books of fish scales, bottles of specimens, chemicals, and other items. Adding to this unbelievable chaos were boxes of foodstuffs and dishes. On the floor, dust and sawdust frosted open sacks of flour and sugar. Large sheets of plywood leaned against the two large bay-view windows, shutting out much of the light. A 3x6-foot table, barely visible through the conglomerate, had no room for plates because every square inch was stacked with relishes, jams, seasonings, unwrapped butter, catsup, Worcestershire sauce, Heinz 57 sauce, Tabasco sauce, horseradish, mustard, and many more such condiments evidently used to add spice to daily living. I deduced that each person must stand to eat. A bucket of water sat near the door, and another bucket of water was beside the sack of flour, giving evidence of the lack of running water. There were no chairs, no cupboards, no sink, in fact, no kitchen at all. The station was only a shell of a building with no partitions for rooms nor an inside ceiling. Why had the exterior been painted so attractively, luring me into false hopes? Reminding myself of the contract made with my facial expressions, I conducted a difficult inner struggle.

One object had recently been added to begin to give order to the surrounding confusion. Claude reached for a rectangular, one-quart, RPM, outboard-motor-oil can sitting on a pile of insulation. He proudly showed it to me as he stated, "This is our new mail box." Now what could be an appropriate reply to such a statement? Claude was so deadly serious, as well as proud, that I didn't dare show my amusement or my frustration. The mailbox boasted a few virtues: the top had been neatly cut off with a can opener and the oil had been washed out, but all I could think was, "Why don't they at least paint it?" Instead of a verbal reply, I managed a faint smile.

I had no way of knowing that conditions on our arrival were much improved from the project's beginning just a year earlier in 1953. Three men—Robert Parker, a hard-working fishery biologist; Leo Thompsen, an engineer; and a Kodiak native, who had been coerced to sign on while drunk—had started the station. They were employed by Alaska Territorial Department of Fisheries and lived first in a tent and then in a hastily constructed plywood cabin. This 8x11-foot cabin, which had first served as a summer shelter and then as a bear-proof tool shed for the 1953–54 winter, would now serve as our summer bedroom. The men had just finished the remaining shell of the station in the weeks before our arrival. My Bob was the first resident biologist hired at Kitoi because these facilities had just become adequate enough to allow a year-round program of research on the sockeye salmon, also called red salmon. Plans at that time called for a separate dwelling to be built for the resident biologist and his family so the station could be used as an office and laboratory. But just as the dairy farmer's new barn must be built long before his new house, so must research facilities be built before living quarters.

Bob and I stepped outside to escape the clutter and for me to exchange heels for loafers. As we peeked into the tiny shack that would be our separate bedroom cabin, the calmness of the evening settled over the bay, soothing both the water and our minds. We walked just one hundred feet over a small rise to the mouth of Big Kitoi Creek where about two hundred silver salmon were schooling. How thrilling to watch them jump! Several at once would leap three or four feet out of water, sometimes in broad jumps and sometimes as acrobats standing straight in the air on their tails. Our fingers tingled for a rod and line, but the trunks containing the fishing tackle that had been shipped by boat would not arrive for about two weeks.

"Chow!" someone yelled.

This announcement took us by surprise. Had dinner been prepared during our short excursion?

Indeed it had. We discovered that the three men were quite efficient in culinary arts. It appeared Claude had prepared the potatoes while Quent Edson had miraculously squeezed five plates onto the crowded table. He had also gathered enough rickety boxes and upturned cans for seats, and tossed a large salad. Robert Parker was engrossed in his specialty of pan-broiling the T-bone steaks that had been flown in on our plane. Expensive cuts of meat were a rarity for us, but we were soon to find that residents of Kitoi Bay consistently put food first, claiming it was their one and only luxury. We had packed vitamin pills in preparation for living on an Alaskan island far from the fresh green vegetables and fruits of the United States. Now we were pleased to learn that even though no refrigeration was available, we could have fresh meats and produce several days of the week. A Kodiak Airways plane, unless weather prevented, brought in groceries and mail each week.

Just after this first evening meal, Robert Parker asked me if I would cook for the group. A scenario of communal living and shared meals had not even entered my mind. Since Mr. Anderson had warned us that conditions were not suitable for a woman and advised that I not even come to Alaska until a few months later, I felt I had no choice. With a confidence I did not feel, I replied, "Yes."

The gas lanterns were pumped and lit for the evening. Water was carried and heated on the oil range for dishwashing. The five of us did dishes while I blindly overlooked the fact that ash trays were being washed before the drinking glasses and blackened skillets blithely wiped with white dish towels.

For me, the most thoughtful and appreciated act of the evening was Robert Parker's offer to loan us a clean, double flannel sheet to use until our bedding arrived. Since our first peek into the tiny, plywood bedroom cabin, I had been dreading crawling into the musty, dirty blankets piled on the bunk. At bedtime Bob built a fire in the little airtight wood heater, giving cheer and warmth to the chilly August night. On the three-quarters-size bunk with a five-foot-long cotton pad (Bob was six foot, two inches), we spread the clean-smelling sheet blanket, stretched out the dirty regular blankets, and then put two of Bob's clean tee shirts over the pillows to serve as pillowcases.

Taking our toothbrushes and a flashlight, we padded unprotected and unafraid the short distance to the river's edge for teeth brushing. Automatically, we breathed deeply in the clean air and looked upward. The stars sparkled as if they were bursting with untold secrets. Lack of haze and smoke from factory-laden cities caused the moon and stars of this northern land to appear much closer, brighter, and more personal. As lovers of fresh air and the outdoors, we decided we would take a nightly stroll to Big Kitoi Creek to brush our teeth rather than walk back to the research station for the task. Besides, the creek gave us the advantage of running water, water so cold it nearly made my teeth ache.

On this, our first teeth-brushing expedition, we could hear the rush of the water and the sounds of the salmon as they continued their jumping display. Then there was a splash louder than the others.

"That wasn't a salmon," Bob exclaimed.

Splash! Splash!

Bob shone the weak flashlight toward the sounds. Two glaring eyes stared back. We gripped our toothbrushes and beat a hasty retreat back to our cabin. We had no wish to prolong our first contact with the Kodiak brown bear while he ate his elegant salmon dinner.

I lay on the hard bed with no springs that night half-laughing and half-fearful of the difficulties that lay ahead in adjusting to such a new and different environment. Could we make our way through these new experiences in this challenging land? Now, as I lay in the darkness, my thoughts returned to my agreeing to cook for the crew. I mentally planned a lunch and dinner menu that I could prepare for the next day and began puzzling over how I could ever find kitchen utensils and food in the heterogeneous clutter of the cabin. At least, I thought, the obstacle of preparing meals amid the workmen's hammering, the sawing, and the flying sawdust should keep any nostalgia away. I did not even have a cookbook. Other than the contents of our suitcases, everything we had brought were in two trunks that had not arrived. As if Bob could read my thoughts and discern my doubts and fears, he squeezed my hand saying, "My wonderful wife, don't be discouraged. Do you remember that David said in Psalms, 'If I take the wings of the morning, and dwell in the uttermost parts of the sea; even there shall thy hand lead me, and thy right hand shall hold me.'"? I was comforted. I thought, too, of all the beauty we had witnessed that night—the stars shining so brightly in the dark, dark night. I remembered this truth, that the darker the circumstances, the brighter God's light. I resolved to trust Him in this place as much as I had in Oregon. With God walking beside us, what difference do surroundings make? With these thoughts, my quiet within soon equaled the quiet without, and we slept peacefully through our first night in a new land.

Settling In

On the third day after our arrival on Afognak Island, I accompanied Bob and Robert Parker on the short mile hike to Little Kitoi Lake for the evening salmon count at the weir. The weir was a concrete dam across the outlet of the lake built to stop and hold the fish so they could be counted, measured, identified as to sex and species and have a small scale removed. (Similar to the rings on a tree, scales tell the salmon's age.) Our inattentive enjoyment of the cool, refreshing evening was suddenly interrupted as we noticed some large, wet footprints on a gravel bar. All three of us, looking up at once, saw a giant brown bear scrambling up the far bank of the stream.

"Howdy, Brown Bear," calmly spoke Robert as he raised his .357 magnum.

Immediately the bear stopped. Not until both it and we were motionless did we realize that two cubs were behind her. This first close, daytime sighting of these highly publicized mammals was truly awe-inspiring. Incredulously, we were standing just twenty-eight feet (we measured later) from a Kodiak brown bear. Perhaps to gain a more-advantageous position, Mama Bear reared erect on her hind legs and was immediately imitated by her twin cubs, who eagerly peeked around either side of Mom for a cautious look at those strange humans. The shaggy-haired trio continued motionless in this erect position except for a slight twitch of Mama Brownie's sensitive nose. Bear seem to have very poor and near-sighted vision, but they more than compensate for this by nearly unsurpassed senses of smell and hearing.

We stood speechless for what seemed like fifteen minutes—although it was no doubt closer to one minute—transfixed by these enormous creatures. One of us finally quavered, "Go away, Brown Bear," and she and her cubs turned, made a nimble leap, and dashed off through the brush.

I think Bob had been eager for me to see these large mammals because he did not think I had a proper fear of their potential. Perhaps his reading, acquaintances, and wildlife management classes had prepared him. Of course, I had heard the usual bear tales, but even they had not produced the desired effect. Bob had explained that it really wasn't fear that one should have but a respect for them and their prior rights. "After all, we are their guests," he had explained. "Should we meet 'His Majesty' while trespassing on his pathway, it is our duty to step off and climb a tree to give him full respect." (Brown bear do not climb trees.) I easily understood this etiquette just as I understood the trail-walking etiquette of men first—with a gun—and women second. Yet, because of no innate mistrust, I would sometimes forget the necessity of always carrying our bear-insurance policy, the .30-06 rifle. To the men's puzzlement, my reaction to meeting the mother bear and her charming twins had lessened rather than increased my sense of possible danger from the Kodiak brown bear. Even though the mother had been a gigantic creature, her face was curiously shy and her ears just like those of a Teddy bear. I could *almost* have run toward her and buried my face in her soft fur.

After this encounter with the mother bear and her cubs, we stopped using Big Kitoi Creek for our evening teeth brushing. However, for the one-hundred-foot trek each evening to our bedroom cabin, we felt safe enough to walk without a lantern or flashlight. Neither one of us thought about meeting a brownie along this short path until one morning we found giant brown bear tracks on top of our shoe prints. Maybe the brownie had been investigating the newcomers who had encroached upon *his* community. After that we carried a lantern to give us at least a moment's warning before running headlong into our noted neighbor. More importantly, the lantern gave the original residents notice that *we* were trespassing. Also, we became somewhat more careful in using our twice-a-day-automatically flushed toilet, a one-holer outhouse built on an outcropping over the bay that flushed when the tide came in.

Of course, indoor plumbing and living in an actual house would have made us feel safer, but hopefully those luxuries would come in the future. Right now the goal was simply to improve the livability of the station, and Bob and I were certainly not going to relinquish our bit of privacy by giving up our bedroom cabin for fear of a brownie on the path.

The days passed quickly as all the men and I were busily engaged in improving Kitoi Bay Research Station. The walls and ceiling were covered with plywood; partitions were put up to create a bathroom, a kitchen, and an office-living room; stairs were built to the upstairs bunks and storage space; plumbing was installed for the future possibility of running water, and pre-fab cupboards were hung in the kitchen. In the midst of this work, meal preparation became a real obstacle course. The simplicity of a canned ham or canned green beans helped, but even in preparing these items, I had to wash sawdust from each pan and dish. Trying to bake a dessert, I would have to dig through eleven boxes to find the salt or sugar, or oil, whatever was needed. Work was equally frustrating for the men because they could never find the hammer, the plane, or the half-inch stove bolt they desired.

Several fretted because a limited budget prevented hiring more construction workers. By the middle of September (1954), the men had started building a high-water dock. Also, a barge was rented to bring out gravel for added foundations or footings on the present station and for the 25x85-foot hatchery portion of the station that would be attached to it. The men even had visions of getting the hatchery portion started and roofed before winter; however, that had to be postponed a year. Delaying intended fishery work was frustrating; the biologists were eager to proceed on their limnological studies, on additional weir constructions and operations to aid in freshwater salmon growth and survival studies, and on lake rehabilitation that would include spawning and hatching of salmon eggs.

Gradually the station became more livable and safe. Our prime safety protection was already sitting in the corner of the main room. This was our mini radio station: four large black objects, all involved with receiving and transmitting, our sole means of communication with the outside world. (Outside the building was a battery charger for supplying the power.) We were learning to operate this unit and quickly learned we could easily eavesdrop on both bush pilot and marine conversations.

At a scheduled time twice a day, Bob would turn on the receiving set for a call from the Kodiak radio station. Calling out was possible at any time, but we usually used this scheduled time to order our supplies. The Kodiak radio station connected us with the phone system in Kodiak. Ben Kraft, the merchant from whom we ordered groceries, hardware, or dry goods, received so much business from our research station that he or his helpers were willing to walk to the post office to get stamps or anything else in town for us.

Some of the work on the living-office-laboratory-kitchen station neared completion. During this time, the five of us at the station became quite the interior decorators as we discussed and visualized suitable colors for our new walls. We finally compromised among the five different opinions, and proceeded to describe the chosen colors to the Kodiak merchants over our short-wave radio transmitter. "Please send us three quarts of soft-yellow interior paint about the color of telegram paper," we would attempt to explain. Then we would patiently wait until the weekly mail plane arrived to find out what shades or tints the clerk had sent after he interpreted our detailed descriptions. Although not perfect, our combinations turned out more suitable than we had expected. I did most of the painting and was satisfied with the results. The cupboards enameled white, inside and out, looked so clean. The soft-yellow walls with chocolate-brown woodwork and the blue bathroom were a remarkable improvement over the bare walls. In the mornings, all we would now need to do was step into the brilliance of the turquoise-blue bathroom and we were widely and pleasantly awake. (But it did seem odd to have a bathroom with no running water.)

Because the kitchen was to be used partly, and sometimes completely, for a laboratory, an acid-resisting, green Formica counter top was installed. Later, many hours of scrubbing made us realize that using white enamel for the cupboards had been a mistake. We counterbalanced this error by covering the steep staircase with black tread and painting the sides black to reduce the need to scrub off so many shoe marks. The painting process, especially painting the plywood ceiling, meant that the wood floor and each of us were soon stippled with dripping paint. But at least some sort of order was emerging from the confusion.

Bob was eager for the messy work to slacken so I could dress normally. My attire had always been important to him. Also, before coming to this island we had made a pledge to each other that we were not going to become seedy. Part of this pledge was our inside dress. At this time women in the States wore pants for outdoor work. Slacks were for recreation, and skirts and dresses were for the house. Thus, I took for granted that I would continue this standard even while on an isolated island in the cold north. Little did I realize that Yves St. Laurent would soon be putting women in pants in a progression that would cause even Bob to accept pants as appropriate feminine attire as long as they fit correctly.

With most of the carpentry completed and the walls painted, I knew the present confused state of communal living could be put to some type of order. This was needed because Mr. Clarence Anderson, Director of Alaska Department of Fisheries, was actually coming to spend two days at Kitoi Bay. I was apprehensive about cooking for "the boss." Actually, I found him to be a most pleasant man, one who could relate to all. Besides chatter on the need for local management of Alaskan resources rather than most actions being controlled by Washington, D.C., lighter talk also ensued. Much laughter erupted when Mr. Anderson commented that he could not pronounce hors d'oeuvres so he just called them "horse's ovaries."

The time came when the liveliness and chaos of the Kitoi group was soon to end. The men returned to Kodiak and Juneau. Extra cold, quiet days had arrived. We did not know what kind of life we would create, just the two of us, but we did send letters back to the States assuring our friends that we were not living in an igloo, dressed as Eskimos, or sitting on ice blocks.

Neighbors in the Wild

Stillness, dense as fog, settled over Kitoi Bay, seeping into every activity. The clattering construction noises, the endless table discussions on the best methods of increasing Alaskan salmon production, and the roar of the Barco impact hammer or the outboard motor had been quieted. Silence. We began to call this the "Silent Season," distinguishing it from the "Noisy Season," which was more meaningful than the traditional labeling of seasons. The Noisy Season was May to mid-October, when other biologists and construction workers were present. The Silent Season was the rest of October through April, when Kitoi Bay's human population consisted of us alone. We moved from the 8x11-foot plywood bedroom cabin into the vast 20x28-foot research station building with the partial upstairs.

Figure 3. A serene view of Pacific waters from our station.

Now in the Silent Season, the only sounds were the lazy lap of the rise and fall of the tide in the sheltered bay; the morning laughter of loons; the occasional squawk of old squaw ducks; and the twice-daily, overhead drone of the engines of the Pacific-Northern-Airline DC-3 as it made the daily Anchorage to Kodiak flights. We journeyed out on the bay in the skiff to gaze at the boundless miles of shoreline with no sign of habitation other than our one small, shiny, aluminum roof. This caused me truly to realize that we were alone. Alone in a wheel-less, human-less world. We knew there were numerous ways to view this solitude but chose to view it as an adventuresome honeymoon rather than an unending imprisonment. During those times when we were already desiring to visit friends, go shopping, or walk to the corner drugstore for a milkshake, we would remind ourselves of the rare privilege we had of enjoying the surrounding expanse of untouched beauty and quiet.

Soon after the men left, the quietness gave us a chance to become acquainted with one of our animal neighbors: Willie the Weasel emerged from a crevice in an old stump. Willie's white ermine coat was accentuated by two, glittering, black eyes and a black tip on the end of his stiffly held tail. His appearance—a long, slender body and low, rounded ears—gave little evidence of his occupation. He was a keen, bold murderer. We never witnessed first-hand what our research revealed—that his favorite drink was warm blood and that he preferred his meat so fresh that it was alive and quivering. Nor could we verify that his tremendous appetite caused him to eat one-third of his weight every twenty-four hours. Had we attempted the same, we would have been consuming seven hundred pounds of meat a week!

Figure 4. Willie the Weasel with food.

We actually began to see Willie several times a day so began to suspect there were many "Willies" around. Winter snow had not arrived, but the weasels had already changed to their white winter coats, making them stand out against the black slate and the green moss.

In human characteristics, we viewed Willie to be a shifty-eyed person who minded his own business and expected others to do likewise. However, a comical action scene was played out when Bob tried to get Willie to drop a mouse he had in his mouth. Bob wanted to see what kind of mouse it was. Willie ran behind a stump and hid the mouse in a hole. As Bob peeked around the stump, Willie came out and began peeking at Bob from the opposite side of the stump. Anyone would have thought they were playing a game.

We had been seeing Kodiak brown bear, the world's largest land carnivore, and now were seeing Willie, the strongest and most ferocious carnivore for his size. What other neighbors would winter weather and silence provide?

Afognak, being an island, had very little native animal population, so most of the animals had been introduced to the area. Deer, elk, and squirrels that inhabited some distant parts of the island had not spread to our part. Therefore, our land mammal neighbors consisted only of bear, weasels, foxes, rabbits, muskrat, beavers, and otter. Of course, there were fish, marine mammals, and birds. Looking out the window, we would see seal pop up their heads. Loons were constantly flying around with their crazy laughter. Puffins and bald eagles were plentiful.

One morning Bob awoke me with an announcement: "Ruth, a new neighbor has come to call. Do come greet him! Hurry, he's really a distinguished-looking gentleman."

I sleepily followed his pointing finger. Outside our window stood a striking silver fox. Every hair of his glossy black fur was in place. The tips of his black fur coat were frosted white, and he sported a pure white V under his neck as a vest. Typical of most red foxes, he had a white-tipped tail. Just as humans are blondes, brunettes, or mixes in-between, so red foxes are born with various color phases of fur. Different colors occur in the same litter. We observed that the rarest on Afognak Island were the pure silver foxes; a few were of the red phase; the majority were the cross foxes, which are a mixture of red and black. But regardless of their color, all are classified as red foxes.

Figure 5. Silver fox.

"We must call him Frosty," I told Bob. "Despite the fact he appears so aristocratic and sedate, he looks as if he had just walked through the bakery shelves rubbing against fresh baked cakes newly frosted with white Seven-Minute Icing."

Frosty stood looking at the big cage of a house cautiously, yet being careful to lose none of his dignity. As we slowly eased the window open to throw him a piece of our breakfast bacon, he could no longer control his lordly stance but fled behind a bush. Hoping he would eat it, we tossed the bacon as near to the bush as possible. Not understanding our quick throwing movements, Frosty immediately disappeared for the day.

Frosty's visits became semi-weekly, and in between times we made the acquaintance of a homely cross fox that we named Dinky. Whether they were strangers to each other or close relatives, we had no idea. Hoping to prevent a later squabble, we fed Dinky at a different kitchen window from the one where we had been feeding Frosty. We waited for the day Frosty and Dinky would both come to their handout restaurant at the same time. Each knew another fox had been invading the territory he considered *his alone* because both Frosty and Dinky would make an extensive sniffing investigation whenever they arrived. Both were beginning to come more often and were becoming friendlier and more at ease with their man-invaded surroundings. Frosty would patiently wait by his window for an hour or more at a time, expecting handouts each ten minutes. Dinky became so comfortable he would curl up in a round, soft ball with his fluffy tail over his paws and nose to keep them warm as he dozed between snacks. If the aroma of preparing dinner were exceptionally tantalizing, I would open the window a crack to watch Dinky perk up, jump to a sitting position, sniff, and twitch his pointed noise. Dinky's actions became so winsome that we were sorry to have given him such an ugly name.

In a week or so the inevitable occurred: Dinky approached with his bouncy trot to find Frosty sitting at one of the windows. Frosty gave a lusty growl as if to say, "I'll have you know that this is my territory."

Dinky, making a low grumbling sound, stood scowling at Frosty as if to say, "So you're the intruder who has been trespassing on my property."

Frosty very nonchalantly curled up to rest, pretending to be oblivious of Dinky's presence. Since Frosty was not sitting at the food-giving window, Dinky no doubt decided that he would let Frosty's presence pass for the moment while he himself took the honored seat by what he knew to be the food-donation window.

But no food was forthcoming. Frosty's presence disturbed Dinky to the extent that he finally made a growling attack on Frosty. Frosty was on his feet by the time Dinky made his lunge, and we were witnessing a real fox fight. Deep guttural growls rumbled. The encounter terrified me at first, but we were later to find that the majority of fox skirmishes are harmless to the participants. Usually each fox rears up on his hind legs and places his forepaws on the other fox's shoulders in a boxing-like clinch. In this position they attempt to push each other backward, the one losing the most ground being defeated. During this same time, each fox stretches open his large mouth screaming, perhaps shouting insults and curses, at the other. Although the struggle sounds and looks fierce, it is really only a game of bluff. Frosty came out the winner in this round so Dinky humbly went back to his window position while Frosty acted as if Dinky had entirely left the region. Finally, we decided to experiment by feeding the two simultaneously. To do our most to help them become compatible, we knew we must feed each at exactly the same moment. Bob opened Dinky's window, while I opened Frosty's window. "Okay, ready." We each threw the cookie at the same instant. With a big gulp Dinky swallowed his and dashed around the corner to take Frosty's away. Again a fight was underway and again Frosty succeeded in backing Dinky down the hill.

Figure 6. Frosty and Dinky fighting.

Each fox began coming and remaining at the house more often in order to have better claim to the territory. Dinky began using a hollow tree a few yards away for his sleeping quarters. Later he decided even that was too distant so he began staking possession by remaining outside the house all the daylight hours, which would ordinarily be his sleeping hours. At night he would leave to do his hunting, returning around breakfast. His daytime sleep, however, was far from restful slumber. He would curl up outside the window, sticking one eye out from his fluffy tail curled over his head so he could quickly flick the eye open should he hear a window latch move. After much patience and time, we finally trained the two to get along with each other. If both were present, we fed them simultaneously; if only one were present, we fed him out of his own window—never out of the other fox's window.

The only time these two antagonistic pets ever joined forces and seemed pleased with the other's presence was when a third fox would start to invade the area. Heavier winter snows, preventing extensive fox-travel and reducing food supplies, caused this to happen. Before Third Fox would come within sight of the house, Frosty or Dinky would scent him and away both would run in pursuit, snarling the intruder away.

Foxes, although shy, nervous, and flighty, gradually became choice pets giving us hours of enjoyment. I had no idea then how much we would rely on these neighbors for entertainment and companionship. They, however, were never actually tamed.

Animals other than foxes kept their distance. Instead of entering our area, the snowshoe hares were content to remain in their brushy grassy settlement. Now that colder weather was arriving, bear were entering their dens for nearly eight months. River otters were nearby but postponed their social calls until midwinter. Few animal neighbors had intentions of making social visits to our cabin.

One dark evening in late October, a visitor other than one of our animal friends startled us. It was nearly six o'clock. The noisy racket of the gasoline engine that powered the battery charger was pounding away as it recharged the storage batteries for our radio set. I was just about finished painting a chair that Bob had created for me. (The boxes as seats were becoming uncomfortable and induced backaches.) Finishing the last stroke, I got up from my cramped floor position and saw, through the window, a light. I was not surprised—even after three months I still could not completely realize how remote we really were.

"Honey, someone is outside," I said casually.

"Oh, sure," replied Bob, engrossed in reading *Pacific Fisherman* as he sat on our homemade sofa (made from twin mattress pads) with his back to the window.

"No, really!"

"Now, don't try to fool me on that one." Bob knew no one could possibly come except by an airplane or boat.

"Honestly, there is a flashlight right outside the window!"

At last Bob turned around to look. "Wow, there *is* someone all right!"

Our front door had been boarded on the outside to keep out the strong easterly winds. The moving light began circling the house to find an entrance. Then a knock sounded on the back door. Bob opened the door cautiously while I held my breath. Two Alaskan native men stood in the light.

"Hello," Bob greeted, surprise in his voice.

"Hello, I'm Pete Olsen," replied one of the men. We immediately relaxed. Although we had not previously met Pete, an Aleut with a Scandinavian name, we knew he was the person who would bring our winter fuel and other supplies in his forty-foot fishing boat, the *Parks No. 6*. Even though our two heavy trunks had been flown in by air, air freight was too expensive to transport everything by plane. Plans were that twice each year canned food, fuel, and building supplies would be brought by boat.

With the stimulus of company, it took only a jiffy to change to clean clothes and cook dinner for the four of us. Visiting with outsiders was a treat, and we especially enjoyed the opportunity of getting to know two of the local men. That first unexpected visit was the beginning of a close friendship with Pete that continued to grow with each contact.

Pete was an industrious man. We were impressed with his pride in his six children and his high regard for his wife. During this first meeting he told us about recently purchasing his $8,000 boat, an exceptionally good buy. He said that as soon as he had it paid in full, he was going to name it *Nina*, for his wife. As Pete and his associate left to return to the boat, he remarked, "That was certainly a wonderful dinner. Except for my wife's, that was the best cooking I've ever eaten."

What fun we had the next morning unloading the boat! While the men did the heavy lifting, I peeked at all our new purchases and supplies for the winter: oil, gas, food staples, tile for the floor, a wringer washing machine on which we would put a gas motor, and—best of all—a light-birch bedroom set complete with bedsprings and mattress. Sleeping in comfort awaited if the springs and mattress could be squeezed up the narrow steps to the attic storage-room-bedroom. Groceries also went upstairs: full cases of six-pound Crisco metal pails, Klim (dried whole milk), Libby's orange juice, peaches, fruit cocktail, tomatoes, and Folgers coffee. Bags and boxes of things like Jolly Time popcorn, Jell-O, hams, large cans of chicken canned whole with the bones, and much more were ready to be placed on the newly built attic shelves.

The larger part of Pete Olsen's boatload was two fifty-gallon barrels of white gas for our lanterns and outboard motors and twelve barrels of fuel oil for cooking and heating throughout the winter. I wondered how these would be brought ashore, as heavy and bulky as they were. Pete waited until high tide, then brought his boat as close to shore as possible. The first barrel was rolled over the stern, then sank amidst bubbles to the bottom. Would it stay there? Slowly, it rose until a small part emerged above water. The others followed suit. Next, a rope was put around the barrels to hold them in place as the tide went out. After they were lying on our gravel beach above the waterline, Bob, Pete, and his helper rolled the barrels up the gentle slope above the high tide mark. Later they were rolled and tipped on end near the big oil tank that had been built up on scaffolding. Then round and round with a hand pump, whenever Bob walked by the next several weeks, each barrel of oil was pumped into the huge tank that held enough oil for our winter's use. The gas was left in its original barrels and pumped out as needed. We felt more secure now having sufficient heating oil for the winter.

All these new items that had arrived were just a prelude to the day's real excitement. The main event was my newfound role as skipper of Pete's boat. After Bob mentioned that I had never been on a boat larger than a rowboat, Pete suggested we go for a ride. Realizing my interest, he let me handle the pilot wheel for a six-mile run out the bay. Bob and Pete's deckhand laughed at the zigzag wake left behind, but Pete encouraged me by saying, "You're doing well for a first timer." The rolling ocean swells coming from divergent angles made it difficult to keep the fishing vessel on a straight course. It takes a while to become used to the delayed action of the pilot wheel, and it must take months to get the feel of the proper technique of turning the wheel according to the plant of one's feet on the deck.

As we arrived back at Kitoi Bay, Pete's instructions enabled me to ease the boat alongside their little skiff. To make my experience complete, he even showed me the engine room and explained the workings of the various gears. I did not have the courage to tell Pete that I could not understand a word of his explanation.

The stimulation of new items to use and eat and the venture as skipper energized the beginning of the Quiet Season. Soon days melted into weeks, bringing changes in weather conditions. October, which usually brought snow to this land, had passed, and now the first goose-down flecks of snow began to fall. On other days the southeasterly autumn winds maddened the sea and beat sheets of rain against the house in a persistent downpour. Occasional calm nights permitted the below-freezing temperature to form a gray skim of ice on our sheltered bay; later we could expect thicker ice cover.

Our time with Pete had made me more keenly aware of the need and importance of relationships. Having always emphasized work and accomplishments, I began realizing that relationships and the atmosphere those relationships produce should be one of life's primary goals. I tucked that thought away for further contemplation. Right now, relationships were limited. A primary goal for us was to survive a new and remote environment. Our life was going to be different. At least I appreciated those two days of contact with human neighbors, instead of just animal neighbors, and hoped they were good preparation for the coming winter of isolation in the wilds of Alaska.

Mail Days

The Silent Season became even more silent as inclement winter weather postponed the arrival of the mail plane. It was to come every Tuesday, but it had been over two weeks since the last mail day. Our anticipation of the plane grew keener morning by morning; our disappointment, greater night by night. Eagerly we would listen to weather forecasts, scan the skies, and add another letter to the outgoing mail can. Living in a sheltered cove of the bay made it hard for us to realize when it was too windy to fly. Other times after an easterly blow, a leftover swell would run into our bay. This lazy swell and glassy water with calm wind made it difficult for pilots to tell where the air ended and the water began. This made landing hazardous. Even when the water was relatively calm, piercing ten-degree Fahrenheit temperatures made it too cold for the small bush planes to take off and land on the water. The bay water would cause icing problems; each landing or taking off in water would add another heavy ice layer in the hull. (A Grumman Widgeon's body is built like a boat hull.) Whenever it was neither windy nor cold in our cove, poor visibility from smothering snowstorms or fog caused non-flyable weather somewhere around the islands. Bob Hall, owner of Kodiak Airways, had many bush pilots[1] to serve the Archipelago. But his crew had to have flexible schedules set by the weather.

We were both exhausting ourselves trying to transform the motor sounds of large airplanes overhead into the sound of a Widgeon about to land at Kitoi Bay. Bob finally suggested another approach. "Whenever Kodiak Airways has a few hours of good-flying weather, we know that they'll first take care of their backlog of passengers. Next, they will probably fly to places like Old Harbor, Karluk, or Lazy Bay because they have more mail and freight. The sensible thing for us to do is to stop expecting them altogether."

"It'll be hard to do, but you're right," I reluctantly agreed.

It was good that we embraced this philosophy; otherwise we would have been living in a state of frustration half the winter. Now we no longer remained home postponing a needed field trip just so we could meet the plane in case it arrived. Instead, we just took for granted that it would not come.

---

[1] Gil Jarvela, Bill Harvey, Al Cratty, Ben Chanham, Tom Belleau, E. J. Lawless, Verlyn Geriene, and Ray Albrecht

Without the mail plane, which also brought the weekly groceries, we ran out of fresh meat and began supplementing the unappetizing canned meats by harvesting clams. Although tides varied depending on the moon and the tilt of the earth at various seasons, low tides occurred about twice a month, usually in the evening or early morning. But this did not mean we had to travel by skiff in the dark because our front-yard beach was abundant with both littleneck and butter clams. Dressed in warm clothing and equipped with lantern and potato fork, we would take the few steps to the beach. First, would come some lantern-light beachcombing in order to admire the colorful sea anemones, starfish, brittle stars, and other unusual creatures. The actual digging for littlenecks became a task similar to digging potatoes in the garden. Looking for bubbles, as we had done when digging razor clams on the sandy Oregon beaches, wasn't necessary—each fork full would yield two to fifteen clams.

The tiny littlenecks, easily identified by the waffle-like pattern on their shells, made excellent bite-sized, steamed morsels. Steamed just until the shells opened, we removed the clams with a fork and dipped them into a mixture of melted butter, lemon, salt, and pepper before flipping them into our mouths. Although steamed butter clams are also good, they do not compare with the tender, succulent littlenecks, so we used the butters for clam chowder.

Frosty or Dinky would often see our lantern on the beach during a low tide and approach for their share of the diggings. Although foxes are not able to open the clams, they love to eat them when they find them with cracked shells—or whenever we opened the clams for them.

Clamming was a pleasant diversion, but still no plane! We continued waiting and watching. Although

Figure 7. Clams dug at low tides were one source of fresh meat. We also ate crab, snowshoe hare, duck, and fish.

ice covered the bay in front of the station, a plane could land at what we called Winter Beach, located just a mile away. The outboard-motor-oil-can mailbox, still a favorite memento of our arrival at Kitoi Bay, overflowed with outgoing mail. Our clam diet branched out to include clamburgers, clam fritters, clam stew, clam pie, scalloped clams, and even clam-potato salad. A hare and an occasional duck were welcome treats.

One afternoon both of us bundled up to wash the outsides of our three windows so we could more completely appreciate the winter bay scenery. Even with the deafening racket of our necessary and faithful gas battery charger, we soon heard the sound of a plane on the water.

The mail plane! At last! How marvelous! Oh, I'm so excited! We will have to hurry and get to the Winter Beach!" I gasped all in one breath.

Such exultation was soon exchanged for woeful deflation. Past our ice-bound bay, we could see the featherweight Piper Cub, which the weather had reluctantly permitted to arrive, skimming the water in a *take-off*, not a landing.

Bob dashed inside to turn on our radio receiver, which warmed up much faster than the old military surplus transmitter.

"KWN4, KWN4, 461 off the water, Kitoi Bay; no one arrived to pick up mail at Winter Beach; arrive Kodiak on the hour," came the frustrating word of Al Cratty, the pilot, as he radioed Kodiak Airways.

Three weeks with no contact with the outside world, and then seeing that vital lifeline vanish from sight when almost within arm's reach caused my stomach to churn. "How could it be? What happened?" I questioned.

"Evidently Al came in without buzzing the station, and we didn't hear him above the battery charger roar. No doubt, he had been waiting for us at Winter Beach for some time and finally gave up."

To ease my deep disappointment, I returned to scrubbing windows. Exchanging the now cold, sudsy water for hot, we began with intense vigor only to find window washing during below-freezing weather a nearly impossible task. No sooner was hot water spread across the pane than it formed a thin layer of ice. Boiling water had to be used to melt the ice layer and a race against the temperature had to be fought to get a section of pane cleaned and dried before it again became iced. FRUSTRATION titled the day.

Five days later a terrific roar boomed down from overhead as Kodiak Airway's Widgeon buzzed our house to announce its arrival. A southeasterly storm had rolled in sweeping out some of the ice in the bay but not weakening the remaining ice sufficiently for a plane to taxi through. We flung on outdoor clothing in rapid, fumbling haste. Finishing a few seconds before Bob, I dashed for the trail to Winter Beach (*see Figure 10*), leaving Bob to put the outgoing mail and some fragile bottles of plankton samples being sent out into the mail sack.

"Be careful and don't hurry too fast. The trail is terribly slick," called Bob.

The southeasterly rain had frozen and thawed on the steep, snow-packed, cliff-side trail making it treacherous. A thin layer of pellet snow on top of the ice acted as ball bearings to increase the unwanted mobility. Only by climbing on the sides of the trail that were not packed and that had a few crevices for footholds could the upgrades be traversed. In places it required crawling on all fours. On the downgrades I would sit down and slide. This method increased my speed, gave fewer chances of falling and helped to maintain my few minutes lead on Bob.

As I got closer, I wondered if I should yell so the pilot would not give up on us. At that moment the powerful engines of the Widgeon started their full power roar. Could I get there before the pilot taxied away?

As if it were life and death, I spotted a fire-escape-like chute at the side of the nearly vertical trail. I sat down and shot to the bottom in a reckless, two-hundred-foot slide, which Bob later made me promise never to repeat.

The wheels of the Widgeon were just rolling into the water when I got to the beach. I could have run and grasped the rudder, it was so close. All I could do, as I stood attempting to regain my breath, was hope the pilot would swing around to take a last glimpse of the beach before taking off. But he never turned to see my frantic waving.

Bob was on the beach in time to see him taxi around the fiord-like point. "By the sound of the engines, the pilot didn't take off. He must be going to see if he can break through the ice to the station," Bob concluded. "Perhaps he'll check back here at Winter Beach before taking off."

"There might be a possibility of getting back to the station before he gives up getting through the ice. If he could only see us and know we were home!"

"We'd never make it back in time. It would be better to wait here in case he returns."

"Please, let me go back and you stay here in case he does return," I urged, knowing that Bob had already had a workout from an early morning's excursion hiking to Root Lake, a small lake several miles from the station.

This is what we did. The constant drone of engines, evidently grinding against ice, sounded through the silent forest when I reached the crest of the divide. This gave me new vigor, and my pace automatically hastened in our game of hide and seek. Just before reaching sight of the station, I heard the engines stop, which gave hope that the pilot had managed to break through the ice and was on the beach. Or could it be that he was unable to break through and had taken off? One more turn on the icy trail and I'd know. No plane in sight. No path had been broken through the ice. He must have given up. Just then I saw Bill Harvey, the pilot, walking away from the house.

"Bill!" I called.

"Oh, there you are. I was getting concerned about you," Bill replied, obviously relieved to see me.

"Where is your plane?" I asked in puzzlement.

"It's in the creek mouth behind the rocky point. The ice was softest to break through there."

We found out that Bill had even climbed out on top of the plane's nose and had broken ice with a paddle in his grinding attempt to break through. When he finally managed to get into the mouth of Big Kitoi Creek and turn around, he had to wade across the icy creek through water over his boots to reach the station. He was worried that something might have happened to us. In true Alaskan-bush-pilot zeal, he had managed to get into the station to find out our status. All the bush pilots were brave souls, men who would risk their lives to save someone else, but Bill Harvey was especially noted for his fearlessness when people appeared to be in need of help. One time he even had to deliver a baby and then fly the mother and premature baby through a heavy rainstorm to the hospital in Kodiak.

"Couldn't you stay for lunch? Bob's waiting on the Winter Beach in case you returned there. If you can stay, I could have it ready by the time you taxied over and got him, that is, if you think the pathway you've broken through is enough to get out and in again."

"Sure. I'll do just that."

After the meal, as soon as Bill left, we excitedly sorted through the mail. We had thirty-two letters from family and friends, plus packages. Parts had arrived from Seattle for Bob to use in repairing the 25-hp Johnson motor. We also received a needed box of 500 envelopes that we had ordered from Montgomery Ward Company. Feeling sorry for our having only boxes for seats, Grandpa William Marr had sent us a pattern for making a chair from plywood. Grandma Mary Marr, at my request, had inserted some lace patterns so I could crochet an edging on my embroidered, hemstitched pillowslips. Only a few items could be put in the to-open-or-to-read-later pile. One was *The Mailboat Monitor*, an eight-page publication Kitoi Bay Research Station received monthly. The paper cost $3.00 per year and was published by the *M. V. Expansion*, a ship voyaging out the Aleutian Chain, mainly from Seward to Chignik. This new service carried both passengers and mail. From *The Mailboat Monitor* we would learn such things as this: "90% of the voting residents of the Chain and lower Alaska Peninsula voted Democratic in the recent Territorial elections according to the canvas made by the Monitor" and many trivial items such as "Henry Erickson and family of Chignik are currently visiting in Seattle. The Ericksons made their first visit Outside last year."

I was becoming used to any place out of Alaska being referred to as "Outside." When we had first arrived "Inside," my reaction to these Outside-Inside terms was a silent shudder as I would visualize either being captured inside or being freed to go outside some enclosed box. Moreover, I would further visualize Afognak Island as being a second, formidable enclosure inside the 586,400-square-mile, territorial Inside. But now, even less than a year as a resident, I found that the connotation of the word "Inside" no longer made me feel we were prisoners in a cage; rather, it was a privilege to be allowed to enter and reside Inside. Truly, the tiny box of Kitoi Bay, even when frozen tightly was likely the most beautiful place within the big box of Alaska.

Figure 8. Icicles frame the frozen ocean saltwater.

As was usual during this first winter, mail day—being such an exciting contrast to our quiet life—was followed by a sleepless night. This night especially resulted in insomnia because we could not clear our minds after entertaining a (human) guest at lunch, reading four weeks' worth of mail, and receiving ninety-five pounds of groceries (which included moldy bread and the outrageously priced eighty-seven-cent lettuce that looked like faded-green tissue paper).

Trip to Surf Lake

We knew the Silent Season would provide extra time for activities such as reading, which was something that we rarely had time to fully enjoy in our Oregon home. So now sitting at the table with the gas Coleman lantern, we appreciated reading and studying. Bob's reading consisted of *Northwest Passage* by Kenneth Roberts and *Far Corner, a Personal View of the Pacific Northwest* by Stewart Holbrook. He enjoyed history, especially northwest history. Then he would often thumb through his well worn copy of *Wild Flowers of the Pacific Coast* by Leslie L. Haskin. I would concentrate on *Punctuation, a Practical Method Based on Meaning* by Robert Brittain. Even though we did squeeze in time for books and board games, we were surprised to discover that the weeks flew by with the same rapidity as they did Outside. The rhythm of daily life continued.

Winter arrived early, bringing with it an inch of ice on the lakes by the first week of November. Contrary to the usual perception of Alaskan temperatures, Kitoi Bay's lowest air temperature during our first Silent Season dropped only to minus-three-degrees Fahrenheit. This mild winter weather compared with the interior of Alaska is the result of the tempering coastal influence of the warm Japanese Current,[2] which also warms the northwestern United States.

But much inconvenience resulted for two who were not accustomed to coping with nearly constant, below-freezing temperatures. It was especially cold on a windy day. (Using the outhouse, located over the bay, was a bitter-cold experience.) We tried to fend off some freezing difficulties by moving outside equipment into the upstairs attic-bedroom of the station, by frequently draining water from the oil tank, and by other preparations. Even so, something always came up. Bob needed a board from the outside lumber pile. This involved a two-hour wrestle with a peavey[3] to remove first the tarp that was frozen to the pile and then to pry off the needed piece of lumber. My mother sent us some hyacinth bulbs to splash a little color into our dark winter, but there was no loose soil to be found—until Bob cleverly found some under the cabin.

---

[2] A wide, warm flow of water starts in the Philippines, passes by Taiwan, and then circulates northeastward past Japan and across the Gulf of Alaska producing a warming effect on the climate.

[3] A metal-tipped, wooden-handled prying device with a movable hook along the side of the metal tip to grip round objects (logs) for turning.

The luxury we most missed was water from a faucet. It soon became obvious that the typical galvanized bucket was just not big enough for carrying water from the creek. Bob cut off an entire end on two square, five-gallon white gas cans, scrubbed the insides, and fitted them with handles from two paint cans. Carrying one container in each hand, he would walk to the creek and then, with the ten gallons, trudge back to the station. A wooden yoke as earlier Alaskans had used would have been helpful. One five-gallon can of water was designated for the kitchen sink and the other for the bathroom. Not surprisingly, it did not take Bob long to figure out that it was easier to keep a bar of soap on a rock and a towel over a limb down by the creek rather than carrying water to the house to wash his hands before meals. Later, though, the frequent rains made that arrangement unworkable. Not only would the towel be drenched, but the soap would be washed thin.

Figure 9. Timed during low tides, our water source was Big Kitoi Creek.

Along with these negatives, the early winter created an astonishing plus for us because of its effect on Little Kitoi Lake. The lake had frozen over before the winter snows, so the ice was clear as glass. We walked out on the lake, strolling on the surface as if it were the plate-glass window of an aquarium. And through it, we could see the sockeye salmon that had returned to spawn. After two-to-three years in the ocean, they had returned in good condition through the same freshwater stream to the lake where they were hatched. Now these salmon were in the brilliant red of their fall regalia. Their lives were ending even as they performed the work that would give life to their offspring. We watched as the females beat beds (called redds) in the gravel to lay their eggs, as the males circled, fighting fiercely for the right to fertilize the eggs. All would die shortly after these final efforts. Just a few weeks previously, I had watched pink and silver salmon spawning in Big Kitoi Creek after their three-to-five-year sojourn in the ocean. But watching the sockeye just under our feet was more dramatic. We stood on the lake watching this life-and-death drama playing out beneath us, and could hardly speak for the wonder of it and the wonder that we could be here to see it.

Some of Bob's winter work consisted of compiling and tabulating summer fish data. He mounted the fish scales and then read them under magnification to determine the fish's age. Later, he made graphs from the recorded data. He also had to inventory everything from stoves to nails. This included every bottle of chemical, every pill in the medicine cabinet, every stick of lumber, every pipe fitting. As a pleasant contrast to this inside work, much of his work still included outside activities. Often his outdoor work required a skiff trip plus several hours of hiking to reach the desired destinations, which were usually one or several lakes. Because the hours of darkness had lengthened considerably, from 3 p.m. to nearly 10 a.m., we would leave the station while it was still dark in order to be able to return in the light. My admitted reasons for accompanying Bob on such trips were the enjoyment of the exercise, the change of scenery, plus the help and companionship I could provide. But a deeper reason was to lessen my concern about Bob's safety.

Our first major trip was to take the skiff and then hike up to Surf Lake (*see Figure 10*) for water samples. "Let's get up at six instead of a quarter to seven in the morning to get an earlier start," Bob suggested the night before.

"Sounds fine," I agreed. Although I am usually not eager to arise early, if an adventuresome day lies ahead, it erases the misery of getting up.

About three o'clock the next morning we were jarred awake by permeating cold. Bob soon discovered the unwelcome cause—both oil stoves were out. Gone were the days when we could merely phone the apartment manager to relay our difficulties! We'd have to fix it ourselves.

"Must have a frozen water lock in the oil line," commented Bob, dressing in the dark and cold.

Bob piled the remaining blanket supply on top of me and then lit the gas lantern to begin his plumbing task. I was thankful to be the "weaker sex" and remain in the half-warm bed. After forty-five minutes of nearly constant tapping, Bob, who was always both creative and persistent in meeting challenges, succeeded in getting the ice-plug out of the oil line and the stoves burning.

Snuggling together in bed, we had not even really become warm again when six o'clock arrived. Had we not wanted to take advantage of the rare, calm weather reported on the marine weather forecast the night before, we likely would have postponed our trip. We could usually take our skiff into the various arms of Kitoi Bay, but to travel seven boat miles into the rough waters of Izhut Bay required calm water that was uncommon during the winter.

Bob filled the packbasket with water-sampling equipment while I put our lunch in the huge back pocket of my hunting jacket and laid out the camera bag for my share of the load. We could always kneel by a creek for water so carrying liquid was not a necessity. On these winter excursions that required a number of instruments and tools, we no longer encumbered ourselves with extras. Only a few weeks previously we had gone on a hiking jaunt with three guns: a .30-06 rifle for bear protection, a shotgun in case we saw a good-eating duck on the lake, and a .22 rifle in case a snowshoe rabbit was eager to supply us a dinner. On this trip, however, the .30-06 rifle had been stored for the winter because we trusted the brownies were hibernating, and the shotgun for ducks was unneeded because the lakes were frozen. But since we were still learning the best places to find snowshoe hares, we made sure to bring the .22 rifle.

Since we were already cold, we did not hesitate to put on nearly all of our outdoor garments, which included down jackets with parka hoods and thermal boots, the ideal boots for the Northland. The bay in front of the house, sheltered from the wind and fed by fresh water, was frozen, so we had to hike to the unfrozen cove where we kept the skiff. This mile walk warmed us in preparation for the hour-long boat ride, which was always numbingly cold in winter no matter how many layers of clothing we wore. As usual, the final layer over all our clothing was an orange life jacket. To make the ride even colder, I carelessly waded into water over the top of one boot while helping load the gear into the skiff. I hoped my wet, clammy foot was not a presage of the day.

As we traveled past pristine beaches with dark gray sand—much more intense than Oregon beaches—and plowed through the bay against the cold, cutting wind, Bob drilled me on duck identification, something I had never had opportunity or time to consider when we lived Outside. With their change in seasonal plumage and the male and female's different marks and coloration, duck-identification, I found, was not easy. But with Bob's help, it soon became a most absorbing game. A heavy, black duck with two white patches on its head and a red-humped bill is sure to be a surf scoter while an all-black one with just a red-humped bill is an American scoter. Should the red be absent but the humped nose still present plus a white-wing patch and a bit of white around the eye, I could recognize the bird as a white-winged scoter.

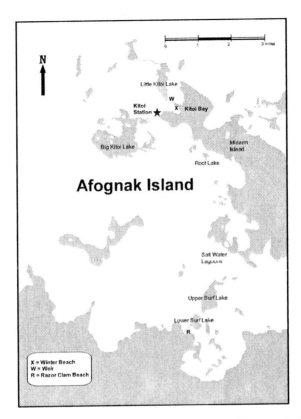

Figure 10. Kitoi Bay and surrounding area of Afognak Island.

The male scaup can be distinguished from a long distance by remembering that his coloring is divided vertically into distinct thirds, making him black on both ends and white in the middle.

But coloring is not nearly as important a clue as size, location, and other characteristics. For instance, black birds with long necks and slightly tipped-up heads, looking like performers on a stage, are cormorants. A long-tailed bird grouped with others of its kind indicates it is likely an old squaw; a large thick-necked bird sitting low in the water, a loon; a crested bird flying straight as an arrow, a merganser. Best of all is the one that jumps straight up from the water and becomes a roasted duck (providing Bob can hit it).

Occasionally, curious seals popped up their sleek, rounded heads to see what was carving such a spume of wake. In addition, this morning some animals seen less commonly than seal were resting on one of the outlying rocky points—three sea lions. They looked much like enlarged seals, so huge that I wondered if they would weigh a ton a piece. Since the approaching boat did not frighten these gigantic, heavy-bodied creatures, we throttled down and continued to ease closer. They held their long necks and pointed heads with small ears nearly upright and curiously surveyed us. After we had approached within forty feet, Bob turned the motor off, quietly placed the oars into the oarlocks, and used the oars to steer the skiff. I hastily snapped pictures. After nearly four minutes, the sea lions decided we were too close for comfort and began to inch their heavy bodies and floppy limbs toward the water. Then with a slow, graceful flop, one by one they disappeared beneath the rolling surf.

At the end of our boat ride, we used a siwash[4] line to tie our seventeen-foot skiff in a calm lagoon. This way the boat was beyond low tide, giving us no worries about having it stranded on the dry beach. Bob was always conscious of the tide stage since in so many ways our lives were governed by the tides.

Although we were chilled from the ride, past experience had taught us that shedding half our clothing layers was the wise move because hiking would soon make us warm. Instead of putting our extra clothing in the skiff where it might have been rained or snowed on, we rolled the two jackets into one bundle and tucked it into the mossy fork of a large spruce. Experience had also taught us that weather changes come quickly near the Gulf of Alaska.

Frozen ground, still without snow cover, provided excellent hiking. The vast acres of Afognak Island were veined with bear trails, and the island road-maintenance crew (the brown bear) had tramped the trails into good condition. Under certain soil conditions, the brownie's method of trail development seemed to evolve through three stages. The newly formed trail usually consisted of two rows of indented footprints. Bear after bear followed in the same tracks of previous travelers, causing the circular foot holes to sink as deep as ten inches. It must be hard for a little bear to stretch to reach the same footsteps of a grandfather bear. In time individual bears evidently stub their toes and miss the step sequence because by the next stage the two rows of alternating holes have merged into two

---

[4] Anchoring with a siwash line is a clever procedure. An anchor with a short rope that will reach the bottom is laid across the bow of the boat. On top of the anchor, a neatly coiled rope is laid, one that naturally has one end tied to either the boat or the anchor and the other end that is long enough to reach the shore regardless of the stage of the tide. A person holds one end of the coiled rope and pushes the boat as hard as possible into the water so the rope uncoils as the boat moves out. When the boat is out the farthest, the rope is jerked so the anchor is pulled off the bow over the edge and down into the water. Then the end of the rope is tied to a tree or a rock on shore that is above high tide. Thus, regardless of the stage of the tide, the boat will be floating (rather than left stranded on the beach from a high tide) and one can have access to it.

parallel ruts much like the ruts made by a narrow-wheeled cart. After many years of travel, the ruts become a two-foot-wide, ten-inch-deep, park-like trail.

We learned never to mistrust the bear's surveying ability. Often the trail appeared to run the wrong direction, but after having hiked out through the woods on our own—often through thorny devil's club—we usually found that the bear had a good reason for his road engineering. Perhaps it was to avoid a hill; perhaps to cut off a point of land. Whatever the reason, it was nearly always one we agreed with on our second trip in a new area.

Figure 11. Evolution of a bear trail: tracks (left), ruts (center), and trail (right).

Bear even erect "signposts" along their highways. These signposts are trees, deeply scarred by bites or by scratches. The highest gouges that we noticed were at nine feet, while the more common range of bites was around the six-foot mark. Imagine the pride that must accompany the biting of the highest gouge! The messages the bear read or smell from these signs would be interesting, but we could not determine what they meant. Perhaps they are a means of boasting "General B. Ears passed here on August 10, 1953."

At last, after tramping these bear highways, we arrived at the first Surf Lake. It was frozen over, as we expected. I reached down to pick up a rock to throw on the ice just for added assurance that the ice was really thick enough for safe walking.

"Bob, I can't budge this rock. Everything is frozen to the ground like cement!"

Even with Bob's help we could not move the rock. "It's all right," Bob assured. "I'm positive the ice is at least three inches thick. I think it will hold us. But remember, if you should ever start to fall through, lie flat on the ice and roll. Then your weight will be distributed over a greater area."

With this comfort, we launched out onto the ice cautiously. The ice suddenly started cracking, crunching, and breaking beneath us. Before we had time to wonder whether or not we were falling through, our feet had stopped on a solid layer of ice underneath the top layer. This under layer was three or four inches thick, but between it and the top half-inch layer were three inches of water and slush. It was a jolting hike to reach the center of this ninety-acre lake. In places I was light enough to remain on top, but Bob, carrying his heavy packbasket, fell through with a sudden jar on each step.

This was only the beginning of Bob's miseries. His next task was to chop a hole in the ice for drawing water samples. It would have been an easy task through the thin ice except for the three-inch layer of water. With each swing of the hatchet, icy water splashed on Bob. Had it been a warm, summer day, I probably would have laughed, but with both the air and water temperature below freezing, I had to sympathize. The water layer also deflected and lessened the force of the hatchet, compelling him to swing many times before the lake water spouted through the hole. (Later we acquired a lightweight ice auger, a spoon-like blade on the end of a metal rod, to use to prevent splashing when cutting through ice.)

Figure 12. Even in the winter, Bob took water samples to determine the water's temperature and oxygen content.

Next, water samples were taken at desired depths with a cylindrical, metal instrument that was closed with a "messenger" (a weighted, metal piece that slides down the string holding the water sampler). Bob took samples at six-foot intervals from the surface to the bottom of the lakes. The water samples were drained carefully into glass bottles to prevent adding any air bubbles and oxygen. One reason the oxygen was measured was to determine if the fish would have sufficient oxygen to supply them throughout the winter. Months of ice cover reduced the oxygen.

Bob taught me how to add the necessary chemicals and shake the bottles to "fix" the samples. In this below-freezing weather, ice formed around the necks of the bottles forcing one of us to thaw them using of an already numb finger. A sacrifice for the cause of science!

By now Bob's wet clothing had frozen stiffly, giving him comical, stovepipe jean legs and a tree-trunk jacket. Even so, this was more comfortable than wet clothing, and it gave protection from the chilling wind that had increased since we had left home.

Next, Bob lowered a scientific instrument to measure and chart the water temperatures from the surface to the lake's bottom. Then, while he measured and charted the acidity or alkalinity of various water samples, I packed the oxygen sampling bottles into the pack, intending to let my numbed fingers linger over the pocket warmers, which were also placed in the pack to prevent the bottles from freezing. (Although the water bottle samples must not freeze, no one cared about *my* human fingers!) The heat of the pocket warmers proved too much of a torturing contrast, however. Instead, I stuck my unfeeling, clenched hands into wool mittens and paced back and forth doing gymnastic exercises until Bob was ready to continue to the second Surf Lake.

While we hiked to the second lake, the air temperature warmed considerably, making the sampling procedure much more pleasant. We had our lunch at this second lake, enjoying the warmer air. But by the time we headed back to the skiff, a southeasterly wind and rain arrived, drenching us.

When we reached the sheltered lagoon where the boat was anchored, we were surprised to see that the calm waters were now rough and choppy. At the same time the wind began to drive snow into our faces, stinging and blinding us.

"We may not be able to make it home with this rough surf, but we'll give it a try," yelled Bob through the storm as he pulled in the skiff.

The possibility of not getting home that night hadn't even occurred to me. Surely we could make it! But as soon as we entered the open water of Izhut Bay, the icy snow hit like thunderbolts of hail, and the choppy, rearing water pounded our boat. Sitting in the bow, I tightly gripped the board on which I sat to keep from being pitched overboard. The powerful, noisy wind controlled the skiff more than the outboard, giving us the feeling that we were entirely dependent on the will of the wind and surf. Worst of all was the driving snow that made it nearly impossible for Bob to see as he attempted to head the bow into the breakers.

Finally, to my great relief, Bob turned the skiff back toward the lagoon. I was thankful not only for his skill and judgment but also for his foresight of having emergency supplies in the boat. The emergency kit Bob had prepared for winter travels included dried split peas, chocolate chips, bouillon cubes, two cans of roast beef, newspaper, matches coated in paraffin, and first-aid supplies. An additional item—one that Bob claimed was the best invention to come out of WWII—dangled on a red string to prevent it from being lost: a can opener. Besides this box of supplies kept in the boat, whenever we left for any distance we always took the precaution of throwing in a duffel bag that contained sleeping bags, air mattresses, and a tarp. All of this foresight paid off for this night's unexpected camping trip.

After choosing a sheltered, moss-covered camping area with a nearby stream, we began the first project, starting a fire. I was cold and wet and knew I needed to keep moving to stay warm. I followed Bob's example and began breaking off the dead, lower, shaded-out branches on the spruce trees for firewood. However, finding that even the dead branches often take quite a lot of strength to break, I began gathering *shecam* wood instead. *Shecam* is an Aleut word meaning "wood-she-can-carry." In this instance it was the bark that had peeled off decaying stumps. Our leftover lunch paper, the dead, wet wood, and the incentive of a little outboard motor gas resulted in a cheery blaze.

Darkness approached too rapidly for us to enjoy the fire's warmth. Instead, we cut and gathered springy spruce boughs and placed them cut end down to help provide some insulation against the cold ground. Bob tied the tarp over the bed area at a 45-degree angle. Taking turns, we blew up the air mattresses and covered them with what little newspaper we had brought in order to add even more insulation from the frozen ground. At last we could unroll our dry sleeping bags, which were zipped together as one. We could hardly wait to be warm and dry under those covers. But first we needed to eat.

Although the snow squall lessened some, the high winds continued to cry through the spruce tops. We sat in the darkness warming chunks of roast beef over the fire, sipping hot soup, and wishing that the tall, winter-whitened spruce could tell us the history of our protected camping area. As the only inhabitants of Kitoi Bay, we had no worries about others being concerned over our failure to return. More than ever before, we realized the depth of the isolation we had chosen.

Campfire chatting and reminiscing did not last for long. We were eager to remove our wet clothing and gain the comfort of our fluffy, dry bed. Bob retrieved the bundle of extra clothing that we had placed in the fork of the large spruce earlier that morning, and we quickly exchanged our wet clothes for dry. What luxury to lay our tired, stiff, aching muscles in the dry sleeping bag! This luxury was dampened slightly by the pungent aroma of my hair.

Just the day before I had given myself a home-perm to give my hair some curl and thickness more lasting than the nightly pin curls, and now the ammonia from the permanent permeated our little campsite. We both wished, smiling, that I could exchange my hair for a wig of a different fragrance! But the solitude of winter was stronger and wrapped around us as we lay listening to the play of the wind through the trees and the breaking of the waves on the usually placid lagoon. We talked about our remoteness, how odd we were to be here—to have *chosen* to be here—in this wilderness. Wouldn't our parents be surprised if they could see us now.

Were we pursuing our dreams? Were we fulfilling our goals? We talked about being unable to serve or give to other human beings, of our lack of having a community outside ourselves. This lack of obligation to others led to thoughts about our—and especially my—increasing desire for a child. At times my desire was so intense, it brought tears.

Around midnight the soft snow on top of our tarp froze, giving Bob relief from an irritating drip that insisted on falling exactly in his ear and forced him to keep his head covered. The soft air mattresses transformed themselves, flattening in the vital places and retaining hard lumps in other spots. Our muscles tightened into stiff unyielding sticks making turning difficult.

"Why aren't you sleeping, Dearest?" asked Bob.

"Why aren't you?"

"Same reason."

We were seasoned, stateside campers accustomed to camping difficulties, but we could not sleep at all that night. "Just think," Bob announced tiredly as we lay awake, "We were paid for this adventure and even all our equipment is supplied. Most people have to pay an outfitter for a trip in the wilds of Alaska." At least we kept warm and dry, which was far more important than sleep. Listening to the howling winds whip the tree tops, we wondered how many hours or days we would be forced to wait for calm water.

At about five the next morning, Bob got up. "It's light enough to get home, I believe. This will be the calmest period of the day."

It still looked completely dark to me. I could visualize huge and violent black ocean waves. And even though I was stiff and tired of lying down, I could hardly think about getting out of the bedding and putting on sticky, wet clothing.

Bob read my thoughts. "You just stay in bed while I run out with the skiff into the open bay to see if the water has calmed enough for us to make it."

In about thirty minutes Bob returned with an affirmative answer. Dressing in the twenty-degree weather was a stark contrast to my usual before-the-stove routine. During vacationing camping trips, I had always dressed in bed, but wet clothing now made this uninviting. I cringed. Shivering, I finally reluctantly pulled on the clammy, half-frozen garments and attempted to comb my matted hair that still reeked of ammonia. "I hope we make it back safely. I would hate to die and have someone discover me in such a disheveled mess," I told Bob.

"What morbid thoughts! Your appearance would be much worse by the time anyone found us in this uninhabited area," Bob replied, cheerfully, not bothering to add any details or the fact that I might be food for Kodiak brown bear, the largest carnivorous animal in the world.

We had no desire to waste any time for a bouillon-cube breakfast, and hurriedly packed by piling all the camping and lake-sampling gear in the middle of the tarp and gathering it by the four corners. It was so heavy, we had to drag instead of carry it to the boat.

"This will be a terrible jumble of stuff if we have to return and set up camp again," I remarked.

"At least we can build a fire and dry things out," replied the practical Bob glancing at the clear but still-dark sky.

The arrow-straight return trip was cold but successful. Dinky peeked over a stump to welcome us home for he had missed a few free meals. After feeding and fox-chatting with him, our first desire was to jump into a hot bathtub and then put on clean clothes. But not having the bathtub or the hot water, we postponed bathing until the cold water was carried from the creek and slowly heated on the oil cookstove.

While the stove heated both sponge-bathing water and soup, we titrated the water samples taken the previous day. The titration process was used to determine the oxygen content of the lakes. Although the water samples had sat longer than desirable, the results would still be accurate enough to give useful information.

After sponge baths and a snack of soup and hot biscuits made quickly from my homemade biscuit mix, we gratefully crawled into bed. We had passed our initiation test of coping with frontier hazards.

Winter Society

At times the solitude became trying. We were isolated not only from people but also from the refreshing touch of sunshine. For two months the winter sun never shone directly on our home. Sometimes we could see it dancing on distant treetops, but the surrounding hills prevented it from even peeking in our direction. During the shorter days and longer nights of autumn, Bob would often initiate a diversion that would be psychologically beneficial to us both. So I was not too surprised when out of the foreboding, dull skies, Bob asked, "Ruth, how about a date tonight? I'd like to take you out for dinner."

"A dinner date at Kitoi Bay? You do think of everything. Where will you take me, to Nick's Steak House? Regardless, I accept with enthusiasm."

Out would come heels, hose, perfume, and other finery. Being ostracized from the kitchen gave plenty of time to bathe and dress with the utmost care, as I again marveled at Bob's thoughtful creativity.

I knew that changing from fisheries research to culinary research was something Bob thoroughly enjoyed since he could let his creative experimentation flow unchecked in this new laboratory, the kitchen. Although not allowed to pass the kitchen threshold, I could visualize from previous experiences the spice cupboard being utilized to the fullest, one fork being washed over and over instead of a clean one being used for each need, and the kitchen in systematic order. I heard the window open. Bob had made a cooler/freezer that used the weather to keep foods either cold or frozen. To do this he had attached a box outside the kitchen window so that all we needed to do was roll open the aluminum-framed kitchen window and reach in. With the present weather, the box would be a freezer. Was he taking something out or putting something in to chill? I knew that even with no refrigeration and no fresh produce, Bob would make our menu excitingly different.

I could be certain of these images because they were the natural result of my husband's two dominant characteristics: good management (especially through neatness) and variety. Bob was neat to a fault. Although orderly, I was not as precise.

Variety, Bob's second pronounced trait entered into innumerable things: in his writing and reading, in his taking new routes to an often-traveled place, and especially in his desire for variety in my dress and in food. Pulling my nylons on over freshly shaved legs, I chuckled as I reflected on the shock Bob gave one of the bush pilots when he made the statement, "The perfect place to live would be in the country within a few hours drive of the ocean, the mountains, and a metropolitan area."

"Just what are you doing out here then?" inquired the pilot—unable to conceive of anyone without a complete abhorrence of civilization living in such rugged remoteness.

Bob's type of variety is not one that produces restlessness in daily living, but one that adds piquancy to any activity. My husband is one of those rare males who actually enjoy a change of furniture placement. Therefore, I knew our "Mother-Hubbard" cupboards would hardly hinder his inventive creations.

All expectations were met. By soft candlelight on a white linen tablecloth, we dined first on a spicy tomato-clam-nectar cocktail. A chilled appetizing salad, without the aid of a fresh vegetable or fruit, consisted of canned asparagus spears placed in a log-cabin-like square, filled with a tuna fish mixture and topped with grated, hardboiled egg. The main course was veal blanquette coated with brown sauce, accompanied by small buttered potatoes with sprinkles of green parsley flakes; red beets; and two crisp, thin slices of dill pickle. The meal and the date ended with a dessert of chilled orange cream, lovely compliments, and kisses.

Sundays usually brought another welcome change of routine. The change helped us visualize time in normal, weekly divisions rather than in the non-calendric days that came with isolated living. Just as Sunday had always been a special day for us on the Outside so, we agreed, it should also be special during our time at Kitoi Bay. After finishing a late eight o'clock breakfast and making preliminary preparations for dinner, we would dress for our morning worship in regular stateside church attire. Knowing that most people would think such Sunday attire in the wilderness foolish, we did not don white shirt, tie, heels, and hose during the Noisy Season but reserved it for the Silent Season. At times it was tempting to neglect such fanciful dress, but remembering our pledge to each other not to grow seedy from lack of social and cultural contacts, we pushed away the thought of not doing so. After we had dressed, we would notice the freezing floor and drafty windows more, but a new atmosphere of ebullience and contentment seemed to prevail. And more importantly, Sunday clothing gave us a more reverent, worshipful attitude during our private church service, as the foxes curiously cocked their heads to hear "What a Friend We Have in Jesus" sung off-key.

After our Sunday midday meal we would relax with the Sunday paper, *The Portland Oregonian*, which had been saved unopened for nearly a week, sometimes longer. Much coverage was given to the testing of the new polio vaccine. Our isolation made exposure to the polio virus of little concern to us, but Alaska as a whole had had 300 cases, the most in the nation, during the past year. The Halloween slant of the comics was incongruous when finally opening the October papers on Sunday, November 27. Nevertheless, the newspaper was read from front to back. Later, the Thanksgiving newspapers that would arrive mid-December would be entirely appropriate since our hearts were always filled with thanksgiving for God's faithfulness.

A biweekly, evening study period also broke up the week and helped to prevent vegetative living in our rustic surroundings. One of the evenings consisted of a typing class for Bob and a mammal-, bird-, and fish-identification class for me. We each taught a class. Then we would drill each other on spelling and vocabulary building. The week's second study evening consisted of two correspondence courses: "Biblical Geography" and "Great Leaders of the Christian Church." These courses were purchased from the Bible Institute of Los Angeles and even included six examinations. After we felt we had mastered the contents of each group of lessons from the books, we would break the seal and take the examination for that section. The completed sheets would then be mailed to the Correspondence School of BIOLA. They would correct the exams and return them to us. We did not receive credit for the courses but especially appreciated them since neither one of us had taken time for any religion courses during our secular college work.

Other weekday evenings were usually spent reading while the gas Coleman lantern sang a peaceful, background drone. We appreciated having the time to relax in this manner instead of rushing to an evening meeting or program. Perhaps such a calm, uncluttered life was turning us into introverts—or could it be that we already were?

On the occasions when the print blurred before our eyes either from exceptional tiredness, a headache, or just poor lighting, we would turn on the short-wave radio set to be entertained by the odd assortment of messages and chatter. It caused the earth to shrink. One evening we listened to a Guam serviceman call a Seattle ham radio operator. He asked the Seattle ham to phone his parents and inquire how his sick sister was feeling. The Seattle ham could not hear him clearly so a more distant ham in Indiana relayed the message back to Seattle. Soon the serviceman could hear his father's voice speaking from the home phone. During the same evening we listened to a ham in Finland conversing with a Canadian and to a husband on a ship at sea calling his wife through the San Francisco marine operator.

Although used sometimes for entertainment, this small radio set was our lifeline to the outside world. Any time of day or night we supposedly could call Kodiak's Alaska Communications System (A.C.S.), although at times atmospheric conditions made reception too poor for our thirty-watt transmitter to reach even this short distance. Long winter nights gave us better reception. An eight-o'clock morning schedule with Kodiak A.C.S. was reserved for us to relay our weather and to receive any traffic they might be holding for us.

Besides our more-or-less dependable transmitter and receiver that gave us entertainment from ham radio operators and pilot conversations, the Department of Fisheries had purchased for us a conventional battery radio from Montgomery Ward's catalog that had the power of connecting us with the news of the world. We were able to receive a New York City station, an English-speaking communist propaganda broadcast direct from Russia, an English-speaking Tokyo news broadcast, and numerous non-English programs. Not being great radio-program fans (we preferred reading), we used this means of entertainment much less than would an average isolated couple. But how we appreciated the value of this small radio during basketball season! Often we had to squat on the floor only a few inches away and strain our ears to pick up a particular game through the interference of a nearby station. When the neighboring station would switch to soft concert music, then we had the privilege of barely hearing the announcer.

One Saturday night was exceptionally tense. Would our Oregon State College basketball team win their game against the USF Dons and advance to the final four? Would they be able to beat Bill Russell and K.C. Jones? We listened closely as we heard, "Robins with the ball is dribbling down the forecourt; a long bounce to Tex Whiteman; he pivots; shoots a left-hand hook; it's in!" Having sat on the hard bleachers in the student section throughout every Oregon State home game the previous season, Bob and I could picture the actions and personalities of each player. Radio static again blocked our hearing, and then "Toole stole the ball, a quick feed to Halbrook...It's in...Score 57-55." Thirteen seconds remained. An unusual technical foul by K.C. Jones put Reggie Halligan on the line and that brought Oregon State within one point of the Dons. Not only the neighboring radio station but the noise of nearly 12,000 people going crazy completely drowned the announcer's words. Time out. What would be coach Slats Gill's decision for this final play? Halligan fired the ball to Toole. Toole whipped it to wide-open Robins, the shortest man on the court. With a two-handed set shot, Robins let the ball fly straight for the basket. Bob and I held our breath. It was in...No, it hit the back rim, and then the front rim. It bounced out. The Beavers came within a hair of a trip to Kansas City; the Dons were the ones to advance to the final four where they won their first back-to-back NCAA national championship.

Back to reality, we again realized our isolation. Day-to-day routine continued, but it was not necessarily dull. One morning as Bob stomped snow from his boots and stepped through the door, he announced, "Our Kitoi Bay select society has now grown to include Icy and Spicy."

Immediately, I had to make a social call, welcoming them to the community. Icy and Spicy turned out to be two river otters who were doing some spicy tricks and adroit movements in the icy water. With frivolous, graceful rolls, they seemed to be enjoying a game of Follow-the-Leader or Fox-and-Geese as we watched from the bank. The wind was in our favor. Unaware of our spying, one otter climbed onto an exposed rock to sunbathe in a brief moment of winter sunshine. His slender four-foot-long, blackish body reminded us of a small seal. Spicy seemed to sense enemies around so stayed near for only a few seconds; then his sleek body and his tapering tail "kerplunked" into the water. Away swam our two new friends with the special aid of their webbed feet.

Our society grew even more when a new fox began making a cautious appearance on the rare occasions when neither Frosty nor Dinky was present. He was another silver fox with glossy, coal-black, white-tipped fur and startled easily. We named him Muffy, but later found it to be an unsuitable name as he was always too worried and frightened to curl contentedly into a fluffy, muff-like ball, tail curled over his sharp muzzle, as Frosty so often did. (In fact, we found ourselves now calling Frosty "she" just because of her gorgeous fur coat; no other fox was nearly as beautiful.)

We tossed Muffy food to help him overcome some of his wary precautions. Muffy would grab the juicy clam or meat scrap and dash away to enjoy a solitary meal. But Dinky, who kept nearly a constant vigil on the house for the much-coveted food, was present too often for us to become well acquainted with cautious Muffy.

Individual foxes' personalities are as marked as humans'. Early one morning, Dinky issued a mournful whine as he sat on the bank three feet from the kitchen window. Having never heard a fox whine to be fed, we fell for it the first time but after that paid no attention to his childlike fuss, knowing we must not spoil him to the extent that he would expect such behavior to bring food and attention. Dinky seemed to enjoy watching us in our house. Although he was not welcome at Frosty's window, Dinky would wander around the house, peek in the bathroom window to watch us brush our teeth, or climb on top of the gravel bin outside the large front windows to observe us while I cut Bob's hair. For Dinky, we became that new stateside invention, television.

The foxes were unnerved when I did the laundry using the new gasoline-powered Maytag wringer washer that had recently arrived at our station. Now I could eliminate the scrub-board procedure where I rubbed my knuckles raw on socks, flannel sheets, and fish-smelling work clothes. Even turning the hand wringer was better than squeezing and twisting out the water. In contrast to my enjoyment, the foxes did not appreciate the putt-putt roar of the washer when it was running. Because of its gasoline engine, the machine sat outside the station, near Frosty's window, making it more convenient to fill by heating water on the stove and passing it out the window.

Figure 13. Dinky curiously peers through our window.

One morning when both the washing machine and the battery charger motors were running, the foxes took their temporary departure. The swishing, sudsy water in the machine brought to mind the lavender smells of my mother's homemade soap that she used for laundry. But in the wake of the new frontier, I now had both a machine and laundry detergent. While I washed, I wondered how long it would take for the clothes to dry inside the station. But most of all I enjoyed the invigorating pleasure of plunging my hands from nineteen-degree air into the hot, steaming water. Heedlessly, I slopped the suds on the surrounding snow—white on white. Suddenly a puff of suds lit on a moving, reddish object. It was a new fox, which we immediately christened Miss Scarlet. Except for the usual black stockings, she was decidedly different from any of our other fox acquaintances.

With her dense, light-red and pure-white fur, this beauty surely would have won the Miss Universe contest of Foxland.

Feminine Miss Scarlet was a real "go-getter" and had a high-strung, nervous manner of sniffing and bouncing. With her nose she read the signs of Frosty and Dinky's usual presence and sniffed into every cranny where they had been. Her fearlessness of human surroundings amazed us. Bob grabbed the camera and a handful of Friskies. As he began to photograph this well-groomed, curiously tame fox, she oblig-

Figure 14. Fox-watching.

ingly advanced in an attempt to lick the camera lens. In response to my invitation, amicable, socially-elite Miss Scarlet placed all four feet inside the door, snatched a red boot, and dashed out, causing us to do some retrieving. We felt it dangerous to try feeding her from our bare hands so attempted to feed her gravy from a spoon. The courageous guest responded with a bite intended to capture the spoon as well as the gravy. Soon our guest learned the spoon was not edible so resigned herself to licking the contents of each spoonful. Then our spoon-fed fox trotted away with a light, airy grace as if she had a thousand and one areas to sniff-out before attending her bridge party. Miss Scarlet did not return until five months later and then in the same hurried but fearless manner.

Another intruder, quite the opposite of Miss Scarlet, was guttural Mr. Boss. A number of times we were called to the window by Frosty's deep growls and Dinky's yapping barks. Both foxes would be scowling at the brush-covered cliff back of the kitchen. After patient searching, Bob and I finally distinguished two triangular ears and a leonine face of a large cross fox (a hybrid between a silver fox and a red fox) peering from beneath a camouflaging, gnarled, uprooted stump. This occurred nearly twenty times before Mr. Boss came out in the open. Through the many hours of spying, he had learned about the odd fox café Dinky and Frosty had been enjoying. We began tossing Mr. Boss Friskies cubes and apple cores, much to the amazement of our two regular patrons. All this time we could not understand why Frosty and Dinky didn't team up and bark Mr. Boss away as they had always done to other strange foxes.

Daily Mr. Boss approached closer to the house. As we had expected, the showdown finally came. Mr. Boss approached within twenty feet of the house; Dinky and Frosty growled. They were alert and tense. Mr. Boss, lying flat, growled menacingly and kicked his hind legs while pawing the ground furiously with his front paws. A flying leap and he was in the air. Frosty, who was farthest away, darted around the corner of the house in time to make a safe retreat. Although Dinky had a head start, the irate Mr. Boss soon overran him and a battle followed at the creek mouth. This was a biting, catlike fight instead of the usual standing, boxing-like clinch where each tried to make the other lose face by giving ground. Mr. Boss even pulled mouthfuls of hair from Dinky's thick coat.

After this episode, the foxes would immediately run upon receiving their first scent of Mr. Boss. They could no longer rely upon the protectiveness of the house. Even when Mr. Boss wasn't around, each fox would lie facing the hillside instead of the house and constantly search for either the smell or the face of Mr. Boss.

Later *Mrs.* Boss began accompanying her mate. Even her presence sent Frosty and Dinky scurrying away so as not to provoke Mr. Boss's anger. Therefore, a five-step social hierarchy was established among our fox friends, with Mr. Boss holding the top rung, then Mrs. Boss. Next (in the order established by their disputes) came Frosty and then Dinky, although Frosty was kind enough to permit Dinky's presence at the free restaurant so long as Dinky kept away from *her* window. Lowest on the hierarchical social ladder was timid Muffy. Though Mr. and Mrs. Boss seldom appeared, I was sorry that we had ever encouraged their friendship. Such aggressive bullies should not be condoned even in the animal world.

Though the presence of foxes hardly replaced human company, their activities and social life helped ease the loneliness we felt at times through the long Silent Season. Foxes had become our friends.

Enjoying Rather Than Wishing

Soon December 25 blazed red on the calendar. Various emotions tugged at our hearts as Christmas approached. What would this holiday be like in the wilderness of Alaska? Because I had always attended the beloved Christmas celebration with my maternal grandparents, William and Mary Marr, I knew that Bob was secretly apprehensive. The Marr gathering always included their five children with their spouses, plus many grandchildren. Bob, married to the oldest granddaughter, had spent the last five Christmases with this enlarged family, so he knew where my thoughts would be and what I would be remembering. Not one of the Marr grandchildren had ever missed this family Christmas, so I was also contemplating the transition my Forest Grove, Oregon, grandparents would be making.

Memories tumbled through my mind. Sugarplum visions danced in my head even though I attempted to submerge them. Bob worried as day after day I pictured and verbalized scenes from stateside Decembers. Before Christmas day itself, my Aunt Thelma Sellers would go to her parents' home to make the fudge and divinity. It was difficult to determine which one was better: the smooth fudge with nuts or the creamy light divinity. Each was made to perfection, because Aunt Thelma knew exactly when the syrup had reached the point when it should be folded into the egg whites for the divinity and exactly how much each candy should be beaten to achieve the perfect stiffness before it was poured onto the buttered pans. Later it was cut into generous squares and placed on platters.

As a child, I excitedly looked forward all year to Christmas, especially the gifts in the morning. Everyone, except the grandchildren, gave presents to everyone else. Perhaps I would receive a book from Aunt Wilma and Uncle Albert, an autograph album from Aunt Marjorie and Uncle Eugene, a game from Aunt Thelma and Uncle Charlie, mittens from Uncle Ernie and Aunt Myrtle. But the nicest gift would come from Grandpa and Grandma. It might be a fountain pen set or perhaps a necklace.

After the excitement of the gift exchange, the women would finish preparing the holiday meal while the men visited about the year's agricultural crops, and the children laughed as they played with their new presents and each other. Next would come the holiday feast. Grandpa always insisted that everyone, even the youngest grandchild, be seated at the same table. Thus, the lengthy table, composed of several small tables placed end-to-end under the white tablecloths, stretched from the dining room, through the entry and into the living room. Usually, we would have place cards identifying the seating arrangement. Grandpa, an Illinois-born Scotsman, always sat at the living-room end and Grandma sat at the dining-room end, closest to the kitchen. Before Bob entered the family, no prayer of thanks had been given. In the years after Bob joined the clan, Grandpa would ask him to say grace.

Each plate held a cocktail glass of red cranberry juice over bits of minced pineapple and bananas. We daintily ate the pieces of fruit from the glasses. It was simple, but, oh, so elegant when eaten with little demitasse spoons and drunk from the small crystal glasses while enjoying the happy faces and attractive table decorations.

Next, would come huge bowls of creamy mashed potatoes, a heavy platter of turkey, giblet gravy, bread stuffing, cranberries, vegetables, candied yams, twenty-four-hour salad, Christmas cranberry-celery salad, and piping hot homemade rolls with butter and jellies. Dessert was always suet pudding covered in brandy sauce, a tradition and recipe brought from Scotland by my great grandparents.

Bob was fearful that missing this large celebration that I had always cherished would make Christmas in the wilderness very lonely for me. What he did not realize was that it was exactly these glorious memories that would make Christmas this year and in future years happy ones as well.

Even so, I peeked inside myself to wonder what it would be like to open presents for only two. No shopping among the pushing throngs in the colorfully decorated stores. No Sunday school Christmas program to attend. No carolers. We were not even sending packages because they had been taken care of early in November. Our gifts to others had been ordered through stateside stores that had been asked to wrap and mail them directly to the receiver. We did not have the pleasure of even seeing them! Yes, the holiday season would be different this year, but we were determined that it would be joyful. Most importantly, the day would be celebrated with emphasis on the true meaning of Christmas. We had each other, and we had beloved past memories.

As we prepared for this event, and contemplated our Christmas menu, we were puzzled by a meat problem. Turkey for two was crossed off as being too expensive. (The Kodiak prices were 95 cents a pound compared to stateside prices of 45 cents or less per pound.) Although it would have been fitting, we did not want mallard duck. Irregular and undependable grocery deliveries had forced us to eat many duck dinners in recent weeks.

"Let's choose a meat that we're really hungry for, even though it isn't considered a traditional Christmas meat," I suggested. We each immediately knew the type of meat I had in mind. With only a laugh passing between us, I wrote "two T-bone steaks" on the grocery list. It was only December 14, but we knew we needed to order our Christmas groceries without delay in case weather delayed the supply plane service.

Four days later one of Kodiak Airway's Widgeons came swooping overhead. Bob had radioed them early that morning to tell them we were frozen in completely, even the Winter Beach, so it would be senseless for them to make the flight. Thus, we were greatly surprised to see the plane circling overhead.

"They probably decided to make the attempt anyway in hopes the ice had lessened," I explained, more to myself than to Bob. It had been two weeks since we had had a supply plane.

The sea was calm, so the pilot landed beyond the ice that was over a mile out the bay. There was no place to taxi ashore because of the jutting cliff-lined shoreline, and, as the pilot soon discovered, the ice was too thick to break through to our beach.

Bob had turned on the radio receiver and transmitter some time before. As soon as the Widgeon was again in the air, the pilot's voice boomed through the receiver, "Grumman 198 to KXA97, Kitoi Bay. Grumman 198 to KXA97, Kitoi Bay, listening on 2512."

"KXA97, Kitoi Bay to Grumman 198. Sorry you couldn't make it. Nice try anyway. Thanks."

'Grumman 198 to Kitoi Bay. Couldn't break through the ice. How's the condition of the lake?"

"Kitoi Bay to 198. Big Kitoi Lake has about twelve inches of ice and two to three inches of snow. Should be in landing condition. No drifts."

"Grumman 198 to Kitoi Bay. Roger, Bob, will give it a try."

"Who is the pilot?" I questioned as Bob hung up the mike.

"I couldn't recognize the voice, could you?"

The only pilot in the area we had known to land with wheels on a frozen lake was Bill Harvey. Such landings on deep, solid ice could be ideal, but if there were tricky air currents or if the snow was either too deep or in drifts, it could be hazardous. Also, blowing snow makes it difficult to tell a lake's ice-snow surface. One time Bill had been circling Big Kitoi Lake and had called our transmitter: "Grumman 198 to Kitoi Bay. Bob, there is enough blowing snow on the lake that it is difficult to tell the lake's ice-snow surface. Could you hurry to the lake and drag a couple green spruce boughs out on the ice to give me a depth perception?" It took more circling time for Bill, but Bob dashed the one-half mile to the lake with his small ax. Later he mentioned that it was easy to get the spruce limbs because they overhung the ice. As a result, the ice was a platform to stand on to chop off the limbs and a skid road to slide the limbs a few hundred feet out into the lake.

Figure 15. Winter mail delivery on Big Kitoi Lake.

With concern for the bush pilot's safety, we now watched him circle twice over the Big Kitoi Lake area and then dip out of sight behind the trees. Since neither of us could identify the voice, I reasoned that it must be a less-experienced pilot.

"I hope you haven't given him a more favorable report on the lake's condition than what it actually is," I muttered as we both hurriedly pulled on our boots, jackets, and gloves.

"Grumman 198 to KXA97, Kitoi Bay," came the rather familiar but unrecognized voice over the receiver that we had left on. "Grumman 198 to KXA97, Kitoi Bay. Have landed on the lake. Where does your trail come out?"

"Kitoi Bay to Grumman 198. In the small cove on the east side. We'll be right up."

"Roger, Roger."

Our bush pilots had extraordinary skill and steel nerves. When we reached the lake, we found the Widgeon in the cove with the pilot, Al Cratty, keeping warm by stamping his feet while he scraped ice off the plane's flaps. Dark-haired Al was young, good-looking, energetic, and perhaps at this moment jubilant from successfully putting his craft down on the frozen lake. The brightly painted plane that had always seemed large on our small station beach looked strangely tiny on the expanse of Big Kitoi Lake. Then we noticed a huge pile of freight piled outside the plane. Surely it could not be all for us! But it was. Two ships, the *Alaska Steamship* from the States and the *Expansion* from Seward, had both come into Kodiak during the two weeks since we had last had mail. The pile included two full U.S. mail sacks, a bushel box of apples with **DO NOT FREEZE** plastered on all sides from my parents, three boxes of groceries, two boxes of equipment, and a heavy 25-hp outboard motor that had previously been sent out for major repairs. No wonder the pilot wanted to land instead of taking the heavy freight back into Kodiak.

After quick greetings, Al hurriedly jumped into the cockpit and taxied away. He had the concern of getting into the air soon enough to clear the tree tops because the hull of the Widgeon had accumulated much ice from the previous week of water landings with no thawing weather to melt any of it. This made the plane extra heavy, but he made it. Clearing the snowy trees, he circled back overhead with a friendly dip of the wings as a parting farewell before winging his way upward and over the soundless, spruce-covered mountains. Later, one of the other pilots mentioned that this had been Al's first landing with wheels on ice even though he had flown for Kodiak Airways for a number of years.

Then came the fun of carrying the planeload of freight down the creek trail to the station. Although this was not simple, it was much easier than packing it on the longer, steeper, cliff-side trail from Winter Beach. On our first trip, I took a bag of mail, and Bob carried the second mailbag along with a box.

"How will you get the outboard down, Honey?"

"I think I'll bring the packboard up from this trip," Bob replied.

Often I dragged the U.S. mail sack behind as a toboggan. Of course, I realize we pay enough taxes without abusing Uncle Sam's property, but under the same icy, snowy circumstances I believe anyone would have done the same. However, this day, for our second trip, after Bob tied the outboard motor on his packboard, I followed with the lightest two boxes. Their weight increased with each step until I decided to leave the heavier one beside the trail until the next trip.

Dinky greeted us when we reached the station. But after unloading and catching our breath for the third trip, we noticed that Dinky was not around.

"Which box did you leave beside the trail?" Bob suddenly asked.

"I didn't notice. It must have been the meat box since it isn't here."

"We'd better hurry back."

"Surely Dinky wouldn't find the meat box. He was here just a second ago. The meat is frozen, so he surely couldn't smell it!" I said, trying to convince Bob and myself of its logic.

As we approached the crest of the first rise, white butcher paper flitted in the breeze. Fifteen feet from the paper and the torn box stood Dinky gobbling up, not the hamburger nor the wieners, but the T-bone steaks that we had purchased for Christmas dinner.

"Dinky, how could you?" I screamed running to chase him away.

He dropped the remaining half of a steak and backed up a few feet, surveying our disgust with a puzzled expression.

After our final trip of carrying in the freight, we found Dinky sitting at the kitchen window begging for a handout! His eyes pleaded with the "haven't-had-a-bite-to-eat-for-weeks" expression. Our cold heartstrings were not pulled in the usual sympathetic manner, so Dinky, even though he cast forth continual eye messages, had to spend the rest of the day outside a restaurant that had

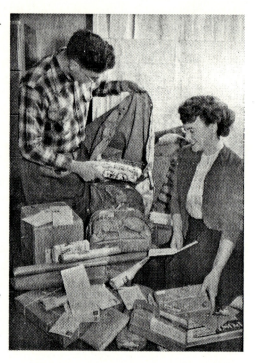

Figure 16. Christmas mail brought news and excitement.

a CLOSED sign posted on the window. He waited, but he waited in vain. It was not until the following day that he had been forgiven sufficiently for us to feed him the remainder of his mauled piece of T-bone in one-inch-cubed bites. Foxes do not chew. They gulp and swallow their food whole, but at least the one-inch pieces made Dinky expend some effort and slowed his eating process somewhat.

Opening the two U.S. mail sacks of packages and letters was an exhausting as well as exhilarating undertaking. The exhaustion came not because of the effort involved but because it was so excitingly different from the usual calm routine in our slow-moving world. To receive so much news at once was overwhelming. To their credit, parents and relatives were not urging us to come back to the Outside. It was just that we could not absorb so much news at once. Thus, we were charged with euphoria. All types of new thoughts ran through our minds. Dave has enlisted in the Army. Mrs. Gardener's lovable kitty has died. The second set of twins, named Dan and Debbie, has been born in the Vincent family. The fire insurance policy on our stored car was overdue. The Castles have purchased a new house. The Christmas-tree rain (icicles, but we webfoot Oregonians call it "rain") ordered five weeks ago did not arrive. Altogether, a seemingly endless array of bits of news over-loaded our minds.

Living in remote quietness made us susceptible to the smallest excitement. Bob and I agreed that we should save our Christmas cards to open throughout the week, but then we immediately opened every one. Every card, every letter, every package was opened except the Christmas presents. The result was another sleepless night, making the mattress feel as if it were stuffed with spruce cones and the pillows with Post Grape-Nuts.

Months before, knowing that snow cover would probably camouflage a Christmas tree's true virtues, we had chosen a beautiful Sitka spruce covered with many cones. It was growing in the open so it was perfectly symmetrical. Choosing ahead of time had been a wise step since a recent snowfall dressed the ground and spruce in an eighteen-inch white coverlet. Now that the time had arrived to cut the tree, we wished we had chosen one closer to the station. After spending the last week glorying in the angelic touch that the pure white snow gave Kitoi Bay and gloating over not having to worry about roads being closed to traffic, the milkman not arriving, or the electric lines breaking, we realized that even in remoteness snow was not all beauty. Our chosen tree was two miles away via land, ice, and water. A boat had to be used, and our seventeen-foot skiff was not near the house. It had been moved to Winter Beach because southeasterly winds usually kept that arm of the bay free from ice. Even there, the skiff had to be removed from the water and put back into the water for each use to prevent ice damage. I am sure Bob would have been glad to exchange our perfect tree for a less desirable, closer one, but knowing that I would be disappointed, he only hintingly suggested it.

The first part of our Christmas tree excursion—tramping to Winter Beach through the continuing feathery swirl of falling snow and viewing the snow-laden scenery—was loads of fun; the second part was miserable. Bob managed to move the skiff down the board chute into the icy water. But after dipping out the snow and then carefully paddling through the ice to the open water, he could not start the cold motor. Pull after pull of the starter rope would not change the mind of the temperamental outboard. By then, I also was ready to choose a tree closer to home, but Bob had decided he might as well make the motor startable then as some other time.

After thirty minutes of pulling and tinkering, Bob managed to get the motor running. Sitting during this time had completely benumbed me so I was relieved to reach land and race up and down the snowy, soft-sand beach to get warm.

Our chosen tree looked so artistic both in its setting and with its snow-trimmed boughs that we hated to cut it. But, of course, we did. A few minutes later with the tree plus some extra, cone-covered boughs for wreaths, we started home. The most difficult part of the homeward journey was cranking the boat out of the water and up its inclined chute with a winch. It seemed like we were always using a winch, wheels, block and tackle, inclined planes, ropes, pullies, levers, or trees to meet needs during the Quiet Season when we had only a total of four hands and four feet. Only by timing our leaving and our returning with the tides made getting the skiff in and out of the water even possible.

Next Bob, ever mindful of treating the tree gently to retain the cones, had the job of dragging the large tree up a two-hundred-foot precipice to the trail. Fortunately, the snow cover gave the tree some protection.

"What sentimental mortals we humans are!" Bob remarked while carrying our "perfect" tree the final icy mile to our Kitoi Bay Research Station.

Back at the station we truly realized the tree's size. The best word to describe it—huge! With much additional cutting and shoving, we finally managed to get it into our unusable (no water) shower, which provided a good place for the snow and ice to drip from the tree since it would have stayed frozen had we left it outside.

Decorations, we decided, should be in keeping with our rustic surroundings, especially since the ordered Christmas rain had not arrived. Even with the cutting, dragging, and shoving, the tree still looked perky. The rightly placed branches with their cones were pretty enough without decorations, but we added the standard decoration of our childhood, strings of popcorn. Additional cones were hung from the branch tips; the larger ones hanging in their natural state; the smaller ones wrapped in aluminum foil to add sparkle. Improvising had become second nature to both of us whether it was something inside the house or figuring out how to move a heavy boat onto shore well above water line. The same kind of improvisation helped us as we decorated the tree. A starfish, dried and liberally sprinkled with gold glitter rubbed from Christmas cards and glued on with clear fingernail polish, adorned the top.

Our winter door was the back door on the wind-sheltered side of the house. Because our front door was boarded against the wintry winds, we placed our cone-laden wreath with its cheerful, red ribbon (made from a piece of yardage material since it was impossible to run to the corner drugstore for red ribbon) on the front door facing inside between the glass door pane and the plywood outside board. Even though the wreath was only visible from the inside, it did not matter because our animal neighbors were uninterested in the traditions and trappings of Christmas. Still it did not show off to its greatest advantage against the plywood. A cheerful finishing touch was added by removing the wreath and painting the board white. This cool compartment kept the wreath in its fresh state throughout the holidays.

A candle centerpiece, a Hallmark-card nativity scene sent by Bob's family, and Christmas-card-bordered windows completed the decorations for our quiet Christmas season of solitude.

Christmas morning came. Secretly, we had both been rather dubiously anxious for Christmas to arrive because, even though we had so many blessings, it could be a lonesome day. But the sunlight dancing in the treetops across the bay was a good omen. The Christmas sky was wrapped in blue and decorated solely by two white, puffy seal-shaped clouds. The sight enticed us to look for vantage points for viewing the sky and the world around us. This was possible only by hiking. The hike in the vigorous air gave us the opportunity to stand in refreshing sunshine. It also stimulated Christmas-dinner appetites and helped us to refrain from package-opening until later in the day. Each of us has always felt that the best should be saved for last, whether it is eating the heart of a watermelon or opening Christmas presents.

After returning from the hike, I prepared Christmas dinner, substituting a canned ham for our filched T-bones, while Bob prepared the ice cream. Having no refrigerator or ice cream freezer required the ice cream to be frozen in a more primitive manner. Bob placed the ice cream mixture in a shortening pail, put the pail inside a larger bucket, and packed the area between the two containers with snow and salt. He then set this homemade freezer outside in the sub-freezing temperature and in a mound of snow. An occasional stirring was all it required.

The aroma of Christmas dinner must have been exceptionally tantalizing because Dinky decided he must make a closer investigation. While we ate dinner, our lovable Christmas dinner thief stood with his back legs on a recently formed snow ledge outside the window and stretched up, placing his front paws on the sill and pressing his little nose flat against the pane. He looked astonished when he found that that he could not push his head through the glass pane.

Dinky had little patience to wait for his share at the end of dinner. He climbed on top of a sand bin, five feet from the window, and acted as if he were going to leap through the window. Afraid that a leap would break the window, we clapped hands, yelled, and stamped feet whenever he was poised and ready to jump. His observation of our entertaining buffoonery was first one of curious interest but soon declined to complete disregard of the actors who continued to distract his thoughts and plan. He jumped. Fortunately, the windowpane did not break; yet it was a strong-enough blow to make another attempt undesirable.

Before going outside to get our dessert, we gave Dinky a bone to enjoy. He eagerly licked it while he watched Bob remove the snow from the bucket, take out the pail, and dish the ice cream.

Foxes, we found, are curious animals. The remainder of the ice cream had been repacked and we were enjoying our favorite dessert when we suddenly became aware of Dinky's absence. Going to the backdoor, we found Dinky had laid aside his bone, tipped over the bucket, pawed out the snow, and was trying to eat the cold ice cream. Not only had he been curious, but he showed a certain intelligence. It was worth the loss of our ice cream just to watch his frightened antics as he experimented with the rolling pail. Apprehensively, he would circle the mistrusted object, paw the ground, and approach the strange object hesitantly, only to be driven back by an unexpected roll from the pail. It took fifteen minutes for him

Figure 17. Dinky eyes the ice cream freezer.

to develop sufficient prowess to paw out a bite. Putting his head inside the pail was evidently asking for it to be bitten off. He nervously pawed out a bite at a time, acting amazed that the substance could be of such a soft consistency and so cold but yet so delicious to eat.

By the time we had finished watching Dinky's amusing performance and had the dishes finished, it was 3 p.m., and darkness had arrived. Instead of lighting the gas lanterns, we opened our presents by candlelight. A long time was spent with each gift, lengthening the pleasure. Flower seeds, film, thick potholders, shampoo, hand cream, miniature game of Animal Rummy, baby doll pajamas, fruit cake, walnut meats, shirt, handkerchiefs, argyles, a metal colored-slide box, books, candy, an Eversharp fountain pen—each gift was appreciated. I had given Bob a belt with his initial, and he had given me a manicure set and a "perfume typer," which was supposed to determine the type I should wear.

Truly, our day had been delightful. Because we had each tried to be exceptionally jubilant so the other would not miss a more traditional Christmas, we had made ourselves merry in the effort. Instead of wishing for what might have been, we enjoyed what we had. Why should a person wish his life away when surrounded by innumerable blessings? Someone else in some other place was likely wishing for the beauty, the time, and the quietness that we had. Truly, contentment or dissatisfaction is usually all in one's point of view.

Two days after Christmas a southeasterly wind warmed the temperature to above freezing, causing the ice to break. After much grinding and groaning from the break-up, the winds blew the ice tabletops seaward to be further melted by the surf. Fortunately, during this brief period of open water, our mail plane arrived, and Gil Jarvela, the pilot, even managed the time to stop for coffee. So, the holiday season did not pass completely without guests. The decorations, the fruitcake, and the Santa Claus napkins were not completely unshared. Despite isolation and the theft of our anticipated dinner, Christmas had been memorable.

Emergencies

Not long after Christmas, the darkest time of the winter, our one and only link with the outside world was lost. The radio transmitter's weak batteries did not have enough power to run it. Bob attempted to recharge them only to have the charger fail. He hoped to repair it, but found that his usual ingenious ability to substitute could not replace the needed parts. Having no means of contacting another human made us extremely uneasy. Also, we more forcefully realized that should I become pregnant (which we sincerely hoped might happen), this island living would not only be unsuitable but dangerous—not necessarily for me during pregnancy, but for the birth and the numerous medical emergencies that might arise in caring for an infant. Yes, if years of longing resulted in such exciting news, we would likely have to leave Kitoi Bay.

Figure 18. Bob running the skiff.

Our general policy about potential emergencies was not to worry about them but, nevertheless, to be prepared. Preparation included a food cache outside the station in case it should burn, an emergency kit in the boat, and small cans of fuel oil at the lakes that we visited most frequently. During our wintertime field hiking, Bob often drilled me on simple safety precautions. "Do you remember where the fuel oil is located at this lake?" he would ask. I would respond by pushing away the snow at the base of a large stump or tree and uncover the cans. Because of Bob's consistency in placing the cans, I am almost certain I could go to a strange lake and find the hidden cans even if Bob had not told me their location. If one of us should fall through the ice, break a leg, or have some other accident during the cold weather, the other would quickly start a fire. To help me operate the outboard, Bob would suddenly idle down and stop the motor on a return trip, saying, "Sorry, I can't take the skiff in so you'll have to." With my strengthening muscles, I would pull the starter rope and proceed. Since I had learned to drive a stick-shift at age fifteen, I related the shifting and choking procedures to this and soon became capable of handling the boat and motor.

Another safety precaution was our rule that we would never kid each other about seeing a bear. Once, Bob was taking the water temperature a few feet upstream from me and suddenly gave a leap and a running charge down the stream. I immediately fled for the nearest climbable tree. Later I sheepishly found out that Bob had merely been chasing his pencil accidentally dropped into the swift current.

But these emergency precautions did little to lessen the anxiety of losing our short-wave radio. The uneasy feeling was somewhat mitigated for a few days when we switched to inside work—tiling the floor—instead of the usual outdoor work.

Two exhausting twelve-hour days were spent laying those little tile squares that are advertised as being so simple to install. The asbestos-tile advertisement with the man dressed in a white shirt with a striking tie and an immaculate lady with high heels daintily placing each square in place completely misrepresented the true picture! Even so, the advertisement succeeded in enticing us. After this "wonderful, economical, long-wearing, and easy-to-install-on-any-floor" tile with its "lasting beauty" had been installed, we had gained a new understanding of do-it-yourself jobs.

Directions emphasized that the tile would not be satisfactory unless wood floors were completely free of dirt, had an underneath subfloor, and were made of boards less than three-and-one-half inches wide. We proceeded even though the station had no subfloor and a year's grime had been ground into the thin, 4x8-foot plywood sheets used for the flooring.

The first quarter of the main room contained no puzzling corners, interfering closets, or door casings with molding strips, so we progressed well. By the time we began the second quarter, we started to worry that we weren't spreading enough of the black cement (glue) on the floor. Because of this doubt, we spread the second fourth a little thicker. The cement, better named tar, oozed up between the tiles. A little of this sticky goop on clothing or hands immediately adhered to the laid tile and was removable only by steel wool and elbow-grease. We had to wash our gummed hands frequently and remove any piece of clothing that became contaminated with the messy, black "stickum." Off would come the left shoe; off would come the right. Shoes, socks, even jeans were slung to the untiled side of the room as we frantically lay the troublesome squares and meticulously measured and cut border tiles and the odd shapes needed to fit around the various obstructions. Unsuccessfully, we tried to wipe the excess cement off with cloths before it coated our few remaining garments. We both thought of Brer Rabbit's tangle with Tar Baby. What spectacles we would have made for a truthful tile advertisement: two nearly bare, chilled tar babies!

Though the outside temperatures were below freezing, we had to disconnect the oil line and move the stove to tile the area underneath the stove. Regarding coldness, the directions read: "The temperature of the asphalt tile itself should be at least 72 degrees Fahrenheit, preferably 80 degrees Fahrenheit. Under no circumstances apply the tile if colder than room temperature because condensation forming on the under sides of this tile will tend to break down the adhesive qualities of the cement."

Despite the instructions, there was no way to keep the house warm during the under-stove operation. Since most of the tile-laying rules had already been broken, we didn't care about any effect the coldness might have on these little squares. Our only concern was the chilled working environment. We covered our goose bumps with several layers of non-cement-spotted clothes before beginning the stove section. Chattering teeth provided background drumbeats for the work. Instead of our former strip act, the winter air caused us to don extra layers, resulting in a massive laundry of gluey garments.

During the second afternoon of tile laying, the ice in the bay began to break into table-sized, jigsaw chunks that ground against each other in an effort for freedom. Bob's thoughts turned to the skiff. It was kept now on a running line at a cove that froze less often than the one in front of the house. After heavy winds or after times when the cove froze and broke up, Bob hiked the mile to check on the boat.

"I'm going to make sure the skiff is all right at the Winter Beach, Dear. How about coming along?"

I sighed. "I suppose I should go to get my mind away from these maroon blocks, but I'm just too exhausted to get my outdoor gear on and hike that far. Maybe I can measure and mark the remaining border tile while you're gone."

Bob headed off. By dusk, he still had not returned. Suddenly, I remembered the dead radio batteries, a thought that had escaped because of our tile project. With true wifely imagination, I could visualize all sorts of things that might have happened to him. My next thoughts: no possible means of communication and no neighbors within thirty, snowy, bear-trail miles. The complete meaning of isolation hammered in my head.

Logically, I knew that I had probably not allowed enough time for Bob's return. But by impulse I felt that I should see if something had happened to him. Hurrying into layers of outdoor clothing and grabbing the smelling salts from the first-aid kit, I dashed out of the house. How foolish, I thought; undoubtedly, I would probably meet him after a turn or two on the trail. Yet I could not help remembering how Bob had fainted from shock when he sprained his ankle just a few feet from the house the previous October. If he laughed at me for bringing smelling salts, I would remind him how valuable they had been at that time.

After what seemed like an hour, but in reality was only a fleeting fifteen minutes, I still had not met Bob on his return trip. Just a few more yards of following his size-twelve boot tracks and I would be able to look out from the cliff and view the cove where we kept the skiff. What would I see?

No boat floated in its customary cove; no sign appeared of Bob lying with a sprained ankle or broken leg. Swirling, floating ice blocks occasionally bumped elbows. The cry of a circling seagull caused me to lift my eyes seaward. There was the skiff! But it was headed out of the bay, along with the eight-inch-thick ice floes. And just as suddenly I saw Bob. My relief turned to fright as I watched him jumping like an otter from ice raft to ice raft in an attempt to reach the runaway boat. One more jump and he was in the skiff.

I climbed down the cliff onto the beach. After examining the ice-cut running line, I waited for Bob to paddle and push ashore.

In answer to my frightened expression, Bob replied, "If I had fallen in, I could have swum out."

"In this 30 degree water, I'm doubtful," I shakily replied.

"I took my two jackets off and unbuckled my boots purposely for that reason. Besides, didn't you notice that I was careful to jump only onto the center of each ice block? Another fifteen minutes and I'm afraid our skiff and motor would have been floating across the North Pacific Ocean."

I was weak with relief that Bob was safe and that we had not lost such expensive equipment. I was not the only one who was fatigued. Our one-mile return in the near darkness took us thirty minutes. When we returned to the cabin, we voted unanimously to abandon the few remaining tiles until the next morning.

Later when visitors or workers commented about the lovely job of tile laying, mental pictures of two sticky tar babies, numbing cold, and Bob jumping over ice blocks flitted through our minds as we would reply, "It was some fun!"

During the rest of our three weeks without radio contact, we were free from emergencies of any serious nature.

One full year later Bob developed right-side abdominal pain and was nauseated. Could it be mild appendicitis? The unusual pain persisted for over two weeks without becoming either worse or better. Because of the expense of transportation and medical consultation, we had not yet made a visit to a doctor. For the last five years, Bob had had bouts of extreme headaches that lasted a week or more at a time. Doctors could not determine the cause and ruled out brain tumor. They could possibly have been from a WWII service injury of a dislocated shoulder and subsequent surgery or from an inherited condition from his mother who had been frequently hospitalized from the same type of headache. These headaches were severe, worse than migraines, and had forced Bob to stop his Oregon State College undergraduate studies for two years. But he managed to return and graduated with a good grade point. Headache bouts continued at Kitoi as did back pains that occurred periodically. Bob was not one to talk about or give into ill health. Yet now we were faced with a pain that could possibly be life threatening. Even so, my campaign talks urging him to let me pack in the groceries and my propaganda speeches on "The Dangers of Strenuous Hiking in Relation to Side-Pains" were to no avail.

It was almost a relief when Bob began feeling worse. This solved our quandary of whether or not he should go into Kodiak to see Dr. Johnson. Bob disliked leaving me alone, but it seemed there was no choice. His work could not simply be abandoned or he would lose all the data and results related to raising salmon eggs in hatchery water, plus there was our obligation to make the daily report of minimum-maximum temperature, precipitation, wind direction, visibility and ceiling to the U.S. Weather Bureau. At this time our radio set and generator seemed to be working reliably, so I did not dread staying alone at the station. However, I was fearful Bob would not reach Kodiak in time.

Fortunately, the weather was clear and calm when Bob used the short-wave radio to call for help. Kodiak Airways responded to the call with, "We'll shoot a plane right out if it's urgent, Bob; otherwise we'll come by in two hours on the way back from another stop."

Although I was not nearly as positive, Bob assured them that there was no rush. Two hurdles had been conquered: radio reception was good so we had been able to contact Kodiak Airways, and the weather was flyable. But a third difficulty was finding a landing place for the plane because even the Winter Beach area had been frozen for the last three days. Bob's increased pain and nausea was not conducive to a long hike. During the next two hours I hiked a total of five miles checking on possible landing spots. Big Kitoi Lake, which would have been ideal because it was only a half-mile from the house, was packed with hardened snow, but the snow was in drifts making it dangerous for a wheel landing. (None of the Kodiak Airways' planes had skis.) Although the Winter Beach had been checked the previous afternoon, I rechecked it and miraculously found that the ice had broken out and been carried seaward by the tide, making it possible for a plane to taxi in on the far edge of the rocky beach.

After radioing this information to Kodiak Airways, we set out at a slow walk for the Winter Beach. We heard the plane zoom overhead when we were only halfway there. Urging Bob to continue his slow pace, I rushed ahead with Bob's overnight case lest the pilot think he had misunderstood our appointed landing area and leave for a more distant beach. Arriving at the cliff that fronted a two-hundred-foot drop to the beach, I was tempted to sit down and use my former chute that Bob had outlawed as too dangerous. But remembering my promise, I refrained and instead grasped at the thorny devil's club stalks to make a record-breaking descent. Standing was not always possible, so the end result was a rip in the back of my jeans and an opened suitcase.

Such a crashing descent notified the pilot of my arrival. He understandingly helped me pick up the strewn contents of Bob's small overnight case while I attempted to keep my eight-inch rip from being noticed.

With Bob's arrival, a tender departing kiss, and the roar of a motor, the departure became real. The bush pilot had come in a little one-engine Piper Cub. This one-passenger craft looked unusually fragile—almost like a model made from toothpicks—as it lifted into the sky and floated close above treetops. I broke the surrounding stillness as I importuned aloud the Lord's safe keeping and gave grateful thanks for the favorable conditions that had made Bob's departure possible.

Knowing that Bob would soon be in the care of a physician lifted my worry load, actually buoying my spirits on the return hike to the station. I was not apprehensive about being alone amid the beauty and solitude of the wilderness. A fox sparrow, one of our few "Dickey" birds, fluttered to a high spruce branch; a small creek gurgled under its ice cover as I crossed. Otherwise, the woods voiced only stillness, an absolute silence penetrating deeply enough to be actually ear splitting.

As I entered the warm but rather cheerless house, the floors creaked, a gratifying silence-breaker and the first of many odd sounds that I had not noticed before. I felt like shouting, "Where is everybody?"

Then as if in answer, I found Frosty and Dinky outside the kitchen windows, a welcome sight indeed. No doubt it was purely imaginary, but their usual fierce-looking expressions on that day appeared sympathetic. Later I decided that their sad faces were probably pure chicanery designed to gain greater food donations. They departed the next day instead of staying to keep me company in my aloneness. Their desertion was understandable because my piece-meal eating and other concerns resulted in a temporary closure of the fox-cafeteria.

The peaceful surroundings unexpectedly became a lonesome land. The house, a product of civilization, seemed incongruous sitting in these woods. I looked on the landscape and environment with an unconscious edge of fear. Even the furnishings inside the house took on a strange and unfamiliar look. Thinking of being alone, absolutely detached from the human race, and in this wilderness caused me to laugh out loud. Then I cringed as the noise of the laughter pierced the silence. During these hours I wondered if the surrounding territory was worth even the two cents per acre the United States had paid Russia in 1867.

The atmosphere was so quiet that even the sound of rustling paper was soothing. In contrast, the radio seemed to be a menace rather than a welcome quiet-breaker. Perhaps unconsciously I wanted to keep my ears tuned for any unaccountable sounds. Reading was helpful, although I dared not read a novel or mystery only to become involved in a second unreal atmosphere. Work seemed to be the best drug for shaking myself away from the unnerving surroundings and back to normalcy. The easily neglected woodwork was vigorously scrubbed—enough scrubbing to eliminate the hidden dust above door and window frames.

Four o'clock finally arrived. This was the magic hour that Bob had said he would radio. Hoping he would be able to keep the scheduled appointment, I turned on both the receiver and transmitter and patiently waited while ALB99 called the various outlying villages that were on the 4 p.m. schedule. We were not usually on this schedule, but I knew Kitoi Bay would be called if Bob had seen the doctor by then.

"KXA97, Kitoi Bay," came the expected signal.

Our government-surplus, thirty-watt transmitter chose this time to have one of its frequent low periods, probably a result of having it on for thirty minutes waiting for ALB99 to finish the regular 4 p.m. schedule. Although I answered, ALB99 continued to call, "KXA97, KXA97, Kitoi Bay. Do you read?"

I heard Bob's voice tell the operator, "We're going to get a new radio out there some day." It was a thrill to at least hear his familiar voice.

The operator then gave me a message in the blind. "Results: mild appendicitis, will stay overnight, see the doctor again in the morning."

After taking the daily 5 p.m.-weather data, checking on water temperatures in the hatchery, and eating an evening snack, bedtime finally arrived. Perhaps tomorrow night Bob will be back, I thought while I filled the hot water bottle as a poor substitute for his presence. I assured myself that I was in no way afraid of being alone, but, nevertheless, even though distance plus an ice-bound enclosure prevented any possible intruder, I flicked the lock on the door before climbing the steep stairs to the bed. The perfect quietness of Kitoi Bay became an eerie vacuum with reverberating thuds and moans. Even the bedsprings howled. First was silence, then a noise, then more silence. And the sequence continued. Between snatches of sleep my ears would tune to the groaning of the ice in the bay, the thud of a limb falling on the aluminum roof, the wind howling in the chimney, or the weird yap of a distant fox.

Morning came as a delight—perhaps Bob would return! Yet, truthfully, I hoped the weather would prevent his return unless he were actually better. Appendicitis is not a welcome accompaniment to isolated living. I decided that the weather would prevent flying since the thermometer-check showed minus three degrees Fahrenheit, the coldest temperature we had yet experienced. Because of icing conditions, the amphibious bush planes usually do not fly when the temperature is below 15 degrees F. As daylight came, I could see that even a Winter Beach landing was not possible because of ice on the bay. I had an invisible front-yard gate securely locked by a padlock of ice. The only key was owned by the weather.

Now that it was daylight, even sound did not echo in the shadowless, smothering snow. I felt my frailty, my smallness, yet my closeness to God. And I was thankful that Bob was locked out instead of in.

The 8 a.m. weather report to ALB99 was transmitted without difficulty, so I anxiously awaited 4 p.m. when I should be able to talk directly to Bob instead of just receiving a message in the blind.

My next problem was how to pass the slow-moving eight hours. Trying to pass time was a strange experience in itself. Usually I never had enough time to do the many and varied things I wished to do. Now I had no appreciation for this time of no-rush, no-run waiting. I ended up yawning away my eight hours by answering overdue letters and filling the outboard-motor-oil-can mailbox. Then, it was time. I eagerly turned on the receiver. But today, profiting from the previous day's experience, I left the transmitter *off* until Kitoi Bay was called.

As I had hoped, we were able to talk directly. Bob said that the doctor could not decide what was wrong and wanted him to stay off his feet as much as possible. He also said that the pain was unchanged and that he had to see the doctor again the next morning but planned on returning the same day. There was no use remaining in Kodiak, he insisted. I was not so sure. Unfortunately, I was not able to ask him all the things I would have liked as speaking over a radio includes many more listeners than even the old-fashioned country telephone line. Talking itself created a squeamish sensation because I had not spoken a word except on the radio for thirty hours.

This brief five-minute talk with Bob, however, was like a potent vitamin pill destroying the narcotic of solitude. The evening and night passed more reasonably.

Early morning brought *real* pain, not the emotional kind I had been experiencing from loneliness. Gripping the kitchen countertop, I was suddenly awash in sharp pain and blood as I experienced a seven-week miscarriage. Besides the exhaustion, weakness, and relief when it was over, it was also devastating because my heart was bleeding from the painful longing for a child: another expectation evaporated.

Later that morning, a lesser shock came. I had not been able to get through to ALB99 with the morning's weather. Suddenly, I noticed that I had left the transmitter switch on. How could I have been so forgetful? Bob had run the charger before he left so the batteries would be well charged, but now after my negligence I was sure the batteries would be low. The lack of reception that morning had obviously been due to low batteries, and not the snow squalls. This meant that I would not have contact with Bob the remainder of the time he was away, and the present weather conditions meant he would not be able to arrive home for a while yet. Another emergency! Knowing our radio set was rather temperamental, we had agreed that we should not worry in case we could not contact each other. Even so, I knew Bob would be concerned, especially since the last two nights had each been below zero. Also, I was concerned about Bob's health. Fortunately, with my own physical trauma over, I was doing better.

I realized that I would have to figure out how to run the battery charger. How foolish that I had never bothered to watch Bob whenever he had charged them. Somehow we had forgotten this in our self-training for emergencies. I would at least make an attempt. Perhaps I would discover some latent mechanical ability inherited from my farmer father. I dug through the immense supply of equipment manuals in Bob's file and laid out the ones appearing to be connected with motors.

Considering that we had seventeen motors at Kitoi Bay, the pile of motor pamphlets made an impressive stack: *Operating Instructions for the Johnson Sea-Horse 3*; *Big Twin 2 Owner's Manual*; *Instructions and Parts Manual, Titan Chain Saws, Inc.*; *Operating and Servicing the Joy, Model 105 Air Compressor*; *Instruction Book, Portable Gasoline Hammer*; *Operating Instructions for Hobart Concrete Mixer*; and many other perplexing titles. Suddenly a title stood out which gave me hope:

Instruction Book for Cyclohm D.C. Generators and Battery Chargers. I began my study session. After floundering through the unfamiliar details, I came to these two deflating sentences: "The primary power source for this unit is a gasoline engine of standard design used commercially for many purposes. See the separate instruction book for the engine." But I had no separate instruction book for the engine.

The only solution seemed to be to study operating instructions for other types of engines. Surely they must start similarly. After all, most cake recipes were only slightly different from each other. How could I have possibly been around motors all my life without paying the least attention to them? I had grown up on an orchard farm with an inventive father who spent a lot of time tinkering with motors in the farm shop. But my motor observations had been limited to the sewing machine. As these thoughts ran through my mind, I vowed that I was going to become more observant.

The starting details for the other engines did not sound exceptionally complicated. But running out in the 10º F. air to look at the charger and motor again thwarted all my hopes because it had as many caps, knobs, valves, and movable gadgets as an octopus has suction cups. How could I ever determine which were the rheostat, choke, starter, and other necessary parts? I would find the choke on two or three different pictures in my supply of pamphlets and then run into what seemed like the outside freezer to look for a similar gadget on the charger. I continued this game of in-and-out, hide-and-seek comparison until I thought I had identified each cap, knob, valve, and gadget. The rheostat was knob-shaped, evidently, and the choke looked something like a prong connected to a sewing-machine stitch regulator.

Previously Bob had asked me to paint red-lettered labels on the various cans and barrels containing oil, gasoline, kerosene, and Blazo. At the same time, he had drilled me on what equipment used what fuel so as I strained gasoline into the fuel tank of the motor, I was not worried about having the wrong fuel. Next, according to my many instructions, it must be necessary to fill the crankcase with oil. I pounded and tugged without success on the cap to what I judged to be the crankcase. I finally reasoned that the motor surely had enough oil left from last time. Yet, how terrible should I do or fail to do something that would ruin the motor!

My hands, although gloved, had by this time become completely numb and immovable from the cold. I warmed my stiff fingers for another session with the puzzling monster by again going inside to continue my comparison of instruction booklets. Rheostat button, needle valve, and other meaningless terms had taken on new meaning. I rechecked the procedure that I had decided to try, again put on down jacket and hood, and again left the warmth of the house.

Armed with a potato masher, I walked courageously to the front of the black demon. Perhaps, I reasoned, the wooden handle of the masher would prevent a shock and enable me to press harder since I could push with both hands. I set the rheostat button and either closed or opened what I hoped to be the choke. (The closed and open positions of the choke varied with the various pamphlets, but it seemed natural that it should be moved to the opposite side from which it was set.) Then, hoping my potato masher would not be ruined, I pushed with it against the starter. The motor ground away, which at least gave me a sand speck of hope. Again and again I pushed the starter with the potato masher. Again and again it ground away, coughed, and suddenly…**it sta-r-t-ed**. What a welcome, grating, roaring sound! After adjusting the choke and needle valve, it began to sound more normal but continued some of its sputtering and coughing rebuttal. I was shocked that it had started. For some reason, perhaps because it was so completely foreign, I received a greater sense of accomplishment from figuring out this simple operation than from anything else I had ever done.

Now, at last, the *Instruction Book for Cyclohm D.C. Generators and Battery Chargers* became helpful. By referring to the proper chart corresponding to the Model 500 stamped on the generator, I was able to turn the rheostat to give the proper number of amperes.

Clear reception and transmission of the words KXA97, Kitoi Bay, at 4 p.m. proved that the two hours with interspersed coughs had succeeded in recharging the weak batteries. Bob gave me the same news as he had previously, that is, the doctor could not decide whether or not to operate. The pain was not much better, but he, being tired of waiting for a decision, was going to fly back to Kitoi as soon as the strong winds permitted flying.

Late Sunday afternoon, after four days of waiting, I heard and saw the Kodiak Airway's plane loop overhead. It was as if the surrounding dead world and I had suddenly come back to life. I had not dreamed the wind had calmed enough to permit flying. Childlike excitement caused fumbling over each button as I put on outdoor wraps. By the time I finally pulled the drawstring of my hood and began the snowy hike, the plane was in the air on its return flight. I could hardly imagine my Dearest being at the other end of the mile. Since Bob, for safety reasons, had asked me not to leave the house area during his absence, just walking through the snowy spruce and hearing patches of frozen turf crackle under my thermo boots gave a new freedom from my lonely isolation and added to my joy. Excited peering around each turn finally produced Bob. With a dash I was in his arms. Tears of happiness began pouring, tears releasing the strain that I had not been fully aware of. An hour and a half later my voice had become a rasping whisper, the result of an hour and half of ceaseless chatter. But this didn't stop our ecstatic reunion and the sharing of every moment from our time apart.

Bob's mild appendicitis caused no further medical emergencies in the following months. He had an appendectomy the following summer to solve the problem, but the next winter pains began from building downstream fish traps on Ruth Lake and Midarm Lake outlets. Then simply carrying water to fill the washing machine brought on a sudden severe episode. For the trip to the hospital, Ray Albrecht, the bush pilot, and I had to lift Bob onto pillows placed on the floor of the plane. Ray kept over water all the way to avoid updrafts that always occur along a shoreline or crossing points of land. Dr. Johnson could feel something but concluded the cause was a severe strain rather than a rupture.

One winter afternoon even I developed a throbbing headache with no idea of the cause. Taking what pain medication we had, I lay on our homemade sofa. Bob was working both in the hatchery and outside. Providentially, he came into the living area before I became unconscious and immediately recognized what might be causing the problem. Window and doors were thrown wide open and cold, fresh air filled the room. We soon discovered the real cause. The battery charger was completely covered with snow. The heat had melted snow and ice that then refroze around the end of the exhaust pipe of the charger. The only way the exhaust from the battery charger could escape was to seep insidiously into the house. Since toxic gas is colorless and odorless, I had not detected it by smell or sight. Without warning, this gas wreaks harm as red blood cells grab carbon monoxide in preference to oxygen. Unknown to me, my blood carbon monoxide was rising, which would have caused a suffocating death except for Bob's rescue. In spite of this scare, I could not complain: I had been the one who wanted the attractive snowbank to accumulate up the windows. Bob shoveled away my snowbank to prevent a reoccurrence.

One more emergency occurred, this one on the water. Pete Olsen offered to let us ride with him on his commercial fishing boat around the island to the native Afognak Village where his wife, Nina, had been born and raised. Bob and I both had wanted to see the only other humans occupying our seventeen-hundred-square-mile world, so we accepted Pete's offer.

Nina's childhood had not been so different from an earlier frontier life stateside. Water was carried from a river or collected from rainwater, and food came from wild berries, fish, and gardens. Potatoes, rutabagas, and carrots were stored for the winter in a cellar; salmonberries were dried and made into jams; fish was dried, salted, and smoked before being stored in barrels. Pete told us that Nina still spoke the Aleut native language and sometimes taught it to others.

Regretfully, she did not write down the stories of her ancestors, which her mother, her grandmother, and others could have told her.

The place where other human beings occupied our island and the place of Nina's childhood were only two of the several reasons we wanted to see Afognak Village. We were curious to see this group of homes because it was often mentioned on radio messages among the islanders. One additional reason was that Bob and I were becoming increasingly interested in the history of Afognak Island. Reading history is more meaningful and deeply retained after visiting an area.

Thoughts of Afognak Village and the anticipation of seeing it abruptly ended because a ferocious storm erupted. Powerful waves poured over the top of Pete's boat, cabin, and all. The savage blasts of wind were coming directly from the Gulf of Alaska. Even though I was holding on tightly, I could hardly maintain my footing. Even more frightening was Pete's face as this life-long fisherman attempted to keep his vibrating craft upright. Responding to Pete's white face, I felt abject helplessness. My only hope was that I knew we were all three silently praying at the deepest level.

Pete loved the ocean, but from years of ocean experience, he also respected it, knowing its power and danger. Minutes seemed like hours as he tensely and skillfully steered without comment while the boat shook, slammed, and pitched through the cruel waves. Pete was anxious about both his boat and our fate. Waves continued crashing overtop, and the wind showed no indications of slackening. Finally, by making the right decisions and skillfully handling his forty-foot craft, Pete managed to get us near to what to us was an unfamiliar shore. Through the noise of the still-thundering surf he said, "I'm going to anchor in this more protected cove for however many hours or days it'll take until the weather calms. My boat is too small for the three of us to spend extended time on it. Do you think you could hike home from here?"

Bob assured him that we could cross the mountainous peninsula (about six to eight miles as a seagull flies), walk over the frozen lakes to avoid some brush, and make it all right. Pete somewhat eased the bow against a low rock cliff, and we hopped onto solid, stable land. Leaving this breath-taking situation, we trudged up and halfway slid down miles of hills. The trees muffled the fierce, shrieking wind somewhat, but still we were almost blown across ice-covered lakes as we continued over the rugged wilderness. Bob had his usual packbasket, but this time it was not heavy. Fortunately our boat ride with Pete had been around a large peninsula that projected into Marmot Bay, so cutting across the peninsula base yielded a much shorter route than following the shoreline. My mind had been so focused, so concentrated on survival, and now we were freely walking on solid ground, breathing the pure air. We finally and thankfully looked down upon gunmetal gray waves slapping the shores of more familiar beaches near our own Kitoi Bay.

Indeed, my heart was exceedingly thankful, yet I had further thoughts to ponder. Today's sea experience had been humbling because I had had no control over the outcome. What about other emergencies? Had I attributed Bob's narrowly saving our skiff as he hopped from ice block to ice block to sheer luck? Had I adequately acknowledged God's providence in helping us through the appendicitis attack, the miscarriage, and the near asphyxiation? For that matter, was I truly thanking God for His daily care and guidance, or was I complacently relying only on myself? In thinking over this day, as well as other times in my life, I breathed the prayer of the psalm, "I trust in you, O Lord. My times are in your hands."[5] As we headed on home, my pondering was replaced with peace and serenity.

---

[5] Psalm 31:14, 15

Bush Pilot in Distress

The long Silent Season was usually a series of peaceful pauses, not exclamation points. Worry hardly whispered. Bursts of excitement were rare. But since the day-to-day, week-by-week routine in peopleless land was so predictable, even relative minor occurrences became major. I cried when we received the telegram from our brother-in-law that Donna, my only sibling, had delivered a 6-lb.–13-oz. baby, Anne Ruth—a major occurrence by all standards. She was not only my first niece but a namesake as well. Then there had been the tingling excitement we both felt when we received a letter telling us that Bob's father, stepmother, and eighteen-year-old brother—Walter, Veneta, and Dave Vincent—were actually going to visit us for an entire week. They experienced some difficult flying because of cold, snowy weather and tasted the adventure we were living. The bay was frozen so we did not even have the sound of water. Dad said, "I like to lie at night and listen to the complete stillness. You don't even have owls to hoot." Yes, the telegram and the visit were major, major exclamation points in our otherwise quiet lives.

Figure 19. Walter, Veneta, and Dave Vincent.

An additional happening—a shattering, grave day and night vigil—came as we turned on the short-wave radio one morning. The short-wave radio had become, over the three years we were there, an artificial substitute for friendships and yearned-for relationships. Even though I felt close to Bob and had stateside friends that I kept in touch with through letters, I wanted to belong to a larger community. Surprisingly, this was partially met through the voices of unseen souls living in the Kodiak Archipelago, ones whose voices we would hear over short wave. Unspoken connections with these strangers strengthened through the months as we listened and empathized. In our imagination, we became the friends of other islanders whom we had never met or even spoken to. Thus, this particular morning we listened not only with the intentness of reading a page-turner novel but with prayer for ones we considered our close community neighbors.

Forty-six hours previously, the pilot of a Kodiak Airways plane had given the first alert as he radioed the 330 miles back, "Grumman 5984 to KWN4. Left engine just quit…full load…cannot maintain altitude…will attempt landing immediately…location north of Chignik Bay." This, the last and only word from the two-engine amphibian, was at 11 a.m. Monday, January 16.

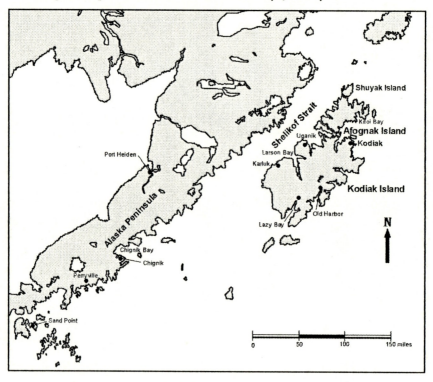

Figure 20. Shelikof Strait area of southern Alaska.

Tense hours of waiting were at last coming to a rapid and dramatic climax. The scattered, concerned islanders, including Bob and me and—more importantly—the various families and loved ones of the missing pilot and passengers, kept their ears glued to radio frequency 2512. No doubt many attempted to still anxious hearts with prayer. The voice of the captain of the *Reliance* came through, "WZA99, the boat *Reliance* to KWC97 Chignik. We can see the plane on the beach. It looks like just a pile of wreckage."

Within minutes a Coast Guard rescue plane from Kodiak and a crab-fishing boat from the village of Chignik were converging on the downed aircraft. But what had started as a quick rescue was thwarted. The Coast Guard plane, after reaching the Chignik area and being forced by the wind to circle at a 4000-foot altitude, developed its own engine trouble and had to return to Kodiak. Furthermore, the fishing boat developed a frozen fuel line.

A call over frequency 2512 was given in hopes that other crab-fishing boats would be able to aid, but none were within even a day's journey of Chignik Bay. It was this call that alerted several of the scattered villages, as well as winter cannery watchmen, throughout Kodiak-Afognak Islands and the Alaska Peninsula. Frequency 2512 could well be classified as the gossip-country-phone-line for these lonely villages as well as for the many fishing boats of the area. Because the fishing boats could help by searching and the islanders could provide weather reporting, it was quickly decided to use 2512, the one frequency on which everyone could broadcast, during this disaster. In the United States, three hundred miles might seem far away, but in this sparsely settled Alaska Territory, an area of much water and small islands, it seemed only next door.

News-less hours passed and the winter darkness descended. Night prevented another Coast Guard plane from replacing the returning Coast Guard aircraft. The wind, which had been steadily increasing throughout the afternoon, suddenly converted from gusts to a full-mouthed gale. Wives, husbands, children, and parents of the Grumman 5984 occupants would have no comfort that night.

Bob and I shook ourselves back to reality. After all, this should not be so personal to us. Of course, we would know the pilot, whoever he might be, for they were all our friends, but we would not necessarily know the passengers. We questioned, "Why has this so affected us?" Living in isolation does have its effect. Unknown people become neighbors if they are the nearest humans. Only ones in our situation could really understand how vicarious experiences truly can seem real.

Tuesday morning finally dawned after a dark night of hurricane-force winds—110 miles an hour at some peninsula points—and driving snow. It seemed everyone now knew that a search was being conducted for one of Kodiak Airways' planes. Instead of the usual gossip jamming 2512 frequency, its traffic that morning consisted only of positions of the searchers, weather reports, amount of fuel remaining, and other facts pertinent to the rescue attempt. Individuals realized that they could help most by not using, and therefore not blocking, the frequency. Battery chargers were run to keep batteries up; outdoor chores were postponed and meals were late while residents listened to the news of the search.

The Kodiak Archipelago people were not listening because the real-life drama broke the winter monotony; they were listening with a fearful personal interest. And so were we. Who was the pilot? Was it Gil, Al, Bill, or Ray? For many people in the bush, the bush pilot was often their only winter visitor and so was valued not only as a friend but almost as a member of the family. Children in the villages looked to the pilot with a Santa Claus reverence as he would arrive weekly, or perhaps once every two weeks if weather conditions were poor, to bring the gift of mail and groceries. Would Kodiak Airways lose their valued reputation of never having lost a life? The search continued as these thoughts and many others swirled through minds.

"Coast Guard 2126, Coast Guard 2126, Coast Guard 2126," came brokenly over the air as Chignik Village, acting as focal point for the operations, attempted to reach the approaching Coast Guard airplane that was replacing the one that had developed engine trouble.

The only answer was the crackle of static.

Port Heiden, located on the opposite side of the peninsula and having a more powerful radio, repeated for Chignik, "Coast Guard 2126, Coast Guard 2126, Chignik reports weather as visibility and ceiling, zero-zero; driving snow; winds, 25–30 miles; temperature, 18 degrees."

Still, no answer.

Weather continued to be reported from southern Kodiak Island and Alaska Peninsula points throughout the day, while the snowstorm persisted in bringing zero-zero weather (zero ceiling and zero visibility, or totally enclosed by fog and clouds). Besides hindering the airplane search, the weather conditions also caused poor radio reception. Kodiak Airways in Kodiak was having a difficult time hearing Chignik even with Port Heiden's help. An interested cannery watchman at Lazy Bay also had a powerful radio set so offered to be the go-between for Kodiak Airways and Chignik. Since constant listening, relaying, and trying to maintain contact was a strain on the batteries, searchers and listeners arranged to tune in every hour, on the hour, to give weather reports and to receive the latest news. Because boats had insufficient time to reach Chignik Bay and planes were gaining nothing because of poor weather, hopes were centered in an overland party crossing the peninsula from Port Heiden. But by 10 p.m. Tuesday it was reported that the overland party had been turned back by deep snowdrifts blown into the pass.

Thirty-five hours had passed since the Grumman had been forced to make its emergency crash. Each hour made the chance of survival less. Were there survivors? If so, would they be able to endure a second night of bitter, zero-degree weather? Had they somehow managed a safe landing on the choppy water with a crippled plane and the turbulent air? If so, had the pilot been able to taxi to shore? In case it had been necessary to swim ashore, would someone have had a pocket lighter or a waterproof-match case? These and many more questions must go unanswered for another night.

At 4 a.m. Wednesday, Jan. 18, Karluk and Sand Point villagers sleepily peered into the dark, pre-dawn sky, in an attempt to guess the weather. They immediately reported to the Coast Guard at Kodiak. Other villagers awakened at the same early hour and turned on their radio sets to keep posted on the search.

When daylight finally came, each one saw that their optimistic hopes and reports were becoming a reality. The ceiling was 3000 feet, even CVU (ceiling and visibility unlimited) in many places. Winds had lessened markedly and snow, to only an occasional flurry. The Coast Guard from Kodiak quickly readied a second search plane to start southward. Fishing boats anchored near Chignik Bay the night before were now beginning to reach the point believed to be near the crash site.

Seven a.m.: Weather reports from each boat and from Chignik, Perryville, Sand Point, Port Heiden, Lazy Bay, Uganik and Karluk continued to be encouraging.

Kodiak Airways was still mainly depending on Lazy Bay to relay most of the information in order that they might receive it more clearly and accurately. Lazy Bay's talkative, friendly operator, who had always before delighted in drawing out Laaaaaaaazy Bay as long as his breath would conveniently last, was refraining from such idiosyncrasies during this emergency. Nevertheless, it seemed strange to hear him say Lazy Bay instead of his usual lazy-mannered Laaaaaaaazy Bay.

"KWC97, Chignik, to Coast Guard 2126; KWC97, Chignik, to Coast Guard 2126."

No answer.

"KWC97, Chignik, to KWO75 Lazy Bay. Report to Coast Guard 2126, Chignik's weather: 3000 ceiling; visibility, 10 miles; wind, 20; temperature, 5 degrees F. *Reliance* nearing Hook Point."

"Lazy Bay, KWO75, to KWC97 Chignik. That I will do, will do. You say you have ceiling 3000; visibility, 10 miles; wind, 20; temperature, 5 degrees F.?"

"Chignik to Lazy Bay. Roger."

"Coast Guard 2126, Coast Guard 2126. This is Lazy Bay, KWO75. Come in please. Coast Guard 2126, Coast Guard plane 2126, do you read? Come in please."

"Coast Guard, 2126, answering KWO75, Lazy Bay."

"Lazy Bay back to Coast Guard, 2126. Chignik's weather is visibility, 10 miles; ceiling, 3000; wind, 20 miles; and temperature, 5 degrees F. Chignik also asked me to tell you the *Reliance* was nearing Hook Point. How soon will you reach there?"

"Coast Guard, 2126, back to KWO75 Lazy Bay. Received the information. Estimating arrival at Hook Point in five minutes."

"Kodiak to Lazy Bay. Thank you. We should know soon. We certainly appreciate your efforts in relaying for us."

"Lazy Bay to Kodiak. Just glad I can help out. Glad I can help out. I just felt it was my duty to do so. Being I have a powerful set here, it is really my duty to do so. Always glad to help out in an emergency. Know you'd do it for me. Thank you for the compliment. This is Lazy Bay clear with N4."

"WZA99, the *Reliance*, to KWC97, Chignik. We can see the busted up plane on the beach. (A breathless pause) It looks like just a pile of wreckage…. There's smoke from a fire. The plane's really smashed up…. Can see three people walking slowly on beach. They walk like they're pretty tired. Will have to anchor boat and row to shore by skiff. Contact Coast Guard plane to land near boat and be ready to remove survivors if hospitalization is necessary."

"'Chignik to Coast Guard plane 2126. Boat *Reliance* has found survivors in Hook Bay. Requests you land and remove bodies…errr, I mean people."

"Coast Guard to Chignik. Roger, Roger, Roger. Are they alive?"

"Chignik back. Affirmative. They can see three men on beach. Not sure about the other two. Perhaps the women are in a shelter."

"This is the boat *Reliance*. This is the boat *Reliance*. Afraid the skiff cannot be landed because of rocky beach and rough sea. Stand by. Stand by."

"Skiff just landed on beach."

"Coast Guard 2126 to boat *Reliance*. We have you spotted. Will land in adjoining cove."

"*Reliance* back to Coast Guard. Please circle. In case skiff swamps when leaving beach, be prepared to drop life raft."

Coast Guard: "Roger, Roger.'

Boat *Reliance*: "Two of the survivors are in skiff. Don't know if they can launch skiff from beach or not. Surf is pounding hard on the rocks."

After a few minutes, the *Reliance* continued, "The skiff made it off the beach and two women passengers are just now coming aboard. Skiff returning for second trip. Be ready to drop the life raft if needed."

"Chignik, Chignik, Lazy Bay calling. This is Lazy Bay relaying for KWN4. Kodiak Airways request Coast Guard plane to return immediately with survivors to Kodiak for physical check-up."

Boat *Reliance*: "The other three survivors are just now leaving beach in skiff. Just a minute, will let you know of any injuries…."

"Everyone all okay. No one frozen or anything. Everyone all okay. Just tired and suffering from exposure. I'll let Ray [*the pilot*] say a word."

"Everyone is fine, but the plane is completely demolished. We couldn't hold it down against the winds Monday night. Passengers are fine, just tired."

Relief came. We could finally breathe freely. Rejoicing and cheers went up by the elated-but-exhausted islanders as we celebrated the rescue. It was another triumph of human perseverance over the forces of nature, another blessing for which to give thanks.

For perhaps the first time, we island residents evaluated our dependence on and appreciation for our one local airway service. We recalled how the pilots had given up their own Thanksgiving Day in order to fly turkeys to the outlying families and villages. A few remembered a family emergency when a pilot had endangered himself by flying through inclement weather to rush Sister Sue or Uncle Tom to the Kodiak Hospital. Among other memories, Bob and I recalled Bill Harvey's zeal to the point of standing on top of the plane breaking ice with a paddle, so determined was he to get through to our cabin because he had felt we might be in difficulty. Others spoke of his courage and competence. Because of Kodiak Airways' small size and friendliness, people who were isolated depended upon them for innumerable non-flying services. Often we had heard these types of short-wave requests:

"What is the address of the Internal Revenue?"

"Say, Tim Katelnikoff is in the hospital. Could you find out how he is for me?"

"Bring down one pair of shoes for my ten-year-old boy when you come, will you please?" (No size, no style requested.)

Whether bush pilots were transporting shoes, people, or medicine, they were vital. As for Bob and me, each pilot had become a dear friend. Fearing the death of a close friend had been the main reason we so vicariously lived the strenuous emergency of the previous hours. The crash was nearly as intense as being on the plane ourselves. We were drained.

Figure 21. Bob at the short-wave radio.

Change of Scenery

By February, monotony had submerged our normal buoyancy. Winter was growing long. Repetitious boredom caused me to ponder how glorious it would be to see a robin or a plain barnyard chicken; to hear a train whistle, the croak of a frog; to smell roses or even diesel exhaust.

Bob must have felt the same. One morning he announced, "We need a change of scenery. Let's take a midwinter outing. In fact, we could even leave this afternoon, camp overnight at the Salt Lagoon (*see Figure 10*), and snowshoe across to Razor Beach early tomorrow morning in time for the minus-one-foot low tide."

"It sounds delightful," I quickly replied as my sense of adventure surfaced. It was nice that Bob was free to set his own agenda.

An easterly storm had dumped thirty inches of snow on us but had opened our ice-bound bay, permitting the skiff to be brought near the house. Within an hour we had hastily loaded the skiff, Bob had attached the heavy 25-hp motor, and we were off through the slapping push of the waves. I felt my spirits lift—how fascinating to be impulsively doing something unconventional even with our lifestyle. Even Alaskans did not go camping just for the fun of camping in February—especially with thirty inches of new snow on the ground.

In forty minutes the outboard zoomed us past the surf-pounded bluffs and into the quiet, sheltered Salt Lagoon. The pounding I had been taking in the bow of the skiff stopped. Our presence ruffled an enormous number of ducks that speedily fled skyward. The distance between the research station and the lagoon was in reality only about seven miles, but since weather usually prevented such distant travel, it seemed like we were a long way from home.

We found a protected area under sheltered boughs and set up camp in our usual manner: first, a layer of spruce boughs over the frozen ground, topped with a tarp; air mattresses next; an insulating layer of newspapers; then our sleeping bags, sheltered with an angled roof made from the remainder of the tarp. The campfire was started outside the front opening of the tarp tent using pitchy wood cut from a large spruce tree bearing older cuts, a strong indication that trappers had used the tree for the same purpose. There were further signs that others had chosen the same sheltered camping spot in the past. We found remnants of what had probably been a trapper's tent frame or cabin. The bottom hand-notched logs had a threshold cut out for the doorway; the remains of a broken bench were nearby, as well as a piece of metal that had likely been a bucket. Behind the site were moss-covered stumps where the builder had cut trees for logs. Scraping first the snow and then the moss from the logs, we exposed a layer of Katmai ash, evidence that these remnants had been used before the 1912 volcanic eruption of Mt. Katmai on the Alaska Peninsula. What interesting stories the few old, old spruce, standing elegantly among their offspring, could tell. Likely, they would be able to describe the settlements of Aleut Indians, followed by the trapping era of Russians and Americans, and then, nearly simultaneously with the trappers, the experiences of wandering gold seekers. Still later, temporary seasonal herring salteries were hastily built in many of these sheltered bays. Now it was fishery research personnel camped on the forest floor beneath their lofty shelter. We felt secure camping under the stately spruce, our own personal sentinel.

Taking advantage of the last hour before dusk, we hiked across a small peninsula to a secluded beach exposed only to the rolling surf. "Think of the property value of this beach frontage if it were located in the States," commented Bob.

The deep darkness of the black shale sand provided a stark contrast to the pure whiteness of the snow. The rolling ocean breakers supplied an energy different than the quieter waters of our nearby beaches. We waded in the foaming breakers as they slapped the sandy beach. Of course, our wading in these icy Alaskan waters was done appropriately—we waded in hip boots.

"I've seldom seen my Grandma Marr visit the Oregon beaches without wading, winter or summer. Wonder what she would think of our hip-boot method?" I asked.

"It won't be a hip-boot method long if we don't head for shore," laughed Bob.

After we returned to the beach, I had another idea. "Let's look for hidden treasures," I suggested.

We wandered through the wave-thrown logs looking for either driftwood or Japanese glass floats. Driftwood, shell, and float collecting are much more rewarding on empty, deserted beaches where there are no competing beachcombers. The snowline prevented extensive beach scrounging, but the recent high tide had melted the snow from a large area. We picked up piece after piece of driftwood, discarding most as not being quite the right shape for an artistic flower-arrangement piece or a lamp base. Yet some artistic driftwood and delicately designed shells openly displayed their unbroken loveliness.

Surprisingly, at the far end of the beach, we found a ship-sized, knurled log against a rock arch that was littered with garbage. Who could litter in an unspoiled wilderness like this? Somewhat abashed, we realized the "litter-bugs" had been Bob and Ruth Vincent because the offending article still bore the bright blue and white label of Avoset Sterilized Cream, a 30-percent-butterfat whipping cream that we always kept on the pantry shelf. Since the lid had been screwed back on, the bottle had followed the whims of the wind and ocean currents instead of sinking as we had intended when dumping the garbage in the outer bay.

"Say, look what I've found," declared Bob. Bob held up a large glass float, nearly eight inches across, enclosed in what looked like the original webbing that had likely broken from a Japanese fishing net. This valuable find would add interest to decorative arrangements. Now I was eager to arrive home—and only a few hours earlier I had been so relieved to leave home—to use the float with shells and greenery, perhaps a candle or three, for a table centerpiece.

Before leaving the beach, I found a surf-smoothed, gnarled driftwood hook on the end of a long, curved pole. It was easy to visualize the animal-like head as a perfect standing arm for a hanging basket filled with ivy. By pointing out its many virtues to Bob, especially its smoothness from years of moon washings, I managed to convince him that it was a "once-in-a-lifetime-find" and should be dragged back to our camp where we had a saw available to cut off the top eighteen inches.

Figure 22. A change-of-scenery outing.

After trudging back to the campsite, we rekindled our fire. Our angled-roof tarp, anchored with rocks at the bottom and tied to trees at the two top corners, reflected the warmth of the fire back toward us and provided a windbreak, creating a cozy climate even in below-freezing weather. We had adjusted to Alaskan coastal temperatures that usually were in the low 20s and seldom below zero.

Preparing dinner was an easy task, and not a single pan was left to wash. Even the most common foods taste delectable in a camping atmosphere, flavored by wood smoke. After punching a small hole in a can of peas to let expanding air pressure escape, we tucked it into the coals. The juice sizzled out the hole when the peas were ready. Along with the overheated vegetable, we enjoyed roasted wieners coated with horseradish mustard rolled in soft, buttered slices of bread and cooked over the coals. Tantalizing aromatic wisps wafted upward. Even a steak would not have tasted better. Our dessert, applesauce and spice cake, was postponed for an evening snack after a moonlight walk on the quiet beach.

As usual, both the moon and stars appeared exceptionally close and bright in the clear night air. Their twinkling animation on winter snow made us feel just a step away from heaven and a deeper reverence for the Lord's handiwork.

Stretching ourselves uncomfortably at 4 a.m. the next morning, we appreciated that the moon and stars had changed from their enchanting, sentimental role to their practical role of providing adequate illumination for us to make preparations and begin the hike to Razor Clam Beach. A breeze murmured and whistled through the treetops. It was cold, but even the drop in temperature had not sufficiently crusted the thirty inches of loose snow. That meant our three-to-four-mile hike to the prized beach would require snowshoes. Snowshoes soon become tiresome for anyone unaccustomed to using them, but without them, we could not have made the hike. As I readied the snowshoes, I was glad that I wore a women's generous size-eight shoe because our two pair of snowshoes were both made for men.

After breakfast Bob put on his heavy packbasket. Off we started in the crisp, biting air, having no difficulty distinguishing the trail because of the moon's reflection on the snow. As usual, Bob broke trail. Following, I unconsciously stretched to reach his identical footsteps and to leave the distinctive path of unspoiled quilted teardrop tracks left by Bob's snowshoes. I remembered, though, my last snowshoe hike. Since my feet were fastened to the shoe only by my toes, I had tensed my ankles with each step, sorely taxing my muscles. Knowing the round trip would be eight miles, I consciously relaxed and stepped with a flexed arch, exactly as I would without the snowshoes. I soon forgot my foolish inclination to leave a perfectly engraved pattern behind and joined Bob as he lustily sang *I've Been Working on the Railroad*.

The need to save breath for an approaching hill stifled our singing, and we soon concentrated on the otter slides, the fox imprints, the weasel signatures, and the 'periods' and 'quotation marks' typed into the snow by the snowshoe rabbits. Devil's club bushes stuck their thorny arms into our path. Even on the devil's club's leafless stalks, nature's crankiness ensures that the thorns are just as vexatious in winter as in summer.

It was a relief to approach the first of the two lakes we needed to cross. Our snowshoes kept us from sinking in with each step, and the flat walking surface was a welcome contrast to the hilly and wooded bear trail. As a high-flying, Pacific Northern Airline's DC-3 flew overhead, we wondered if the passengers noticed either our trail or us as two tiny specks dotting the expansive lake. In the past, whenever we had used snowshoes on a lake, and even when we had walked only with boots, the bush pilots would spot our trail. On mail day they would comment, "You were evidently across the southern ridge on that narrow lake this week."

The smooth-walking surface of this large unnamed lake made it easy for us to stop concentrating on the trail and look about us as we wished. The breaking light of dawn showed us that a new day had arrived. Morning light skated on the distant mountains of the Aleutian Chain.

Through the dimness Bob pinpointed a fox on the opposite shore and then discovered that it was not a fox but a river otter heading in our direction. He slid and hopped, slid and hopped, in a repeating pattern across the flat, snowy lake. Likely, he intended to follow its outlet stream to pursue his daily occupation, fishing, after crossing the sixty-acre lake. Fortunately the wind was coming toward us, so after turning to get the best view, we stood as statues as the otter loped closer. We had always wondered how otter were able to hop in such a unique way to make the consistent six-to-eight-foot slide-and-hop patterns. Now we waited nearly breathless hoping to observe his movements. His playful progress was spellbinding to watch. With a long, sleek back hunched like a Halloween cat, he would bound for a few steps and then slide on his stomach through the slushy snow with all the natural exuberance of a child on a sled. After each playful slide, he raised his head, sniffed, and again started off with a running hop. Several times he looked in our direction, but he was either nearsighted or unafraid of stationary objects because he continued in his direct course undisturbed, passing within seventy feet of us. We enjoyed an excellent "fashion show" of the dark, sleek fur on his slender figure. After he passed us, he suddenly caught our human scent and fled in an efficient lope.

We followed this otter's sliding, hopping trail, which was along the same creek as our own, for a mile. I could not help envying his effortless skimming locomotion since my snowshoes were becoming increasingly heavy. Stopping to bang them together to shake off the heavy snow, I fervently wished to exchange my man-sized heavy duty shoes for a pair just large enough to carry my one-hundred-twenty pounds.

We soon crossed the second lake and were only a small rise away from the ocean again. "I can't hear the surf yet, so the sea must be fairly calm," remarked Bob during our brief pause.

"Good, then we'll have no difficulty getting home tonight."

"You don't mean home sounds good already?" kidded Bob.

"Perhaps. Anyway, I feel as if it were noon. Let's eat part of our lunch for a second breakfast."

Figure 23. Otter trail.

"We're only a short distance from Razor Beach," replied Bob. "Let's have a snack there."

Sitting on a log at the edge of Razor Beach, we hungrily ate two of our sandwiches and watched the rolling whitecaps so seldom seen on the protected beaches near the station. Had people been added to the scene, the beach before us would have been a diminutive Rockaway, Oregon. After our food, Bob spotted some markings further down on the smooth, wave-erased sand—fresh elk tracks, we decided—proof that the Roosevelt elk planted on Afognak Island were finally beginning to multiply and disperse.

Our brief rest had to be cut short because it was nearly low tide. Again, our schedule was controlled by the tides, not the clock. Time to dig! Clamming on the Oregon-Washington beaches was a different sport than clamming here. There, we would drive to the beach in the nightly procession of car headlights shining like a double strand of fluorescent beads. The dimly lit beach was always crowded with people, from two-year-olds to graybeard Methuselahs, milling up and down the beach in search of bubbles. The sand bore the telltale streaks of many dragged gunny sacks. No wonder this peopleless, pristine clam beach looked unnatural to us! There was no one to jovially ask: "How are you doing?" No competing to rush for a hard-to-find bubble—bubbles on this beach were everywhere! Many of the razor clams had their necks well up in sight, creating rings that enclosed a white stub of lengthy neck. The fun and sport of digging clams was surely gone.

We soon discovered otherwise. Despite the amazing number of clams, they were much harder to catch than we expected. As soon as we touched the sand with the point of our long, narrow shovels, away the clam would burrow, often making us dig an entire arm's length before we could grab its shell. I seemed to do better digging with my hands; rubber gloves kept the sand from being painfully pushed between the nail and skin. Occasionally, when a clam's foot outdistanced my fingers, I would find my arm buried shoulder deep in the wet sand with not even as much as a pulled-off clam neck for my effort. Bob would then come to my rescue with his shovel, and we curiously dug deeper to find out what large monster could have disappeared so rapidly. Usually we ended up not with a razor, but a large gaper clam. (One gaper is enough for chowder to serve four.) This day we also found some large Alaska surf clams, but most of our digging resulted in razors, the most savory of all clams. Even while we dug, we noticed that our mouths watered for their succulent goodness hot from the frying pan. Many of the razors were larger (six inches in length) than any we had ever dug.

Looking toward the breakers in between digs, Bob and I noticed that we were not alone. A seal popped his round head out of water to stare at us. We could imagine how his eyes must be straining and how the wheels of his mind must be turning—who were these two strange beings who were digging up the beach?

Finally tiring of our sport, we stopped, shelled the clams, put the meats inside a cellophane sack, and then placed the sack of razors in the packbasket. Winter weather made the packbasket function either as a refrigerator or a freezer. Leaving the packbasket on the sand, we took time to collect a few large shells that I wanted for serving seafood salad. This desire had come two weeks previously after having found an unbroken, unchipped clam shell that measured 15½ inches one way and 14 inches the shorter way.

Bob then hoisted the packbasket onto his shoulders, and we left regretting that Razor Clam Beach, with its many clams, was mostly inaccessible to us. The surf was far too rough for a skiff most of the time, and the smooth beach landing strip far too narrow for even a small plane to land and turn around. Because this beach was mostly unknown and seldom accessible, it gave abundant rewards. When the beach had been shown to us the previous August, three of us had dug 144 razors in fifteen minutes. This time we quickly dug 84 razor clams. Bob said that if crab fishermen knew of this spot, they would likely deplete the population by digging them all for bait.

After an eight-hour-day of snowshoeing and digging, we stumbled back to our camping site just at twelve noon. Regardless of my best efforts to snowshoe with a relaxed, natural walk, my ankles ached miserably; and Bob's, likewise.

In a few minutes we had broken camp and were on our way home. The porpoises put on tumbling displays in our honor, and we were even heralded by the occasional spouting whale. Whales—even killer whales—often followed our skiff when we were outside Kitoi Bay waters. Then, as an addition to our marine harvest of the day, Bob shot a seal. Although seals are the natural enemy of commercial fishermen, such that the Territory of Alaska placed a bounty on them, we did not shoot the seal for an elimination measure but because of its delicious, large liver. Liver has always been a favorite meat with us, and seal liver is unrivaled by beef, pork, or even veal. It is juicy, not dry. We felt fortunate for having hit our target and securing the seal before it had sunk. Putting it into the skiff, we anticipated the fresh liver meals to come.

As we entered Kitoi Bay that afternoon, Bob explained how the bay had been carved from layers of black shale by faulting and glacial action. It had only been twenty-four hours since we had so gladly left for a "change of scenery," but we gazed fondly on the beckoning research station so protected by the strength of the spruce-mantled peaks and glistening white Duck Mountain. The twenty-four hours had been enchanting, exhausting, and exhilarating.

Figure 24. Razor clams sizzling.

Both Frosty and Dinky were present as a welcoming committee, which gave us even greater delight to be home. What a feast they had as Bob and I, propped up on stools at the kitchen sink, tediously cleaned each razor clam and presented the unwanted bits to Dinky and Frosty as a banquet. After cutting off the shell, we were careful to wash the sand off completely before further cutting; otherwise the sand would cling to the cut edges. It took three hours for the two of us to clean the 84 clams. The arduous digging and tiresome cleaning made us feel more than justified in claiming our own banquet that night of succulent, golden-brown, egg-dipped and butter-fried razor clams, each as large as or larger than a hand.

Loss and Gain

Only two weeks after our camping trip, a catastrophe left us in an unsettled state. By this time, Dinky and Frosty had become dearer to us than any pet we had ever had. They had practically become family. The foxes were not actually trained or domesticated because that would take breeding over generations. But these two had become more superficially tame than we ever thought possible. As we became acquainted with these and others, we were surprised at the character divergence among foxes. I especially felt close to Frosty. It was only natural to stop while preparing dinner and visit with Frosty on the other side of the windowpane. Bob fell into the habit of always carrying Friskies in his pocket and habitually rewarded Dinky with Friskies for his faithful, trotting companionship around the immediate area. They each remained consistent in a routine that had been settled months before.

One afternoon, Dinky, who had acted perfectly normal and healthy during the morning, suddenly began having difficulty walking. Each time he tried to take a step, he would fall on his right side. How difficult to see him suffer before our very eyes. How could we help him? Finally, he crawled under a lumber pile out of sight. Bob soon followed and found him near death, eyes closed and unable to move. Regretfully, Bob realized he must help in the only way possible. He returned for his .22 rifle and mercifully shot Dinky. Even though I seldom cry, tears were close. I had never been an intense animal lover. Of course, I had always been against fox farming and fox hunting, but I had not fully realized how attached I had become to Dinky.

Since the ground was frozen, his body had to be put into the bay. I was glad this was Bob's task and not mine. Putting the carcass in the bay was unwise because it could wash up on shore and other animals could become sick from eating the carcass. But we had no choice. All of the station's non-burnable garbage was taken out in the skiff and thrown overboard just as the troop ships did in WWII. Everyone just accepted the practice.

While we were still in shock over losing our friendly Dinky, Frosty returned from one of her three-day absences and trotted up the path in her usual lively bouncing trot. Her presence helped mitigate the pain from Dinky's death. She enjoyed the graham crackers that we fed her and then followed Bob on his routine 5-p.m. weather take. On their return Frosty lay in her usual spot while I

Figure 25. Our fox friends were like pets.

chatted with her during meal preparation intervals. Rolling open a window, I tossed her a fourth graham cracker. She started toward it and fell on her right side. Frantically, I called Bob and we watched as she got up, fell, and then lay looking up at us with pleading, pathetic eyes, making no attempt to rise again. How difficult it was to watch as her agony increased. We were devastated. Finally, we could not stand the acute suffering her eyes revealed. We became convinced that she also must be put down.

The experience of both Dinky and Frosty dying of no apparent cause within a three-hour period was ghastly. We knew that we had not fed either fox the same food for the past three days because Frosty had been away. Also, we were quite certain that they did not have rabies since neither gave any indication of being mad. Bob observantly stared at me and I stared at him: which one of us would be next?

"Frosty had such a beautiful silver pelt. If we were not so sentimental, we would pelt her," said Bob.

I exclaimed, "Oh, no, we couldn't possibly! It would be just like skinning a person!"

"I'm afraid so. I'll put her in the bay."

When he returned, Bob said, "You know, I should have left her outside to freeze so we could have shipped her out to determine the cause of death. I wonder if it's some kind of shock disease that strikes at the top of the population cycle. Maybe something poisonous was available to both of them. And, by the way, instead of 'she,' I should be saying 'he'! I know she looked like a feminine beauty, but she was a male. And Dinky, with his unruly hair and homely looks, was a female."

Nevertheless, to us Dinky will always be "he" and Frosty, "she." Although we had a number of fox pets since, none ever ingratiated him- or herself into our favor the way Frosty or Dinky had. We grieved and continued to be lonely without them. Sometimes we would catch ourselves saving a good scrap for Frosty or Dinky, only to find no pet to donate it to.

Longer daylight hours and less-frequent periods of imprisonment by the tightly frozen bay attested to spring's approach. The longer daylight was invigorating; the open bay inspired a sense of freedom. On a few occasions this open waterway to the world even brought us a much-appreciated human visitor. Sometimes with the arrival of an unexpected storm, passing crabfishing boats would seek shelter in our bay.

Representing frontier hospitality as we did, we always tried to invite visitors in for dinner—probably a selfish invitation on our part, since we undoubtedly enjoyed the presence of guests even more than they did a meal. Our first spring guest was Hiram McAllister, a leading crab fisherman. The king crab fishery was expanding rapidly in the Kodiak area, and the shrimp fishery had also begun and was increasing. Both were providing a boost to the economy.

Figure 26. Soon I stopped envisioning an Alaskan king crab as a monstrous spider.

Hiram was an exceptionally jolly, likeable man who immediately caused me to visualize him dressed in a red suit playing the role of Santa Claus. While Bob was in Kodiak with his appendicitis attack, Hiram had taken him to visit a crab cannery,[6] introducing Bob as the pure food and drug inspector. During dinner Hiram was still chuckling over the effect this misrepresentation had produced.

Before leaving, Hiram gave us a huge king crab. King crabs occasionally reach as much as twenty pounds, and one spidery leg may be stretched to a span of five feet. The ones that we caught in our crab pots did not run this large, but the heavy iron pots were still difficult for Bob to pull to the surface. Many times the pots were empty; yet at other times, seal heads for bait attracted not only Alaska kings but even a few Dungeness, the more delicate type that are caught off the Oregon coast. Our large crab-boiling kettle was not big enough for our gift crab, so it had to be broken in half and boiled in two installments. Then, because we could not eat all of Hiram's gift before it would spoil, we ate only the large sections of the leg meat, giving the remainder to our new fox pets, Mr. Boss, Mrs. Boss (who was growing noticeably heavy), and bashful, cautious Muffy.

With each bite of Hiram's crab-meat gift, we recalled some of the stories Hiram had told us. One was a harrowing experience he had had nearly at our backdoor. His boat, *The Sue*, had capsized just fifteen miles north of us across the island in Perenosa Bay (*see Figure 1*). The main cause was a heavy load of crab pots on the deck and a plugged bilge pump. Water-filled tanks add to the load for all crabbers but are necessary in order to keep the crabs alive. Hiram had related this event with gestures and detailed suspense:

> *We had just pulled off our wet boots and outer clothing and stretched out on the bunks, when the boat began to list. With a yell to arouse the sleeping deck hand, we scrambled on deck only a moment before the boat rolled over on her side dumping the three of us into the ocean. Jim dived under the side of the floundering boat, cutting loose our small skiff with his belt knife. So there we were—wet, cold, Jim without his shoes, no food, no matches, not even an oar for the skiff, and it was snowing and stormy. Aboard the ship was every type of survival gear imaginable: rations, flares, sleeping bags, etc., all under twelve fathoms of water. Ripping the seat from the skiff, we paddled to shore, spending a cold, miserable night huddled under the skiff. Even this layer of fat [patting his stomach] didn't help. For breakfast a few raw clams were a little, but not much, better than nothing. After a second day of raw clams, we faintly remembered that the Alaska Department of Fisheries had a rustic cabin somewhere on Paul's Lake, about five miles*

---

[6] Freezing crab was soon discovered to be superior to canning. The Port Wakefield fishery processing plant on Raspberry Straight soon became the one preferred by crabbers.

away, so we started hiking in what we hoped was the right direction. Late that evening, we found the cabin equipped with a stove, matches, food, and bunks. Boy, it really looked good! We felt like kings.

The strong westerly winds prevented even the commercial airlines from flying. Then when the westerlies did subside enough for flying on the sixth day, the wind was still so strong that it laid the smoke from our fire signals flat against the white ice. Finally on the seventh day, we were able to attract P.N.A.'s attention. [Pacific Northern Airlines is the commercial airline whose daily flight pattern was directly over the cabin] And do you know, when I came home that evening after a quick pickup by the Coast Guard, my wife thought I was kidding about my boat sinking! Not until I phoned the insurance agent did she believe my experience.

Three weeks after Hiram's visit, we again had real human neighbors for two days when rough water forced the *Juno* to anchor in Kitoi Bay. Disturbed goldeneyes, scaups, marbled murrelets, and harlequin ducks plowing through the waves and flying from the bay indicated the arrival of the boat. After the *Juno* had anchored, Bob went out in the skiff to meet the newcomers, but afraid that our meal for two would not stretch for six, he did not invite them in for dinner. Later, he took them one pan of yeast rolls that I had just taken from the oven. We had not intended the rolls to cause indebtedness, but that evening when two of the crew came to visit, they brought with them a much-appreciated sack of fresh produce—lettuce, tomatoes, and an avocado.

Even though we felt somewhat primitive with our lack of running water, no electricity, homemade davenport, and painted box chairs, the two men looked at the waxed-tile floor, painted walls with huge windows, desk, four-drawer file, bookcase, and the white kitchen cabinets with Formica counters and exclaimed in amazement about our lovely accommodations. The evening was spent discussing fisheries: king crab, red salmon, silvers, Dollies, pinks, flounder. I had finally learned a few facts about fish, I thought, as I embroidered and listened, because that's all anyone who comes to Kitoi Bay can think of or talk about. Silently, I wondered if red salmon were more valuable because they had to be in a lake for a year, then the ocean for three years, and then back to the lake to spawn, or was it that red salmon were more valuable because their higher oil content made them taste better than pinks? And just why, I continued to muse, do you suppose each fish has so many different names? The men referred to red salmon, sockeyes, and bluebacks—all three are names of the same fish.

April brought even more company. To have three groups of visitors during the spring—so different from the previous ice-bound months—made us feel very social. Yet like the first two groups, neither a lady nor a child was present. The third group was a party of bear hunters rather than fishermen: two guides and their client, Dr. Holmes, a physician from Omaha. Not that I expected a female, but seven months without seeing one made me wonder how it would seem to see someone of my own gender.

After meeting the guides and the doctor, Bob came in with a description of the boat's occupants and an announcement, "Dr. Holmes is extremely eager to meet you. He's curious to meet a wife who would live out here all winter alone with me."

"Having met handsome you, he should have no doubt about the reason," I flattered. "Well, this should be fun. Are they coming in right away?"

"No, I knew it would be more fun for you to visit in their cabin so I accepted their invitation. This way I can take you out for the evening."

I carefully applied my lipstick. With feminine vanity, I noticed that my hair was curled in an especially attractive manner. Also, I was pleased that this had been Bob's day to shave. At Kitoi he usually enjoyed the luxury of leaving the razor in the medicine cabinet of our waterless winter bathroom every other morning.

We rowed the few yards to their small boat and entered the spotless but tiny cabin. Dr. Holmes could not hide his puzzlement and amazement. Just what did he expect a wilderness wife to look like? An unkempt, backwoods hermit's wife?

Wishing to welcome us with friendly hospitality, the doctor first offered us cigarettes, and the guide offered us some John Barleycorn. After we politely refused both, Dr. Holmes appeared even more intrigued and curious. Perhaps he was analyzing us as ascetics, or perhaps as alcoholics isolated for a cure; it would have been interesting to have known.

If Dr. Holmes were curious about us, I was equally curious about him. Kitoi Bay, you remember, offers no back-fence gossiping. However, I learned little, only that his wife went to Mexico each year for her vacation while he came to Alaska to hunt big game. When possible, the doctor continued his psycho-therapeutic analysis by addressing a question to one of us.

"What do you do to pass all the wintertime hours, play Scrabble?" questioned Dr. Holmes as he envisioned what he thought was a luxury of time.

"We're usually too busy for that. I don't think we've played Scrabble more than twice this winter," I replied. Then, as we each accepted a steaming cup of coffee from the head guide, I realized that to Dr. Holmes "being too busy" was a weak explanation. I could have explained that we kept regular daytime work hours and maintained a regular, evening study schedule. That would account for Bob's time, but he would still wonder what I did with my daytime hours. No doubt he was visualizing the hours I saved by not answering the telephone, shopping, caring for children, or attending the local garden club meeting. Should I explain that instead of doing business and visiting over a telephone, I did the same thing through the time-consuming means of letter writing? Should I mention that I did hand-mending, such as recently having to use blue denim to patch Bob's tan down jacket? Should I explain that shopping was not eliminated, only changed to choosing carefully from Sears Roebuck or Montgomery Ward catalogs? Should I say that instead of social meetings I accompanied Bob on his hours of fieldwork? No, all these would be such endless explanations. Likewise, it was doubtful if a man would understand the many small things that consume a woman's time when labor-saving devices are lacking: washing kerosene lamp chimneys; continual checks on the thermometer inside the unregulated oven to keep a halfway constant temperature; ironing with a temperamental gas iron; daily mixing both powdered whole and powdered skim milk; keeping forty-nine panes of window glass partially clean from the rapid accumulation of scum caused by oil heating; and living without running water. Neither would he realize how rapidly the relaxed minutes that Bob and I spent together in talking, laughing, identifying ducks, making candy, or just gazing at the stars added into hours. So I hastily added a short, logical explanation, "Our evenings are usually spent reading."

Further puzzlement and obvious amusement registered on the physician's face. Now I wondered if he were analyzing us as reading introverts. Well, perhaps we were. Reading completely relaxed us from the routines of daily living. It is just as well, I thought, that he doesn't know that we never get what we consider sufficient time to read. Evening reading light was poor even with the curved piece of leftover roofing tin we put behind the lantern to reflect the light onto our books. Often with the dim light and the singing hum of the gas lanterns after a day of physical outdoor exercise, we were ready to go to bed by nine-thirty.

Dr. Holmes' final analysis of his two case studies would have been most interesting. No doubt he penciled in his mind the diagnosis "abnormal" or else "healthful attitudes must be preserved by an immediate change in environment" because he spent the final forty-five minutes indirectly giving us his method of treatment. Significantly, he told of three cases that he had had in his professional career where isolation had led to insanity or suicide.

We appreciated his kind concern and his free professional examination but decided we wouldn't let his advice spoil our experience in this new country, America's lingering frontier.

Big City

Quent Edson came in late April to help with the spring biological work. Since someone had arrived, we could now plan a weekend in Kodiak to dust off the snowflakes of winter. We planned the trip for Saturday, May 1. The day dawned bright and clear with only a mild wind. Bob radioed Kodiak Airways at eight. They said a Widgeon would be right out. Now it was three in the afternoon. My emotions ebbed and our carefully pressed clothes had begun to wrinkle. Our shopping day was nearly gone.

On our first arrival at Kitoi Bay, we had passed through Kodiak but had little time to see the town. From my memory the town lay rather awkwardly on two narrow, paved streets along the waterfront. It was almost-less-than-a-town that stretched and squatted between the bay and the mountainous backdrop. A few scattered houses perched like birdhouses at the bottom of the mountain. Two or three miles of gravel road and paths led into town. My most vivid memory was of one or two intoxicated men stumbling down the street. Soon I would know whether my memories were correct. But why were we not hearing a plane buzzing the station so we could soon be on our way?

Finally at four o'clock Bob phoned Kodiak Airways to find out if they were still planning on coming to Kitoi for us. Bob Hall, the owner, answered, "Sorry, but we're afraid we won't be able to make it. I started out for you myself at nine this morning but lost an engine so had to turn around and come back. We've been working on it all day. The other planes have been tied up also."

"Okay, Bob. Sorry you had the trouble. If you can, we'd like to make it into town in time for church tomorrow morning," my Bob answered.

"Roger, Roger. We'll see you early tomorrow morning, weather permitting. KWN4 clear."

As Bob hung up the mike, I heaved an Eeyorian sigh, but then I relaxed and commented, "At least my excitement has worn off from all this waiting. Tomorrow I'll be able to emerge from our hibernation more composed. It's good the engine broke down *before* we were aboard instead of afterwards!"

Not really expecting the plane early the next morning, Bob still had some shaving-cream lather on his face and I, the bed to make when the Widgeon came roaring overhead circling the station. Its thunderous announcement of arrival was the aviation equivalent of ringing the doorbell. After a dash into our Sunday finery and a quick cup of coffee with the pilot, we were off.

Figure 27. A Grumman Widgeon landing in Kitoi Bay.

How easy and effortless flying seemed. A mile that took an hour of difficult, winter walking flashed past us in seconds. We soared above the rough terrain, the still-frozen lakes, and the rippling sea as effortlessly as seagulls. Soon we could see Kodiak Island and Kodiak itself because the entire flight was only thirty minutes. Yes, the town was tucked between the water and mountains, but it appeared larger than I had remembered. There were more than two streets.

Figure 28. Departing for Kodiak.

Houses were not as scattered as I had thought. Seeing Kodiak after living in Corvallis, Oregon, was different than now seeing it after living in complete isolation.

As we got off the plane, our pilot casually pointed out Benny Benson, the one who designed the Alaskan flag for the Territory. When Benny was a young teenager in an orphanage in Seward, the American Legion organization ran a territorial flag-drawing contest among all Alaskan school children. Benny drew eight stars representing the Big Dipper and the North Star, and this young Aleut boy won the contest. He was now a Kodiak man working as an airplane mechanic for Bob Hall's Airlines.

Probably not many people fly to church on a Sunday morning, but before we knew just what had happened, we were joining in the singing of "Praise God from Whom All Blessings Flow." The church service had begun. Although we had yearned for this privilege of uniting our hearts with others in formal worship, we each had difficulty keeping our thoughts from wandering and our minds from whirling. Sitting in a pew brought back memories of home, and yet it was so dreamlike. It seemed ages since we had experienced a real church service. We were in a sea of unfamiliar faces. Did we stand out as strangers? Were we overdressed? Clothing was more informal than in our former churches. The morning Sunday school attendance registered on the wall was 287, a surprising number since Kodiak's population was measured in the hundreds, not thousands. After months of living alone, I found great pleasure in just watching people and observing clothing styles rather than listening to the minister's announcements. Many young married couples sat in the pews. Most likely they were from the nearby naval station. Children, who had been absent in our lives, seemed everywhere, radiating an endearing charm. I continued to be distracted.

While we stood singing another hymn, a little, curly-haired boy standing in front of us turned to sneak a sly glance at Bob, the owner of that deep, bass voice. Many of the children were of mixed racial heritage, descendants of the Aleuts, Indians, Russian fishermen, fur traders, and others. The children were adorable and captivating. Then, while the choir sang an anthem, my unruly mind pushed the words and the music into the background as my eyes flitted throughout the congregation picking out the women and more of the precious children. The pastor's words marched on while I carried on an internal monologue with God.

"Lord, you do understand, do you not? I haven't seen a female for seven months! And oh, how I plead for a child of my own. Bless each of these dear children."

As the pastor led us in the morning prayer, my straying thoughts, feelings, and emotions finally settled into the American Baptist Church service, and I thanked God for the privilege of coming again into His house. After so many months away from church, I felt a deeper appreciation for corporate worship than I had ever felt before.

After the service, we leisurely strolled down the crooked, almost meandering streets in search of a restaurant. We soon found that the Kodiak pedestrian has to be cautious in crossing streets since the drivers take the right-of-way even at the intersections. Or was it just that we were unaccustomed to trusting the screeching brakes of those four-wheeled monsters?

Although we couldn't find the type of restaurant we had visualized for a Sunday dinner celebration (our first meal out in months), we did find the Polar Bear Café, a small, clean, four-booth restaurant. It was built so close to the street that the sidewalk had to make a jog around it. The owner, an attractive native lady, eyed us curiously during our meal. Evidently, she could tell that we were not residents of Kodiak, and yet we didn't fit the profile of the typical bear-hunting party, common visitors to Kodiak this time of the year.

Just as we had attracted the interest of the café's owner and waitress, so the people on the street fascinated us. From our corner booth, we could look directly down the sidewalk. In fact, had the sidewalk not turned around the corner of the café, we would have been sitting on the sidewalk! As each pedestrian approached, we became aware of the wide variety of social types: the elaborately dressed socialite; the coarse fisherman; a naval officer and his well-dressed wife; an unshaven, swaying drunkard; a trio of uniformed sailors followed by a group of giggling girls. Because of Kodiak's mixed-culture population, the class identity of the approaching individuals was varied. The occasional drunk staggering down the street was no more likely to be an Outsider than an Aleut; the attractive young girl was no more likely to be fair haired than brown or black haired. Girls with an Aleut heritage and skin ranging through all the various shades of brown had dark eyes and beautiful, black, glossy hair. The few older Aleut men had no baldness or gray hair. Besides observing the variety of types and the distinguishing racial and cultural features of the passing parade, we noted again the greater percentage both of younger adults and of men, so typical of Alaskan cities. We were sorry when we had finished our meal because that required us to leave the interesting moving picture show of Kodiak residents.

Bob had arranged a visit with a fellow biologist from the Alaska Department of Fisheries, Reed Stevens, and his wife, Ri. Since we hadn't yet had the opportunity to meet many families in Kodiak, we appreciated the few we were beginning to meet. Reed and Ri suggested taking us for a forty-five mile drive through the Kodiak Naval Station and around Chiniak Bay to Cape Chiniak, nearly the extent of the macadam and gravel road on Kodiak Island. The prospect delighted us both for the opportunity to ride in a car (the first in many months) and to see some of Kodiak's barren, rolling-hill grassland that appeared undressed compared to Afognak's spruce-green foliage.

Snow still clothed the peaks of the hills—or mountains, as some called them—while the lower reaches were dressed with spring's greenery. This mountainous shoreline rose abruptly to our right. Looking back across the bay and the winding road, we could see treeless Near Island (*see Figure 30*), Kodiak, the city dock, the naval base, and the airport. We could pick out occasional fishing vessels, reminding us of Kodiak Island's number-one industry, salmon fishing.

Our interest in the surroundings suddenly ceased as Bob and I both became miserably carsick. Even though Reed was not making paperclip curves, the winding road, the swing of the back seat of the Stevens' station wagon, and our lack of recent automobile travel upset our equilibrium. Not being able to conceal our nausea, we asked Reed to stop at the far side of Women's Bay. The fresh air and brief cessation of movement brought little relief to our woozy and swirling insides. By the time we had reached the head of Middle Bay, we were forced to ask the Stevens to take us back to our hotel room. How disappointing—especially after the anticipation—to find that we were just not ready to resume travel on wheels. We had become accustomed to the rocking and bouncing of a small boat that traveled straight, not the swaying and turning of a land vehicle.

After three hours of lying in bed with our headaches and churning stomachs, we gradually began feeling better. Yet because of some lingering queasiness, we decided it best not to eat for at least a few hours.

Soon we dressed and left for the evening church service. Several people who had spoken to us that morning again welcomed us, but we did not know a single person in the congregation. After the service a Mr. Bill Stone noticed our desire to become acquainted. He introduced himself and introduced us to his wife, Zelma.

"Are you new in town?"

"We're new to Kodiak, although we've lived at Kitoi Bay for nearly a year."

"Kitoi Bay. I don't believe I know where it is. Is it near Uganik Bay?"

"No, Kitoi Bay is a new fisheries research station located on Afognak Island."

"Oh, near the village of Afognak, I suppose."

"No, Kitoi Bay is as far from the village of Afognak as it is from Kodiak. We're in town for our semiannual visit."

"You don't mean it? Zelma, did you hear that? How long did you say it has been since you've been into town?"

We laughed and Bob replied, "Seven months. Ruth has spent the last seven months without even seeing another woman or a child."

"You just must come home with us for a cup of coffee. Can you? We'll bring you back into town."

We gladly accepted their friendly invitation and deduced from Mr. Stone's last statement that they lived out of town. However, his next remark really puzzled us.

"Hope you won't mind riding with the children. The bus is rather a jolter, but the group is a merry one."

We soon found "the bus" was not a nickname for an old car. It was a regular yellow bus. Many darker-skinned, dark-haired children were boarding it along with several adult ladies, one with a tiny baby in her arms. (Emotions welled inside as I yearned to be holding a baby of my very own.) It was not until we were on and seated that we realized just whom we were going to visit. Our new acquaintances were the superintendent and his wife of the native children's orphanage, the Baptist Mission, founded in 1893. Bob suddenly remembered putting pennies in his childhood Sunday school collection envelope for the Baptist Orphanage in Alaska. Now, twenty-two years later, we were on a bus with these children.

Driving the two graveled miles north of town and into the mission grounds, we were immediately attracted by the Kitoi-like spruce. At that time the town of Kodiak was the approximate dividing line between the southern, grassy mountains and the northern, wooded mountains and islands. Mr. Stone parked the bus, and the children and adults made an orderly exit, seat by seat, and then away the boys and girls scrambled to their various cottages. We accompanied Mr. and Mrs. Stone and their two daughters, Zelanna, age thirteen, and Nelda Jane, age eleven, to their station wagon and rode the remaining mile to their private, rustic log home tucked among the spruce.

I gasped in admiration when I entered. The rooms were neither modern nor elaborately furnished, but the modest interior fit with my expectation of how an Alaskan living room should look. The room was captivating. Alaskan paintings hung on the knotty pine walls; Aleut artifacts occupied two shelves of an open bookcase; hand-braided rugs and a bearskin lay on the varnished hardwood floors.

I purposefully chose to sit in a rocker near the Kodiak-brown-bear rug so that I could reach down and feel the deep fur and the Teddy-bear-like ears of the cub brownie. Worn parts of the rug gave evidence of hours of romping and enjoyment by children during the ten years the Stones had lived in Kodiak. Seeing this rug and all it added to the warmth of their home made me hope for a bearskin rug of our own. In fact, it was Bill Stone himself who would come to Kitoi in a later winter to join Bob on a bear hunting expedition[7] for just such a trophy. Bob, with a friendly cat purring in his lap, noticed my attention to the rug.

---

[7] For a Kodiak brown bear hunting experience during our third year on the Island, see Appendix A.

"You are really charmed by him, aren't you?"

"I'm enchanted."

The conversation then continued with various bear experiences. I could not help but wonder on how many previous occasions the bear rug had been a conversational piece, yet I realized that around Bill Stone one did not need a conversation starter. His suitability for being superintendent of a children's mission was plainly evident by his sense of humor, jovial nature, and genuine friendliness in addition to his love of children. "Bill and Zelma" were almost unconsciously exchanged for "Mr. and Mrs. Stone" as we continued to visit and enjoy their hospitality.

Bill told us the history of the orphanage and of its founding on Woody Island in 1893. It had been located on 640 acres with a large garden and many buildings, including a power plant and even a hospital. Many of the orphans were there because their parents had died from epidemics. It was not until 1937 that the American Baptist orphanage was moved south to Kodiak, mostly because the main building had been destroyed by fire in 1926 and again in 1937.

Zelma soon had coffee, lime sherbet, and cookies prepared. As we sat around the table enjoying these refreshments, Bob and I could not resist commenting on our pleasure in eating from fine china placed on a pink linen tablecloth instead of the Navy-surplus, heavy handleless mugs and thick, white dishes we used at the station. Of course such dishes were only practical for our summer influx of workers, ones who would soon be arriving. Yet I could not help feeling a wave of nostalgia for the years when Bob and I had followed the ritual of eating Sunday dinner with china, cherished pieces of sterling, and our Heisey crystal, now all packed carefully in a barrel while we were Alaskan pioneers.

Throughout our visit and even on the short ride back into the lights of Kodiak, Zelma and Bill showed great interest in our isolated situation. It was always surprising that even Alaskans seemed astonished that anyone would live without others within walking distance. But unlike people whose reaction to our isolation was "How can you stand it?," the Stones were intrigued by our novel life. After learning that our Kitoi Bay accommodations were pleasant except for lack of electricity and running water, Bill and Zelma expressed complete approval, if not envy.

Arriving back at Kodiak Hotel (the only lodging place in town), we eagerly anticipated the climax of our interesting day: a bath in a real bathtub. No water to carry from the creek; no need to heat it; no cramped, sponge-bath procedure—merely a turn of the faucet and there it was—a huge tub of hot, sudsy water! Bathing was luxurious. This day had been as welcome as fresh strawberries in the spring, but we both realized we had no desire to exchange our life at Kitoi Bay for city-dwelling in Kodiak.

Since we had arrived in Kodiak a day late and missed our Saturday shopping, we scheduled Monday for our shopping day and set Tuesday for our day of return. Monday's shopping included looking through every store in town, which was not a great chore considering the town's size.

While Bob visited oil and gas companies, a welding shop, and other stores for research and construction needs at Kitoi Bay, I strolled through the dress areas of Kodiak's two general merchandise stores and also visited the two dress shops. Not that I intended to buy a dress, but I just wanted to see the styles and feel the textures. The limited assortment surprised me. In the four stores combined, I counted a total of only fourteen dresses and not one of the fourteen was of a style I thought to be appealing. Of course, each clerk assured me a new shipment was expected. It is understandable that residents of Kodiak usually go to Anchorage or even Outside to Seattle once a year for shopping and for dental and medical needs.

Bob and I met again to continue shopping together along the bar-lined streets for the many items on our list. The feel and jingle of coins seemed strange since we had almost forgotten the need for them. As we chatted, I mentioned to Bob, "A clerk asked me if we were on our way Outside. She must have realized that I did not live in Kodiak."

Although not Kodiak residents, we were beginning to feel like Alaskans because of our use of the terms Outside and Inside as unconsciously and glibly as others. Even so, others seemed to know that we were not residents in this small community.

As we had during our Sunday café meal, we again noticed that Kodiak had noticeable distinguishing characteristics. Although the oldest town in Alaska, it still looked like a frontier: drunken men staggered along the sidewalk in mid-day; many people on the streets appeared coarse, practical, and with an indifference to usual social restraints or approved etiquette. The wide variety in dress and attitudes was typical of a frontier where individualism rather than a culturally established pattern rules.

Unlike Kitoi Bay, Kodiak could hardly be considered "in the wake of the frontier" because it had progressed and modernized. Military construction during the past fifteen years had changed Kodiak from a small cluster of homes into a town. These years brought electrification, a hospital, and an adjacent military base with a road built to it.

To our bewilderment, nearly every third car seemed to be a taxicab. Checking later on the exact number of taxicabs, we found that Kodiak had twenty-six, or an average of one taxi to every ninety people.[8] Since there was a bus that ran both within the town and to the naval base at a lower fare than the taxis charged and since a person could easily walk any place in the small town, the predominance of taxicabs was a complete mystery. Later, after becoming acquainted with a former taxi driver, I asked what constituted the majority of his business.

"Why, taking people from one bar to the next," he answered seriously and without hesitation. "Lots of times I've been called to the B & B (Beer & Booze) just to take a passenger across the street to the Belmont."

Figure 29. A Kodiak street.

As was the case with the taxis, there seemed to be an unusual number of bars and liquor stores, fueling the traffic of drunks. Many fishermen in the area squandered most of their paychecks in bars to the detriment of their families. While walking down the streets, we counted six times as many bars and liquor stores (18) as grocery stores (3). The incidents of crime, including murders that occasionally took place in a Kodiak bar, reminded us of the lingering frontier-like character of the town.

The streets and sidewalks were overrun with dogs. "No Dogs Please" signs were posted on the doors of nearly every store. Often a large dog would be lying outside the front entrance of a store waiting for his owner. Many others, apparently shifting for themselves after being left behind by a family who had moved,

---

[8] Population was around 2300, which included about 600 out-of-town residents.

prowled the streets and sidewalks. It did not surprise us later to read that the city council was putting various dog ordinances into effect.

Our most enjoyable shopping—grocery buying—had been saved until last. Roaming through supermarkets had always been a favorite activity for us, so we were thrilled that Kodiak boasted a modern supermarket, in obvious contrast to the other aging storefronts. Because we had been doing our grocery shopping over the short-wave radio set for the past seven months, pushing the grocery cart down the aisles among the stacks of self-service foods of O. Kraft & Son provided immense pleasure. Besides groceries and meats, they had hardware, clothing, engine and boat accessories, and furniture. Taking our time, we looked at nearly everything and especially enjoyed finding recent additions since our last grocery shopping tour, which had been eight or more months ago before we entered the Territory. The change was astounding. TV meals had just arrived (never mind that television wasn't yet available in Kodiak!), frozen soups, miniature marshmallows, breadcrumbs, and even canned pie fruits and berries with thickening added.

"If we stayed isolated for ten years, grocery shopping would be like touring the store of the future," I suggested.

"Yes," Bob replied. "It actually would be culture shock, and I suppose we would appear as Rip Van Winkles."

"Perhaps we had better continue our annual or semiannual trips to town."

If we had been willing to pay our own airfare, we could have flown into Kodiak more than once or twice a year. But to us, the $72.00 (round-trip cost for the two of us) was prohibitive. Besides, there would have been the cost of a hotel in Kodiak, not to mention missing a day's work and having the uncertainty of being able to return to Kitoi due to weather. But this trip was especially enjoyable because Bob's employer, the Alaska Department of Fisheries (territorial), paid the airfare and hotel costs. In the early evening, we again ate dinner in the Polar Bear Café, sat in our favorite sidewalk window booth, and again observed our two-legged neighbors before returning to our Kitoi Bay four-legged variety.

Just as we finished our main course, Pete Olsen, the native fisherman who had let me operate his boat the previous fall and who had later attempted to take us to the village of Afognak, came up the street from work and recognized us. Immediately, he entered the restaurant, sat down, and visited with us for a few minutes. As I looked across the table at Bob dressed in his sport jacket and overcoat sitting next to Pete with his darker skin, tattered, dirty work clothes, and tin lunch bucket, my mind focused on how superficial and camouflaging clothes, race, customs, and even education can be when it is character that makes the real person. The conversation began to wind down.

"When will you be going back? On the Tuesday mail plane?" Pete asked.

"Yes, we plan on leaving sometime tomorrow, weather permitting of course."

"I'd sure like for you to meet my family. We have a birthday party tonight—not that I like parties—but it's one of those things you have to go to, I guess. If you don't leave tomorrow, we'd like to have you come see us tomorrow evening, that is if you think you can stand the children. They're awfully noisy."

Bob and I both told him that we would be glad to come if the weather prevented our leaving.

"I'd just love to visit an Aleut home," I told Bob after Pete had left. "I hope tomorrow is really windy or else soupy with fog."

But Tuesday dawned clear and bright, some wind but not enough to prevent flying. Airplanes were already in the air by the time we phoned Kodiak Airways to find out the departure time for Kitoi Bay.

"Probably about eleven," Bob Hall informed us. "We'll come by the hotel and get you so you won't need to carry your baggage down."

We had time for a last shopping excursion. When we arrived back at the hotel to pack the few remaining articles, we found a message had come while we had been shopping: our flight would not depart until 2:30.

At 2:30 the phone rang. Bob Hall spoke, "We can take you as planned, but so much wind has come up we won't be able to land at Port Williams or at Point Banks (two points on Shuyak Island north of Afognak Island). It would be better for us to go tomorrow. Is it okay with you to wait until eight fifteen in the morning?"

"That'll be fine. We'll be ready first thing tomorrow morning."

Turning to me, my rather pleased husband said, "Well, your wish came true, Ruth."

That evening Bob and I walked to the street that we remembered as Pete's address and then counted to the third house. We hesitated at the corner wondering if we had remembered the correct directions. Knowing that the Olsens had six children, were expecting their seventh, and that Pete had had his share of bad luck in fishing, we hardly expected the largest, newest house on the road to be theirs. The lighted interior showed a native woman at the sink, so we decided that perhaps this was it.

A chubby-faced, black-haired little girl answered our knock. Her sisters and brothers were playing house with a blanket draped over an empty baby buggy for a prop, and an older girl, around ten, sat on the davenport reading. The aroma of homemade bread filled the house.

"Is this the Olsens?" Bob asked.

"Yes, I'll get Mamma."

Mrs. Olsen came from the kitchen, her slight limp nearly unnoticed because of her bright, friendly smile. She immediately invited us inside.

"Just sit down and I'll call Pete." We could tell our visit was a surprise, and no wonder because Kodiak Airway's planes had been taking off and landing in the channel in front of their home throughout the day.

Pete, who had evidently been resting in a bedroom, came into the room, warmly greeted us, and then informed the children—Ruth, David, Lydia, Kathleen, and Mark, who ranged in age from eleven to five—that they would have to do their playing in the bedroom because their play in the front room made it too noisy for visiting. I was sorry to see the merry troop leave. Mrs. Olsen shyly excused herself to finish the bread she had been making in the kitchen. I wondered if her oven, like mine, heated mainly from the top, making it necessary to place aluminum foil over food to prevent burning.

I now noticed that their oldest girl, Ruth, was reading from a set of Child Craft books. The other children, although intent on their bedroom playing, wandered into the front room often enough for us to get to know them by name and for them to scrutinize their visitors. One of the boys let their parakeet out of the cage for us to see. Pete then brought out Christine, their youngest child who was sixteen months. She was just awakening from a nap. Pete's pride in his healthy nice-looking children was evident even though he said, "Sometimes we wish for just five minutes of quiet."

Soon Mrs. Olsen rejoined us, and the topic of conversation drifted to their home. I had already glanced about the living room and into the cheerful blue and yellow kitchen. I saw an automatic clothes washer, electric mixer, large refrigerator, upright freezer, and an oil range with a top that shone as bright as new. Having an oil cookstove at Kitoi, I fully realized the labor necessary to keep the grease and oil from collecting. Everything was clean, and the home was larger than the average Kodiak home.

Pete explained that when they bought the house it had only two rooms. Gradually he had converted the two rooms into the present kitchen and built the rest. "But we still can't keep ahead of our growing family," Pete laughingly said. "As soon as we get the upstairs finished, we want to add to the living room and make it larger."

Nina Olsen's six children plus her birth handicap of a limp made her appear twenty years older than I was, but actually she was only age thirty. As a little girl of eleven, she had been sent without relatives in a government health boat to Seattle for hip surgery, but it had not eliminated the problem.

Bedtime arrived for the children. Each well-behaved child washed and prepared for bed without help and with a minimum of confusion. Eleven-year-old

Ruth, the oldest, took the responsibility of bathing and preparing baby Christine for bed, allowing Mrs. Olsen complete freedom from bedtime duties. Much later I learned that almost all native children did this. What a sharp contrast to my culture.

Our evening at the Olsen's came to a close with ice cream, coffee, homemade cinnamon rolls directly removed from the oven, and some of Mrs. Olsen's delectable, wild-salmonberry jelly. We left with warmth of inspiration from having visited this industrious family and a temporary desire for six—yes, even seven children to bulge the house seams outward.

By eight-thirty the next morning we were in a Widgeon taxiing through the waters of the channel between Kodiak Island and Near Island. The morning was bright, clear, and calm. Bob had given me the choice seat in the cockpit with Gil, the pilot, while Bob sat with the groceries, folding chairs, galvanized pipe, and other departmental supplies in the back. I was pleased that we were soon to have real chairs instead of boxes.

Unexpectedly, this flight turned into a mountain-top experience in an above-mountain-top setting. As soon as we reached a comfortable altitude and I was again experiencing the newness and elation of flying, Gil leaned across and shouted above the motors' roar, "Now flying an airplane is really very simple." And he began to explain the rudder controls, the control of the wings, nose, and other details while I,

Figure 30. Aerial view of Kodiak, Dog Bay, and Near Island.

completely puzzled as to why he was explaining each instrument so explicitly, listened intently. Even though detailed, the directions were clear and concise. Gil, a former flying instructor (and surprisingly, a former beauty-salon operator), gave a reason for each instruction.

He leaned back in his seat. "Okay, now you fly it."

To my astonishment he took his feet and hands off all the controls, automatically forcing me to operate the co-pilot's controls. Although startled, I was delighted. I tried to remember all of his concise instructions.

Amazingly enough, I was not just flying; I was piloting! The needed actions seemed to be the natural ones. Whenever I felt the right wing tip downward, I raised it by turning the small half steering wheel to the left, but not much or the plane would roll too far on its left side. As I turned the wheel, I pushed my corresponding foot with the same amount of pressure that I used on the steering wheel to control the rudder correctly. The inclination seemed natural. Even so, it took complete concentration for me to maintain control of the two-motored craft because besides the plane's side action and the rudder, I had a third part to watch: the nose-tail tipping. "By keeping your eyes on the distant horizon," Gil had said, "you can tell not only if the plane is tipped sideways but also if it has its nose up or down." I soon found that a pilot automatically feels any lack of levelness and that the horizon verifies these feelings. The wheel used for controlling the side action was attached to a stick for controlling the nose. If the nose was downward and should be leveled or tipped upward, I would pull back on the wheel and stick; similarly, if the nose needed to go downward, I would push forward on the stick.

For several minutes I had been keeping all three parts of the flying in control. I wished that I could turn and see Bob's expression or even Gils' but dared not take my eyes from the horizon. Even such momentary thought-wanderings caused my downfall. I forgot and pushed forward on the stick when I had wanted to bring the nose higher. The nose dipped and the plane began a downward plunge. I screamed and took my eyes off the controls, turning to Gil in panic. Naturally, I expected him to take hold of his controls and get us out of the dive. Mr. Gil, as he was often called, continued to sit back as if he were only a passenger. Desperately, I struggled to capture my frayed senses and to get the plane under control. I pulled back on the stick—we leveled out. I now concentrated even harder on managing the side action, the rudder action, and the nose-to-tail action. Five or ten uneventful minutes of smooth flying passed, improving my crestfallen self-image.

In a short time we began crossing some of the rocky headlands jutting into the sea. The wind updrafts rocked the plane making it nearly impossible to prevent the teetering ups and downs.

"See those two clouds below," Gil shouted. "Lower the plane and go between them."

Now that we were completely over land, the air currents had again steadied, freeing me to concentrate on how to maneuver the plane downward between the two puffy clouds. Down, down, down. I discovered that distance in the air is deceiving. Finally, by the time we reached the two cloud markers, I had the plane at their level and glided between them as easily as driving a car between two Highway-138-Crater-Lake snowbanks in Oregon's early spring.

"Keep lowering the plane."

It already seemed that we were clipping the mountains. But I followed instructions and continued to concentrate on keeping the wings level and the rudder in control.

As the research station came into view, Gil took hold of his controls and said, "Just keep your hands and feet on the controls and you can go through the landing with me to get the feel of it." (Such trust!) Again, he explained every move during the landing, but there were too many instructions and I was too dazed to grasp everything at once, as he surely knew.

Our floats touched the water, and white spumes of sea foam rose on each side of us. Now instead of pushing on the rudder controls in the direction of the wheel, Gil pushed his opposite foot in a remote control maneuver that slowed the plane to taxiing speed. It was days, though, before my ecstasy from flying slowed to a 'taxiing speed'!

While we were airborne, before I had taken the controls, I had gazed below me at the archipelagic shorelines, thinking of my life. Like those shores, Bob and I were slowly undergoing change. Life's experiences deposit and erode, improve and deteriorate, to shape our vision and character. Every experience—even this, my first piloting of a plane—moved and marked me.

The Noisy Season

Summer was noisy. As soon as weather permitted, a small crew of workers and a few biologists joined us at the station. They came to build, add on, supervise, and/or do research. While at the station, they joined us almost as part of our family. We called summertime the "Noisy Season."

The construction workmen were colorful. Some were troubled, aimless souls like clamshells rolling with the tide, not having discovered who they were and what to do; others were outgoing and jovial. Still others were serious and intense. A portrait gallery would include Jack, a former beggar who stole picnic baskets in city parks; John, always quiet except for a sharp wit displayed at well-timed intervals to bring peals of laughter; Von, a blackballed Kodiak bartender; Leo, a good-natured fellow who dieted by avoiding potatoes but stuffed himself with hot breads and pastries; Claude, who entertained us with his southern drawl and accentuated hillbilly speech; Molly, a male Montana State University graduate who was a miner, politician, and construction engineer—but greatest of all achievements—a grandfather; Shorty, who jealously guarded his imported wine; Gene, a jokester whose labels of "coffin nails" for cigarettes, "puddling sticks" for spoons, and "landing gear" for feet kept conversation confusing and amusing; Ed, a recent high school graduate who was homesick for Juneau and his girlfriend; Milt, who would pull his huge, bushy eyebrows over his eyes as blinds to keep out the glare of the morning sun; and Milt's twelve-year-old son, Pinkie, a welcome catalyst for the group of adults. This sample of Alaskans kept us constantly entertained as they filtered through Kitoi Bay. I learned to appreciate their individualities: a generic sameness would have tasted like unsalted oatmeal, but their differences combined for a flavorful mulligan stew.

Bob and I again moved into our toy-sized "summer cottage on Kitoi Bay Heights" or our "shack on the hill," depending on our mood at the time of reference. It was the same shed we slept in on our first night at Kitoi, but since then it had been moved to the top of a small embankment. This little house-bedroom provided us some privacy. Lack of both space and kitchen equipment required that the whole noisy season group eat together at the main station, which was our wintertime home. This shift from the wintertime Silent Season to the summertime Noisy Season had been abrupt but not exactly unwelcome. At times Bob and I played the role of host and hostess for the heterogeneous group; at times we were Father and Mother; and at times we were just two observers watching actors and comedians produce a real-life drama. Other biologists (such as Quent Edson and Robert Parker) and a few construction workers were present much of the summer, but Bob and I were the only ones privileged to watch the complete performance from the entrance of the first players in Scene 1 to the final curtain drop in the fall.

We were already veterans since this, the summer of 1955, was our second Noisy Season. Some workers came for only a week or so and others for the entire summer to construct a 25x85-foot hatchery (attached directly to our station) and a large ten-inch-diameter, wooden pipeline to carry water from Big Kitoi Lake to the hatchery. It was the first time I had seen pipe made entirely of wood. Constructing a pathway for laying the pipe required a lot of digging and blasting.

Figure 31. Completed wooden pipeline.

The pipe itself was put together by the muscle power of two men (one on each side) using a T-shaped wooden rammer. The rammer was fitted with a cone-like tip to evenly drive the tapered end of an eight-foot pipe section into the already laid pipe that was held firmly in place by ground stakes. When wet, the wood would swell so the joints were tight. The wood also provided a certain amount of insulation. Having water for the living quarters was a great side benefit of the water's main purpose, which was to supply water for the hatchery. Eggs and small salmon would now be reared in the hatchery for research studies being conducted on several of the nearby lakes. Thus, the following fall (1955), sockeye were held in a holding pen at Little Kitoi Lake and artificially spawned. The eggs were put in the new hatchery to await hatching in the spring.

The new steeply sloped gravity pipeline that had been placed higher up on Big Kitoi Creek, however, did not prevent Bob having to carry water from the creek that following winter. Although the water came through the hatchery and then into the house, keeping the water running smoothly was nearly a full-time job. Bob fixed the toilet so it would run continuously and told me to keep faucets running so the water line to the house would not freeze. How much we appreciated the modern convenience of having water from a faucet. Naturally, we wanted to keep this luxury as long as possible. It was perfect in above-freezing weather. But now my problem was learning to keep faucets on instead of off. Bob said I was adjustable in every other way, but not this. Something so simple was extremely difficult. Any husband other than mine would have thrown up his arms in frustration and ceased keeping the pipeline open long before Bob finally conceded. Time after time, he had to patiently thaw the lower sections of pipe by using hot water, a blowtorch, or both. Once he had to thaw the line three times in one day. Finally, the faucet was accidentally left closed long enough for nearly the whole line to freeze. He had to unscrew the various pipe sections to prevent further freezing from bursting the pipes. Ultimately, Mother Nature took control and we reverted to carrying water from nearby Big Kitoi Creek. Dipping water from the creek had to be timed with the low tides when the water was not salty from the influx of ocean water. Oh, well, I reasoned, even open faucets would not keep the pipeline open all winter. Carrying water for drinking, cooking, cleaning, bathing, and washing clothes was inevitable.

But in the Noisy Season of 1955, these future difficulties with the pipeline were things I did not envision. Molly McSpadden headed the project and the construction workers labored hard at building it, even building a trestle in one place to carry the pipe. The influx of so many workers required some adjustments. A hastily constructed bunkhouse helped provide sleeping quarters and a ping-pong-sized dining table facilitated the eating arrangement.

Pinkie, Milt's young son, added interest to this new group of personalities. He had been at the station scarcely ten minutes before he vanished through the dense spruce into the network of bear trails. As his name implies, Pinkie was a freckled, red-haired lad just bursting with energy stimulated by freedom from a sixth-grade classroom and by the surrounding miles of forest so well adapted for running, fishing, and hunting. Twenty-five minutes after his sudden disappearance, Pinkie breathlessly arrived back at camp (the name that was gradually taking the place of "station") and announced, "I found a lake. That's a nice little red pram[9] you have on it." He was as confident as a weasel is skittery.

"Did you meet Mr. Bear along the way?" Bob asked.

Pinkie looked rather surprised, while a doubtful, concerned expression crossed Milt's face.

"That's right, Pinkie. You're not in the city limits of Juneau any longer. Remember 'thar's b'ar in dem 'dere hills,'" Gene cautioned.

"That red hair would really attract bear," further admonished Ed.

During the following evening and throughout the next day the men spun bear yarns in an attempt to frighten Pinkie sufficiently to cause him to remain at the station. However, Pinkie did not swallow all the tales, at least not to the extent of confining himself to the small station area. But Milt, after taking a Sunday afternoon walk and finding bear tracks on all sides of the station, became convinced that bear were nearby. Reluctantly, he told his son that he would have to remain at the station and not wander into the woods unless with an adult.

This restraint was difficult for a twelve-year-old with a natural desire for exploring and an unlimited curiosity. But Pinkie obeyed.

Figure 32. Preparing dinner in the kitchen/laboratory.

---

[9] On Little Kitoi Lake we had a lightweight 14-ft boat with a 15-hp motor.

Since I was the only woman, and supposedly not busy, it was taken for granted that I would continue cooking for the group. Cooking for eight to ten hardworking laborers would have been very tiring except for the men's help. Their help had increased over the months so soon they were washing and drying all the dishes as well as preparing what I consider the most difficult meal, breakfast. Not having more interesting activities, Pinkie became my assistant in the kitchen. His company, as he stood or sat in the kitchen inhaling the tempting aromas and licking all the mixing bowls, was pleasant. Although I liked to cook, I also missed outdoor exercise, especially now that wrapping like a mummy was no longer needed for protection from the cold. So during the next month when Pinkie began plotting such plans as, "If I help you, can you hike someplace with me this afternoon?" I attempted to arrange my schedule to include a free hour or so for walks with Pinkie.

On these hour excursions I carried Bob's .30-06 against the one chance in a hundred that we would meet an unfriendly bear. Pinkie often carried his .22 rifle. On one of our first trips, we left the station on the century-old bear trail and started toward Little Kitoi Lake. With the disappearance of the snow, the moss covering logs, hillsides, and spruce limbs had deepened in color and in many places had given the woods a lush, green carpet. It was fun to leave the trail just to walk on such downy softness. With each step our feet sank three to four inches, making it easy to imagine we were touring a luxuriously carpeted castle. Ferns and plants grew out of this swank covering with graceful poise. Only the thorny devil's club bushes and some tangles of salmonberry thwarted our steps.

Noticing that Pinkie was keeping his rifle pointed to the ground, I complimented him on his caution.

"Boy, Dad wouldn't let me have it if I didn't keep the shells out and be careful with it," he replied.

Reaching the weir at Little Kitoi Lake's outlet, we found Bob and Quent counting and measuring the tiny smolts migrating from the lake. These tiny fish, ranging from two to four inches, slid over the screens of the weir and swam down the board flume into a holding pen. From there Bob or Quent would then dip them, quickly measure and count them, and record the number on their hand tallies before flipping the wiggling little creatures into a basin of water and pouring them into a smooth eddy of the outlet creek.

Certain samples of the smolts were counted and placed in a special bucket and anesthetized. Then, one by one, they were removed and placed on a graph-papered board with their nose against the edge that had a side abutment. A quick, deft puncture with a "teasing needle" was placed through the paper at their tail to determine their length. The recorded fork length was used for later computation. Some of the anesthetized fish were put in formaldehyde for dissection and microscopic examination at the station.

"What kind of fish are they?" Pinkie asked, as he watched the whole procedure.

"Most of them are tiny red salmon—the larger ones, like that one flipping down the trough, are young silver salmon. They've been living in the lake for the past two or three years and are now on their way to the ocean."

"You mean those little minnows are two years old?"

Figure 33. Little Kitoi weir.

"They aren't very big after two years in the lake, are they? But they'll be five to seven pound salmon when they return from spending two to three years in the ocean. They stuff themselves in the ocean just like you've been doing the last few meals."

Being used to such teasing, Pinkie didn't let it hinder his questioning. "Why are you counting them?"

Quent took his turn to explain. "That's a good question. A simple answer would be that we are trying to find how many eggs live until the fish go to the ocean and then how many of the ones that go to the ocean return."

"Why do you want to know?"

"So we can tell how many fish the lake can support. The lake has food for only a limited number. By the way, would you like some target practice with that .22 you have in your hand?" Quent asked.

"Sure would."

"A raven has been feasting on the downstream smolts for several days now. He's down near the mouth of the outlet. There he is now. Do you see him?"

With boyish glee, Pinkie was already sneaking up on the black intruder. The raven, being used to Bob and Quent working at the weir, was fairly tame so Pinkie cautiously approached to about eighty feet, balanced his gun on a protruding rock, aimed, and fired. To his amazement, the raven fell.

"I got him," he yelled.

He rushed to get the dead bird and then ran back to the weir to show us his success. After due praise for killing this predator, he spread the raven on top of a huge rock so that later his father, Gene, Ed, and the rest could see it.

"We'll have to leave now, Pinkie, as it is nearly time to get dinner," I reminded him.

"So soon?"

"So soon."

But just as Pinkie picked up his rifle to accompany me, his face became white, and he began slapping his pockets. "I've lost my clip. The clip isn't in my gun, and I don't have it in my pockets." All the joy of his hunt had vanished by this calamity.

"Are you sure you don't have it? What about your shirt pocket?"

"No, the clip is gone," Pinkie moaned and then rechecked each pocket. The clip was not to be found.

"We'll go back and hunt for it now before the tide comes in."

"Oh, that's nice of you, Ruth. I can't use my gun all summer if we don't find it. Besides, Dad won't like it if I've lost it."

We searched up and down between the weir and the mouth of the outlet. Finally after twenty minutes of searching, I spotted the black clip wedged among the dark rubble. Pinkie was overjoyed.

"Thanks so much, Ruth, for coming back and hunting it. I'll help you with dinner if we are late."

"We are late, but we will have time enough. We should hurry though." Then as an added incentive, I added, "You may walk just as fast as you want home and I'll keep up with you."

"You'll keep up with me? I noticed you walk real fast. Dad always makes me walk so slow when I'm with him, but I still bet you can't keep up with me."

Away we sped, much closer to a run than a walk. I tried to match Pinkie's high energy. In seven minutes we had covered the crooked mile and were at the station. Although Pinkie didn't leave me behind, he did reach the station a few yards ahead of me. My lungs ached. I was breathless and exhausted. In fact, I had to lie down for twenty minutes to get breath enough to change into a housedress and begin dinner preparation. (Bob did not appreciate seeing me in work clothes unless I actually needed outdoor gear.)

Each evening after dinner Bob and I would leave for our own miniature bedroom. This plywood abode would have been little protection against winter's snow, chilly rain and whipping winds, but a tiny oil space heater easily coped with the summer's airy wisps of wind. We appreciated being tucked into our private and romantic "shack on the hill." Bob had even created a space to hang our clothes—a rod directly over the foot of the bed.

These evenings were pleasant contrasts to the gravel chatter from the mix of drifters, drinkers, yarn-spinners, "gripers," and planners who occupied the main building and the newly built bunkhouse. Their colorful conversations ranged from the ranting words of radicals to the musings of intellectuals. We preferred evenings alone. At high tide we were lulled to sleep by the ocean waves swirling around the cabin's knoll and into the river's mouth, sounding like a cat lapping milk. At low tide Big Kitoi Creek sang to us as it splashed and splattered over the rocks below.

During the richly checkered conversation in the bunkhouse one evening, some of the men told Pinkie that I was a schoolteacher. I had not realized that any of them knew that. Previously, I had asked Bob not to mention it to Pinkie, preferring a mother-son relationship or just a friend-to-friend camaraderie.

The next morning Pinkie in wide-eyed wonder asked, "Ruth, are you really, really a schoolteacher?"

"Yes," I chuckled. "How did you know?"

"The fellows were saying you were last night, but I just couldn't believe it. You don't act like any of my teachers. I can just see Miss Stimpson running a race with me," and then visualizing the ludicrous scene, he convulsed with laughter.

"Schoolteachers must be schoolteachers in the classroom, but that doesn't mean they aren't like everyone else when they are outside the classroom."

"If you ever taught at Juneau, I'd tell the kids what you were really like." Some tittering and smirking resulted from the thought of the fun that would be. "How long did you teach?"

"Four years."

"And I thought," Pinkie continued disgustedly, "I was getting away from schoolteachers when I came out here."

For several days Pinkie was abnormally reserved around me. His usual teasing grin had been erased. But a couple coconut cream pies later he again accepted me as a non-schoolteacher.

One morning he approached with a badly crumpled piece of paper in his hand and a gleam in his eye. "I wrote a letter to my friend, Clark. He's Clark Gruening. His grandfather[10] used to be governor of Alaska, and Clark would even take me into the governor's mansion."

---

[10] Ernest Gruening was the longest appointed Territorial Governor (1939–1953) of Alaska. Later he served as U.S. Senator. Because of his leadership in the drive for statehood, he is known as the Father of Alaskan Statehood.

"That must have been exciting," I replied. Yet, I could tell it was not the governor's mansion Pinkie really wanted to tell me about. Something else was up his sleeve.

"I said something about you in the letter."

"Well, I suppose that is permissible."

"Do you want to read it?"

"If you want me to read it."

"Well, don't look at the messy writing and the misspelled words. I may copy it over before sending it," Pinkie mumbled as he handed me the short, penciled letter.

I soon discovered the phrase he was so eager for me to read: "I'm stuck out here all summer with a schoolteacher."

After dinner Bob often took Pinkie and me with him to Little Kitoi weir when he made his evening smolt count. Being twilight, we usually went by boat instead of walking on the trail. We had made a contract with the bear that if they would allow us to use their trails in the daytime (payment for our share of the trail upkeep), we would let them have complete jurisdiction at night.

Whenever I accompanied Bob, I always saw interesting, unusual things. In fact, when I first became acquainted with him, I wondered if he were not animal-magnetized: a deer would peek out of its forest cover as we watched, or a squirrel would fearlessly sit on a limb munching a fir cone as we passed. But when I found out these interesting occurrences carried over to inanimate objects as well—he would point out geological earth distortions or tell me why a blue elderberry is found on a certain spot—I realized Bob's natural curiosity and wide interests had made him more observant than the average person. Bob would keep notes while on Afognak Island: "On May 2, 1955, ten bald eagles were feeding on a sea lion carcass that had washed ashore." He made notes on geology, history, land mammals, birds, and plants of our area. He published some of his observations in academic journals, even though they had nothing to do with his salmon research work.[11]

On one of the twilight trips to the weir with Pinkie and me, Bob stopped the outboard so we could observe the mating antics of a pair of loons that had flown from one of the lakes down to the bay to spend the twilight hours. Their court-

---

[11] Vincent, Robert E. "The Larger Plants of Little Kitoi Lake," *The American Midland Naturalist*, (Vol. 60, No. 1) 1958.
Vincent, Robert E. "Observations on Red Fox Behavior," *Ecology*, (Vol. 39, No. 4) 1958.
Vincent, Robert E. "The Origin and Affinity of the Biota of the Kodiak Island Group, Alaska," *Pacific Science*, (Vol. XVIII, No. 2) 1964.

ship was a clamorous, spectacular affair: screeching, squalling, swerving. The male loon paraded on tiptoes—how that is possible in a liquid substance I do not know—to lift himself out of the water, displaying his large, white breast and vigorously flapping his wings.

Then Bob noticed two black spots on a distant, indented beach. Giving a long pull on the 25-hp Johnson outboard rope, Bob, standing as usual in the stern so he could see over the bow, shifted through the gears to high speed. We rapidly headed toward them. As expected, the objects turned out to be two brown bear, the first Pinkie had ever seen. They looked at us curiously until Bob throttled down and slowly nosed the bow toward shore. We were getting too close. The two brownies turned and shuffled off. Heading the skiff toward the weir, Bob again spotted a bear on another beach. He was an enormous creature, probably around three quarters of a ton, and lumbered into the brush before we could approach closer than two hundred yards. All three of our furry neighbors had been enjoying a spring meal of beach rye, roots, and crustaceans dug from under the rocks. After this excursion, Pinkie decided for the first time that his father's ruling on not leaving camp alone was for his protection instead of a restraint to curtail his freedom.

Although the construction crew had been at Kitoi only a few weeks, they had become restless, like clothes pinned on a clothesline. Frustration arose from having no activities other than working, eating, and sleeping. The typical early summer weather of rain, fog, and mist ("missed Oregon and hit here," Gene would describe it) did not help their melancholy. Each other's favorite stories had already been exchanged; the spinning of tales grew less colorful. The married men declared that they had written everything to their wives and that there was nothing else to say. "This isolation gets to you after awhile," they would complain. We were amused by their complaints about the quiet isolation because to us this season was so different from the Silent Season.

In their boredom, the crew began dreaming up a Swedish steam bath. It was not many days until they had completely convinced themselves not only of it as an asset to Kitoi Bay but even of it as a necessity.

The men began their project on a day too rainy[12] to allow regular work. Spirits soared. Gene, who repeatedly sang "The Yellow Rose of Texas," as if it were a top-ten-hit song, throttled it to full volume. Perhaps the psychological benefits of this new project counterbalanced the time their employer (the Alaska Department of Fisheries) lost in hatchery construction. Immediately, the fellows (fifty percent of whom were of Scandinavian background) became placated and quite content. Even the ones who had put little effort in the planning and building of the bath-

---

[12] Over 70 inches of rain fell annually.

house became eager for its completion so they could also try this extraordinary beneficial type of bath, the sauna. "Bathhouse," "sauna," and "steam baths" were vocalized and glamorized sixty to eighty times during each meal's conversation. These words replaced the former dominating word, "salmon." I actually appreciated the topic change since I often tuned out the salmon discussions, although I had absorbed that pinks were humpies, reds were sockeyes, silvers were cohoes, dogs were chums, and kings were Chinooks.

Finally, the 12x16-foot, two-room building—huge compared to our bedroom house—was finished and ready for Saturday night bathing. Without question, the bathhouse was the most sturdily built building at Kitoi. The first small entrance room, with one window, a bench, and nails for hanging clothes, was the dressing room. The large bathing room, also with one window, had a tier of three benches across one wall providing a choice of steaming at any of three desired levels. In one corner was an oil-drum stove covered with another split oil drum for a jacket. Small hard rocks that covered the stove were kept from falling off by this outer jacket.

These instructions were posted on the wall in the dressing room:

1. *Fill bucket with lukewarm water.*
2. *Fill coffee can with hot water for tossing on rocks.*
3. *Wet down top bench with water and sit.*
4. *Toss water on hot rocks, sparingly at first; then sit. Do not use cold water on hot rocks.*
5. *Using previously prepared lukewarm water, soap and wash, using rest of the water to partially rinse yourself.*
6. *Draw a bucket of cool water for final rinse.*

Don'ts:

1. *Do not try to overdo the heat.*
2. *If you begin to feel woozy, return to cool dressing room for awhile before resuming bath.*
3. *Don't sit in a draft after leaving steam room.*

That evening the men bathed in two groups of four each. Next, Bob and I took our turn and followed the posted instructions. Foggy puffs of steam wisped upwards, coating our outsides and probably our insides with moisture. We continued to sit.

Soon we were prostrate (from bleary fatigue) on a bench perspiring from head to toe. According to our propagandists, the perspiring would not only cleanse our pores but would completely relax us. Personally, I felt that I was keeping company with the biblical characters of Shadrach, Meshach, and Abednego. Instead of being relaxing, the half hour of steaming left me feeling weak and unnerved. And far from receiving the best sleep I had ever had, I was so tired and exhausted that I suffered through eight hours of insomnia.

For some, steam bathing is an extreme sport. The authentic Scandinavian ritual, as well as that of the native Aleuts of Alaska, was to end the sauna with a plunge into the icy bay. I noticed that none of the men did this. Yet in spirit, they were "in the pink," whereas I was much past the pink since I felt my blood might boil.

Bob and I took more steam baths during the summer, learning as we went. Even so, they did not compare with the hot shower that we could enjoy now that we had running water in the station. The majority of the workers and biologists continued to be enthralled with their saunas and eagerly awaited Wednesday and Saturday, the two scheduled bath nights, practically transforming the occasions into social events.

Probably because there was nothing more interesting to do, or perhaps because of his love for pastries, Pinkie began taking a genuine interest in cooking. I let him attempt anything he wanted, so the final result usually ended up as chocolate cake, coconut cream pie, or chocolate cream pie. (I made the crusts.) Thus, our lives mixed richly, especially in calories!

Much time was spent on the cooking classes, but we each enjoyed them. And the men especially enjoyed the results of Pinkie's new interest; neither were they blind to the advantages of congratulating Pinkie on his creations.

One morning when I was busy kneading bread as Pinkie entered the kitchen, he hopefully inquired, "May I knead?"

Figure 34. Pinkie at the barbershop.

Soon he was covered in flour as he happily poked and prodded the dough. "Oh, this ushy, gushy stuff. Wouldn't it be fun to squeeze it through your toes?" Immediately after this exclamation, Ed walked by the window and spotted Pinkie working away with my red apron nearly up to his chin.

"Hi, Cutie-pie, you'll sure make somebody a good wife some day," Ed teased.

For a second Pinkie was lost for an answer, but only for a second. He made a dash for the door. By this time, because of Pinkie's floured cheeks and flashy apron, Ed was in fits of laughter. Pinkie reached into his right-hand jean pocket, pulled out a water pistol, and made a direct hit on Ed.

Ed was surprised speechless. Not dreaming that Pinkie had a water pistol, much less a full one, I was equally astonished. The men working near enough to witness the scene doubled over with laughter. Pinkie grinned as if he had a mouth full of pudding.

"Where did you ever get a water pistol out here, Pinkie?" I asked later.

"I've had it all summer but kept it hid since I wasn't supposed to bring one with me."

Such incidents lightened the men's days. Pinkie was a tonic for all of us. Regardless of effort, it seems that any heterogeneous group living in a confined, isolated place becomes impatient and irritable. A sense of humor and much give and take is necessary for congeniality, and despite the circumstances, each worker at Kitoi did well. Sharp edges seldom emerged. The group was especially considerate and thoughtful of me. In fact, with nine men graciously treating me with undue favor, I was in danger of being spoiled. As a token of appreciation (or else as added incentive for me to keep good things on the table), the fellows asked Quent, who flew into Kodiak one Monday for construction needs, to purchase twelve carnations for me. Quent said that he had been an object of real interest dashing around shopping with a pick under one arm and a yard-long floral box with ribbon under the other arm.

Molly McSpadden, who kept a fatherly watch over all of us, was especially concerned about the way I would run outside in a sleeveless dress and no coat. He continually reminded me to put on a coat. If Molly were in sight, I would often put one on just to relieve his concern. Having lived in our germ-free paradise through a gale-whipped winter without a single cold convinced Bob and me that germs, rather than exposure, were the real gremlins. Nevertheless, I appreciated Molly's concern.

From the first time that I heard the name "Molly," I had been curious to meet him. I had had the intuition that I would especially like Molly McSpadden, and how right this turned out to be. Intelligence, taste, education, and common sense were mixed together in this unusual man. I have never known a person with such an enviable combination of cultural polish and unaffected plainness. Probably he would have been as much at ease conversing with President Dwight D. Eisenhower as chatting with a roadside tramp. He was always interesting as he leaned back in one of Kitoi Bay's newly acquired folding chairs, puffing on his pipe and telling us about his new grandson. Meticulously cleaning his fingernails with a fingernail brush after work each day was as characteristic of Molly as demonstrations on the correct manner of using a pickax. Molly's face bore the mark of leadership; his expression, kindness; his speech, graciousness; and his actions were a combination that revealed a man of thoughtfulness, self-reliance, and unpretentiousness. He was years deep in warm understanding. Although not tall, truly he was a gentle giant.

Figure 35. A mealtime snapshot (Leo at end of table; Molly at far right).

Molly's one great problem at Kitoi Bay was despondency that grew deeper each week at having to be separated from his wife. In contrast to this, after a trip home to Juneau, he arrived back loaded with fresh produce, gliders for Pinkie, and chocolates for me. He was cured of homesickness for a few weeks and became his natural, genial self once more.

My seven-day-a-week cooking responsibilities coupled with Molly's exceptional pancake-making ability made breakfasts become his responsibility. I accepted this without complaint. Though I could have slept in every morning, I usually joined the noisy breakfast clatter and chatter that went something like this:

"Cheer up, Ed. Not hearing from your girlfriend last week isn't that bad," Milt would admonish with a stretch and yawn.

"Fifty-one more days, just fifty-one more days, and I'll be out of this isolated place."

"Claude, how many eggs can you eat with your pancakes this morning?" Molly would likely yell from the kitchen.

"I'll take about half a settin'," would come the responding drawl. Claude had been lengthening his southern drawl and emphasizing his hillbilly jabber ever since a dinnertime conversation on the pros and cons of correct grammar. You would never guess that he had completed three years of college.

"Will you eat a couple more pancakes, Claude?" asked Molly, flipping his light, airy, plate-sized hotcakes that he cooked directly on the stovetop.

"Naw, I'm gettin' too fer b'tween the hip pockets."

"Milt, give the smearcase a heave, will you? Ruth needs some on her graveyard stew," Gene might boom out. (Translation: "Milt, would you please pass the butter? Ruth needs some on her milk-toast.")

"Leo, how many more pancakes for you?"

"One more is enough."

"Now, Leo, remember your diet. You'd better apply that elbow bending exercise of pushing yourself away from the table," Gene would caution.

When Molly was through filling everyone's tremendous appetites and sat down with his own plate of steaming pancakes, the fellows would begin washing the dishes.

"Who's volunteering as pearl diver?"

"I'll wash this time," Claude volunteered and proceeded in his sloppy but rapid dishwashing.

Besides the much-appreciated help from the men, Pinkie continued as my main assistant. Since one of his responsibilities was setting the table for each meal, he would, regardless of my cautions, reach into the cupboard shelf at his eye level and lift down ten of the heavy, roadside-diner-type, crockery plates to carry to the table in one tall stack. Surprisingly enough, he passed the complete summer without a broken dish, while I broke several. Pinkie also prepared the coffee (two pounds consumed daily) for the workers' mid-morning and mid-afternoon coffee breaks and even washed the cups afterwards, although he greatly disliked my insistence that the cups must be washed in soapy water instead of by his under-the-faucet method. But most appreciated of all his help were the miles he must have run for me to the upstairs grocery supply and to the outside cooler, a hundred feet away.

To speed my cooking, I would make huge batches of biscuit, pie crust, muffin, and cornbread mixes in a large aluminum dishpan purchased for use as a mixing bowl. These mixes would then be stored in five-gallon cans for quick use. Another big help was my planned month of menus along with the corresponding grocery orders (*See Appendix B*). Although the planning had taken hours, the menus and grocery lists proved their value by giving me much more time. After a month I would repeat the same menus with only slight variations, so I never had to be concerned about what to serve or what perishables to order on the weekly Monday-morning grocery orders over the radio. Because the bread was stale by the end of our grocery week, Mondays often meant toast. All cookies were homemade, and I tried to keep the cookie jar constantly full. The men loved not only cookies but also rich milk gravy, which they would overly load on their mashed potatoes. Pinkie especially devoured the homemade sweet rolls.

I had been accustomed to cooking for two, so the grocery lists now seemed immense in both number of items and in quantity: one five-pound can of baking powder, one case of the three-pound-size cans of Log Cabin syrup, one case of catsup, etc. The radio-broadcasted grocery orders entertained our Kodiak neighbors and other islanders who often picked up island communications over the short-wave channel on their regular radios. They usually knew whether we would be having T-bones or wieners during the coming week. To Bob and me, T-bone steaks were like lamb chops to hungry wolves since, having spent most of our married lives as students, we had always budgeted groceries and everything else stringently. The men decided that food was their one luxury in such a deprived location so expected to eat like kings. They set an extravagant amount (at least to us) that each should pay. Cost of groceries was only a third more than Outside prices. Had we been living in interior Alaska, groceries would have been even more expensive. We paid $100 a month for Bob's share of the bill and $50 a month for mine since I did not eat as much as the men. Of course, Bob and I could have lived on a third of our grocery payments, but it was nice having roasts, steaks, real butter rather than mixing a yellow glob of coloring into white oleo, and three times as many fresh vegetables and fruits as we had ever purchased in the Outside. Moreover, such groceries made cooking easier. The biologists, when present, paid me $1.00 a day for cooking, but the hired construction help paid me nothing. The men also helped with the dishes.

Although we had begun to find a rhythm to life in the Noisy Season, the arrival of other short-time laborers gave the permanent summer workers some welcome changes. There were new stories to hear and old ones that could be repeated. In the future no one will ever be able to convince me that women are more loquacious than men. Men are talkative!

As new arrivals came, we again sensed that in Alaska you did not ask questions that pried into a person's background. Some of these men had left the problems and pain of their stateside lives to come to this remaining frontier. In this new land, would they make use of their time, talent, and treasures, or would they submerge themselves in alcohol without coming up for air? Some came from the fringes of society. But other Alaskan drifters had once been famous—Carnegie Medal holders or Olympic Stars—but having achieved success and recognition, they then became content to float as if their fuel had been completely consumed. Several of our summer helpers had cut off all connections with relatives or friends on the Outside for one reason or another as their lives in the United States had gone awry. Alaskans accepted each other for who they were, not for who they may have been. Underneath the workmen's rough, coarse coverings, I could always detect an inner gem. Bob and I developed a deep appreciation and gained much from each one: not one left Kitoi Bay without our having added a friend.

With us during one time were Bill, Archie, and Gill, three unpretentious men who were intellectuals. Bob and I suddenly became more aware of the growth we needed to achieve. Poems and literature gems were often quoted; the dictionary was used about three or four times daily by each. Archie was a biologist from Juneau. The other two had Ph.Ds, an accomplish-

Figure 36. Our "shack on the hill."

ment we especially admired at that time. One of them, Bill Smoker was a new fishery biologist hired by Alaska Department of Fisheries. Since he had ten or more years experience and a pleasing, affable personality, Bob looked forward to working with him and learning much from him. (I liked the fact that he shaved every day.) Gill, an engineer, had been hired to do estimates on various possible projects. He was from Iowa and constantly wrote letters: to his wife, to a son and daughter in college, and to a son and daughter in grade school. To our surprise, one Sunday he appeared wearing a white shirt and tie. This was incongruous with Noisy Season Sunday attire. Other than us, no one ever brought dress clothes to Kitoi Bay. We made Sundays a special dress occasion during the Silent Season, but not even on anniversaries did Bob wear a white shirt and tie during the Noisy Season.

Perhaps the newcomer having the most difficulty melding into the ways of the group was Shorty, a short, quiet Italian around fifty years of age. His sad countenance and his lack of having anything in common with the rest immediately touched my sympathy and concern. His conversation, which was infrequent, consisted of praise for his wildcat rifle and the problem of getting good wines in America. Other than on these two topics, Shorty was silent.

Leo Thompsen, the engineer, and Molly McSpadden, the construction foreman, soon found that Shorty's greatest skill and greatest joy came from digging. He appeared bewildered with any type of machinery, but with a shovel or pick in hand he seemed at home. He did not dig as an average person might. He dug scientifically and efficiently, accomplishing more than any of the others would have in the same length of time.

Sometimes the men would be through with their coffee break before they realized that Shorty had not joined them. They would find him still digging. They then began inviting him to quit work for coffee breaks. He sometimes accepted and sometimes refused depending on his interest in his work. There was no problem in finding sufficient digging for him to do since part of a dirt and rock bank had to be scraped away, hatchery footings had to be dug, and a pipeline bed had to be prepared. A Skagit—an old-fashioned dragline operating on cables and buckets—was used to dig away the bank, but Shorty would not dig near the Skagit while it was running. So Molly gave Shorty the job of building rock steps to our plywood bedroom cabin," while some of the others did Skagit excavation near Shorty's digging site. Shorty turned the steps into a major project, a work of art that won the admiration of the group and pleased him immensely. He filled many a wheelbarrow (one machine he would use) with large, flat, shale rocks from the beach and made trip after trip to his own construction site. Soon he had formed regular, patio-sized steps from the dock to our tiny bedroom home. This improvement stimulated us to paint the outside of the cabin. After that, I mixed odds and ends of paint and painted the inside as well. With all these improvements, "the shack on the hill" became "the mansion on Kitoi Bay Heights."

One morning Molly practically had to give up his day-to-day ritual of cooking pancakes because the oil stove in the kitchen had filled with so much soot that it almost stopped burning. This was a frequent occurrence due to the lack of electricity to run the fan for forced draft. When this happened, I always preferred for either Bob or Quent to clean out the soot since they seemed to be the only ones capable of doing the task without leaving the floor and white cupboards in a sooty mess. However, on this morning Quent and Bob were anxious to set a fish sampling net in a distant lake, so they asked Shorty to clean the kitchen range. During the hour it took for the stove to cool, I remembered that Shorty would probably forget to put newspaper on the floor, so I hurried down to the station and covered every inch of the floor and counter tops. Two hours later when again I ran down to the station expecting the stove to be cleaned and burning, I was in for a shock. Of course, I had expected to spend a half-hour cleaning up black smudges, but I never imagined the disarray that met me. The floors, the white cupboards, and Shorty were all coated with soot. The stove was still open, cold, and in the process of being cleaned. The papers on the floor had been trampled and torn, and soot had been ground into the tile. I felt as if I had become part of a charcoal painting. Shorty was muttering and looked perplexed and worried.

Figure 37. Our shack became the "mansion on Kitoi Bay Heights."

"Is anything wrong, Shorty?"

"Yes, this stove is dangerous. I should not even be fooling with it. Something is wrong with the carburetor, and it is likely to blow up any minute. You certainly won't catch me lighting it. As soon as a match is put in there, it is going to blow."

He had me thoroughly convinced, but he continued.

"No, I'm certainly not going to put a match in there. I'm going to be clear out of the house. There's your husband just coming back. I'll go get him to light it."

My knees felt weak.

Bob took a look at the stove while Shorty, still muttering to himself, hurried outside. Bob then assured me there was no danger and dropped in the match. Nothing happened other than the fire started.

Shorty amused us again one afternoon when I asked him if he liked garlic. I had been planning on having garlic bread for the evening meal and did not wish to bake the loaf unless everyone would eat it.

"Oh, excuse me, excuse me. Haven't I offered you any?" he exclaimed as he ran up the stairs. To our amazement he came down with a large bulb of garlic and passed it to each of us. He was surprised that no one took any. "Why, I chew it all the time," he said. Surely enough, we then began noticing that he sucked and chewed the garlic like most people suck and chew old-fashioned, hard candy. Little did we imagine that decades later many people would consider garlic valuable for preventing infections or lowering cholesterol.

Jack, John, and Von were three other workers who arrived for three weeks' work each. When they came, they moved into the empty bunkhouse. The other men were staying upstairs in the station. Because the population of Kitoi Bay had gradually become a collection of fishery biologists instead of construction workers, the dinner hours had become seminars on the best methods of doing salmon research. The three newcomers joined me in noting the monotony of meal-time conversations. They took steps to change the discussions and to have a little fun with the college graduates. One mealtime Jack asked, "What in your opinion were the major factors contributing to the Boer War?" At the next meal Von nonchalantly asked, "What do you think of Ernst Amadeus' works?" Soon Jack spoke up, "How would you relate the Dred Scott v. Sanford case in 1857 to the present racial problems?" These were only the first in a series of erudite questions that poured forth. Initially, we were all amazed at Von and Jack's keen memories and ashamed of being so uninformed ourselves. Later their secret was revealed: the ones at the bunkhouse had a pocket book of facts that they consulted before each meal.

But Claude, who had now become shaggy-haired with broken glasses resting on the end of his nose amazed us in his own right as unique talents began to emerge. He could quote long passages from Shakespeare and, in comparison with the rest of us, was an authority on all of Shakespeare's writings. His familiarity was a result of spending a complete winter alone in an isolated cabin with no books except an old set of *The Complete Works of Shakespeare*. Another favorite topic of Claude's was the Alaskan statehood question. "If they want to live in a state, there're forty-eight states to choose to live in without trying to make Alaska into one," he would say. In such discussions Molly, an Alaskan resident for twenty-five years or longer, would also take the anti-statehood position but reasoned differently than Claude. His opinion was that Alaska was not economically ready for statehood. Others would talk in depth on Alaska being the victim of colonialism and self-interest groups. Another would emphatically say, "Statehood would enable us to have the local power to direct our own fishery management and regulations. It is time to get rid of those fish traps that prevent salmon getting upstream to spawn."

So went the summer: an interesting mix of personalities, a privilege of living among and appreciating people that Bob and I in different circumstances would merely pass on the street. A few of these "different" types, Bob himself had hired out of the saloons of Kodiak as they sat with a glass of whiskey. Bob would describe the construction work needed, the surroundings, the pay, even the lack of hard liquor, and they, surprisingly, often accepted. When the men sobered up, Bob found that he had chosen well. They were pleasant men when not tormented by drink.

What had brought us together in this unique setting? Was it career advancement? Stateside conflict? Frustration with life? Money? Regardless, each one of us was cut from a different type of fabric—soft cotton, smooth linen, scratchy wool, strong muslin, fragile silk—colorful personalities quilted together by the house called Kitoi Bay Research Station.

Anniversary Adventures

"Honey, does this type of living come under the "for better" or "for worse" in our vows six years ago?" Bob asked in a relaxed mood one Sunday at the breakfast table.

"Whichever, this certainly didn't enter our vision at that time, did it?" I replied.

"Does today happen to be your wedding anniversary?" inquired Ed.

I nodded and was silently aware that this would be our first anniversary without some type of special celebration.

"Did you think this bright sunshine with the temperature soaring into the sixties was only a happen-chance?" Bob cheerfully responded.

Immediately, I was ashamed of any inner sulkiness because from Bob's reply to Ed I could detect an attempt to make the day as special as circumstances permitted.

"Well, if today is your wedding anniversary, you deserve the day off," declared Molly, again demonstrating his thoughtfulness. "Ruth, you're banished from the kitchen today. I'll get dinner. Since it is Sunday, we only need one meal anyway, and we'll have it about 4:30."

I could have hugged Molly! How understanding he could be, and no wonder the men working under him admired him so greatly. His taking over the cooking for the day was visible love.

Freedom from the kitchen in itself was a luxury, but added to that was Bob's suggestion that we take a four-hour excursion to explore new places and to see some old places that by now were blooming in their summertime garb. The calm bay, the warm air, and the unfrozen land were in sharp contrast to their wintertime appearance. Ordinarily in June the weather was cold, cloudy, or rainy. Today the world was inviting and full of enchantment. Nature beckoned us to explore each cove and each mossy projection of land.

The highlight of the day turned out to be the tufted puffins, commonly called sea parrots, perched and nesting atop Midarm Island. These chunky, black-and-white birds have eye-catching red feet and proudly sport outrageous beaks (colored by a rainbow of reds) that are compressed sideways to make it possible for them to eat mussels and other hard-shelled marine life. Above each white cheek, the tufted puffin wears a silvery feather tuft curving attractively over the eye in a long semicircle that emphasizes its unusual face.

The "apartment houses" that these spring-and-early-summer-residents had made dotted the rocky cliff more compactly than stores on Market Street. Because the steepness of the bluff made it almost impossible for man or large animals to climb, the puffins had well-protected home sites.

We anchored the skiff on a sheltered beach at the other side of tiny Midarm Island and hiked to the top of Puffin Cliff, as we coined it. The skiff and motor had already frightened most of the occupants from their deep-burrow homes, causing them to color the sky in flight. On one side of the cliff, a few struggling trees gave us foot-and-handholds as well as cover as we slid down parallel to some of the nests. From this natural blind we watched the puffins swoop back to their homes and make a flying beeline into their nests. Many of the wary parents, when approaching their nests that were close to us, would make a turn and dart seaward again, but patient waiting finally rewarded us as a puffin landed just ten feet away. She landed on her doorstep and did a good deal of scrutinizing before entering her two-foot-deep nest to settle back on her one mottled-brown egg.

More surprises were in store for us. The next stop was Sea Gull Rocks, another geographical place name that we created that day. These two ship-sized rocks jutted seaward from an exposed headland, where we were able to anchor the skiff safely while we explored.

Figure 38. Baby seagull in the cleft of a rock.

We easily found the seagulls' well-made grass nests in the grassy nooks and sheltered dips of the steep rocky slope. A few clung camouflaged and unprotected on the bare, wind-swept rocks. Bob had stopped to inspect these island seagull nurseries only two days before, so when we found three of their huge eggs laid since his first visit, he kept them to eat. He was curious to sample this Aleut food staple. (His later response to the scrambled eggs was completely favorable. If I had been blindfolded so I could not see the reddish yolks, I too would have enjoyed them.) I protested such unkindness to the poor mother seagulls that were circling overhead crying at us to leave their nursery, but Bob explained that each mother would lay another egg to replace the one taken. Just as a puffin never sits on more than one egg, so a seagull never nests on more than three of her giant, brown-speckled, buff eggs.

After enjoying this gull-eyed view of the world, we boarded the skiff and Bob announced, "Our next stop will be at Ruth Lake."

"And just what do you mean?" I asked, puzzled.

"Exactly that. I waited until today to tell you, but yesterday we named a fifty-acre lake Ruth Lake. We can't continue talking about these many lakes when they have no names to designate them. Each biologist is officially naming one after a daughter, but since we haven't a daughter, this lake shall be named after you."

I was thrilled by the thought of having my name immortalized on future maps.

The many glacial depressions of the late ice-age retreat had formed numerous lakes on Afognak Island, an asset for fishermen, research biologists, and those who appreciate picturesque beauty. During the year we had hiked into several of the unnamed inland lakes and looked at them in awe as we realized we could easily be the first white persons to have viewed that particular body of water from the ground. Even on the lakes near the coastline, we were no doubt often the first to break the calm of the lake's surface with a skiff. Nearly all these lakes were flanked by the soft, blue-green beauty of the spruce-clad hills. Ruth Lake was no exception, but now on this wedding anniversary day I was humorously deflated when Bob said that it was soon to be poisoned, providing a counterpart for study in relation to a natural control-lake. Poisoning was used to rid the lake of undesirable fish such as Dolly Varden or stickleback before planting salmon fry or young fingerlings to establish a new adult red salmon run.

I continued to enjoy my escape from cooking as next we took advantage of the low tide to gather shells of all types: mussels, whelks, limpets, periwinkles, and—by far the most numerous—clamshells. Whole shells had always been at a premium in the States and here they were as common as wastepaper. We were even paid richly in unbroken sand dollars.

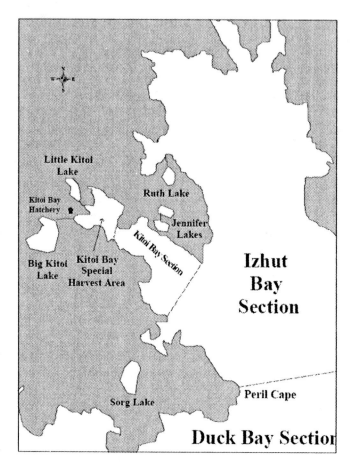

Figure 39. Kitoi and Izhut Bays showing Ruth Lake and Jennifer Lakes. © Alaska Department of Fish and Game. Used by permission.

During the winter I had begun a clamshell collection as a means of learning to recognize the various types of Kitoi Bay clams: gaper, Alaska surf, red neck, cockle, butter, razor, soft shell, bent nose, and littlenecks, our favorite variety for steaming. Soon the array of shells and my interest had expanded to include more of the treasures cast up from the sea. Top shells, scallops, sand dollars, chitons, and sea urchins were added to the collection, while I became more befuddled than ever in my search through Bob's pamphlets and books in an attempt to identify and attach their scientific names.

Figure 40. Our sixth wedding anniversary at a typical flat-slate beach.

Such good collecting grounds could stimulate a gathering instinct in anyone. Bob and I enjoyed wading in tide pools and turning over rocks to collect new specimens. Later would come the more disagreeable part: boiling the live specimens and carefully removing the smelly animals from their outside skeleton. And then, while still hot, the bivalves would have to be shaped in the desired open or shut position and secured while they cooled.

On the return trip, we saw a few violets on the nearby soil-less, slate rock bluffs. Not wanting to be late for Molly's dinner, we stopped only once. This last stop was for a mass of wildflowers. Having the full benefit of the long hours of summer sun, the flowers on this hillside had burst into blooms nearly twice as large as their more southerly relatives. What a show! All winter I had regretted not having plants for a summer flower garden, and here we were on our knees picking dollar-sized violets and big monkey flowers that were painting the hillside purple and yellow with their colorful blossoms.

We returned from this delightful anniversary excursion just in time to witness Gene's most exciting experience of the summer—an experience that would likely live and grow over the years as the story was told and retold. Our complete group of summertime personnel had congregated near the back door of the station, enjoying the warm sunshine before entering for dinner. Gene, who had been doing some painting, was washing his hands in a can of gasoline about seventy-five feet from the rest of us. Behind Gene, a yearling brownie strolled into the station area. Molly was the first to see the visitor.

"Gene, look behind you," he calmly called.

Gene, expecting Pinkie to be attempting some joke from behind, turned and gazed into the face of the bear standing only fifteen feet away. He froze. None of us went inside to get a gun since the sight was so comical that we, as Gene's audience, didn't even think of the danger. The cub, which was having his first encounter with a human, darted back a couple yards and stood curiously staring. Our eyes were focused completely on Gene. The Gene who had never before been at a loss for words continued to stand motionless and gaping. Then as he finally began to regain composure, his mouth moved but no words came out. His laughing audience still did nothing to help. The cub was first to relieve the situation by detouring around the station instead of following the bear trail, stopping to sniff and peer through the trees every few yards.

"I've never been so frightened in my life!" was Gene's trite but honest first statement. "He was breathing right down the back of my neck!"

We all laughed, the spell broken, and moved inside for the meal. Dinner conversation was lively as we ate Molly's delicious corned beef and cabbage, complete with potatoes and carrots that had also simmered in the flavorful juice. I had wondered what menu Molly would create from the groceries in stock and had not anticipated any surprises. But he did manage to surprise me with pies: two chocolate and two butterscotch pies with graham cracker crusts showed that Molly had cooking skills far beyond his usual pancakes.

The bear experience was relived several times during the meal, and the yearling cub soon was named Charlie. His unruly fur reminded us of the advertising ditty, "Use Wildroot Cream Oil, Charlie; It keeps your hair in trim…." We didn't know then that Charlie would become a frequent guest at the station. Molly poured the remainder of the corned-beef-and-cabbage juice outside the back door, which evidently attracted Charlie. He approached the house the next day to find the source of the smell. Although the men had agreed Charlie should not be fed nor urged to become a pet, they really were not sorry that the corned-beef juice had unintentionally called Charlie so near. Cameras were hurriedly dug out of duffle bags and cupboards, while Gene quickly grabbed Quent's rifle from the corner gun rack. He stood in the doorway with the gun pointed directly at Charlie, just as a safety measure so those with cameras could be free from the worry of danger. The camera fans moved to within fifteen feet of Charlie, who was sprawled on the ground licking the corned-beef juice that had soaked into a board. Twenty minutes passed with Charlie good-naturedly posing for the cameras.

As the photographers came into the house, Gene relaxed his vigil, took a look at the gun with which he had been protecting the rest of us, and exclaimed, "This gun doesn't have a single shell in it!"

"Why, that's my gun," Quent noticed for the first time. "I never keep shells in it when it's in the house."

After this pleasant visit, eighteen-month-old Charlie, probably recently booted out of the family circle by his mother, never bothered to detour around the station area but continued to follow the ancestral trail, diverting only to sniff at our back door and at the fire pit where the garbage was burned. We had no difficulty knowing it was Charlie, and not a cousin, because beside his nonchalant, yet curious, personality, he had the distinction of a bare back. With summer shedding, his back became more ragged on each appearance.

We never knew when Charlie might come lumbering up the path, day or night, but we soon could guess. Making a six-mile circuit and then retracing his route, Charlie would stop at each beach to hunt for dead fish, to eat seaweed, or to tumble over rocks in search of invertebrates. When full, he would half bury himself by digging a nest on a high lookout point and snooze. This weekly circuit became so predictable that we began expecting Charlie to appear every fifth day. We would often spot him on a nearby beach and could accurately estimate the length of time it would take for him to reach the station.

Figure 41. Charlie, a Kodiak brown bear cub, appears at our back porch.

On various occasions I would look out of the kitchen window to see him approaching in his slow, shuffling gate while the men working on the hatchery at the back of the station had no knowledge of his presence. I would hurriedly run through the house and give the familiar yell "Charlie's coming!" from the back door. They would then be prepared for cub Charlie's three-hundred-pound bulk (eight to ten years are required for a brown bear to reach full size of 1000 to 1600 pounds) to emerge around the corner of the building and make his supervisory investigation of the project.

Once, he even came to oversee my end of the work. In his usual, nose-reliance method, he lumbered to the side kitchen window. After sucking his nostrils in and flaring them out, he decided a closer look was needed. He raised up on his hind legs, placed his front claws in the putty of the window frame, and peered inside. My laughing eyes were pressed against the opposite side of the windowpane. When Charlie's nearsighted eyes focused on mine, he hastily fled. Later I was reminded that had Charlie been of a different temperament, instead of running, he might have slapped out the pane of glass separating our eyes.

Charlie's next kitchen investigation was conducted at night. Outside this same side window was a small barrel for empty tin cans, conveniently located to be reachable from the open window. Because of the station's temporary overpopulation, Robert Parker was sleeping in the station's eating area. On his first night of a planned week's stay, he was awakened by a noisy rattling of tin cans. He thought that foxes were causing the disturbance, so he got up to frighten them away. As he rolled open the window and leaned out to do so, he was suddenly shocked into full wakefulness by his first meeting with Kitoi Bay's supervisor, investigator, and intelligence agent: Charlie.

Finally, after Charlie prowled two nights in a row, ripping the screen off our outside cooler, removing the cardboard box of meat, and stealing the blood-soaked box, his conduct was no longer charming. True, he was generous enough to leave the packages of meat and steal only the container, but our stock of screening material was rapidly disappearing under the swats of his paws.

The next time that Charlie appeared in the daytime, Molly used an age-old method of frightening bear. The trick consisted of simply putting pebbles in a tin can and shaking the can vigorously as the bear approached. Charlie immediately turned and actually scampered, instead of lumbered, into the forest. Few of us had confidence this trick would actually keep him away, but to our surprise he began again to detour around the area as he made his weekly circuit.

As they prowled the beaches and creeks, Charlie and his relatives would take just one or two bites from salmon and leave the rest. The bite would be taken from the backside, just at the nape of the neck between head and back. I decided this must be the easiest, the most nourishing, or the tastiest part of the fish. The bear ate the fish the same way that I would like to eat a watermelon: eat the heart and discard the rest.

As the excitement of Charlie's visits ceased and as the end of summer approached, Pinkie became restless. The early enchantment with Kitoi Bay had disappeared completely.

Realizing the dullness of our daily routine to an active boy, I attempted to spend more time outside with him. In June after the frost danger had passed and the ground had finally begun to warm, we planted a tiny plot of garden. The aster, poppy, and snapdragon seeds had been planted in cans inside two months previous, so I transplanted them along with some potatoes and some lettuce seed. It seemed late to be planting a garden, but I reminded myself that the long hours of daylight offset the weeks of freezing weather. Instead of fertilizer, we carried kelp from the beach to enrich the soil. Because tall spruce surrounded the handkerchief-sized plot, the plants had difficulty competing for sunlight. Pinkie and I had unrealistic visions of great success so spent a number of hours nursing the plants along. We even transplanted some of the flowering plants to a new rock garden Pinkie had created. The worst part of working in dirt was the hordes of mosquitoes that would swarm up from the soil into our faces with every scrape of the hoe or dig of the shovel. I usually wore a face-covering mosquito net even though it hindered my vision.

Figure 42. Twelve-year-old Pinkie carefully cleans his catch of rainbow trout.

At other times the two of us would observe fish: Dolly Varden at the mouth of the inlet to Little Kitoi Lake, silver salmon at the mouth of Big Kitoi Creek, or pink salmon off the dock. The silver salmon were still in good condition and would jump a yard or more out of the water as they waited for high water to go on up the creek to spawn. Waves of emotions thrilled through our veins when we were able to see six to ten pink salmon gracefully leap in midair at once, hear their resounding splash, and watch the dark schools mill around. Their fins often stuck out of water. In addition, we would fish for both Dollies and rainbow trout in Big Kitoi Lake. Lack of fishing pressure made fish abundant so Pinkie or I never thought of throwing in the line unless we saw the fish first. To get a bite we needed only to dangle the egg or lure in the clear water in front of a big rainbow. Such ease in catching soon took away much of the challenge and excitement.

On sunny afternoons, Pinkie and I would cover face, arms, and legs with mosquito repellent and sit a few yards from the station on the numerous, large, flat rocks at the mouth of Big Kitoi Creek. The creek was typical of the area: clear, short, and swift. While I wrote letters, Pinkie would build practical objects with the shale rocks. Their flat surface made them intriguing and ideal as building stones. With childlike glee, he energetically and imaginatively built me a throne complete with arm rests. It turned out to be so comfortable that I used it and appreciated it throughout the rest of the summer. His other rock projects included a chair for himself, a chair for Bob, two beds, and a patio.

Typical of Alaskan children, Pinkie had never picked an apple from a tree nor seen a snake. (No snakes and very few frogs exist in Alaska.) In describing a visit to his grandparents in the state of Washington, he emphasized the startling fact that they had apples in a box on the back porch. "You know they have boxes of apples on their back porch, but they never tell you that you can have an apple. They just expect you to eat them without asking." Such luxuries as bushel boxes of fruit are seldom experienced in Alaska because of the high cost of transporting perishables. But Pinkie's inexperience on subjects of reptiles and fruits was counterbalanced when I questioned him about what he meant when he spoke of "planing a skiff." Such ignorance was preposterous to Pinkie, as it would have been to any boy living in close contact with water, boats, and fishermen. He patiently explained to me that this was getting the boat going fast enough to lift the bow out of water, leaving just the stern on the water. Less of the boat in the water makes less resistance so it can skim instead of plow and thus go faster.

At nights Pinkie would absorb and be entertained by the men's conversations in the bunkhouse. Most gossip would eventually be passed to me with Pinkie as the tape recorder.

"The men think it is strange that you run so much, Ruth. Why do you always run from your cabin to the station instead of walk?"

"Oh, I just like to run. It gives me good exercise."

"Dad, and Gene, and the rest of the guys were real surprised you and Bob were having your sixth wedding anniversary Sunday."

"I wonder why?"

"Well, don't you know? You act like you've just got married." A child, like a mirror, can reveal astonishing surprises.

Mmmm! During our two-year courtship, Bob and I were careful never to act like love birds. Holding hands was as much as we indulged in publicly. Now that we had had six years of marriage freedom, six years of love roots that had grown abundantly, were we flouting our married state in front of these lonely men? Pinkie's remark was a reminder to me that we should be more careful. Bob and I must not forget that during this Noisy Season our focus should be on group relationships. But containing deep love is difficult.

Digging into the Past

Although we had no deed to property on Afognak, we found ourselves beginning to look on the Kitoi Bay area as "ours." Historically, others had undoubtedly felt the same. Even in the year 1955, few Aleuts owned land. Many still considered that land belonged to everyone. What type of people had formerly occupied our seemingly virgin nook? Had men, women, and children hunted, fished, danced, fought, loved, worshiped, and mourned in this primeval forest we now considered so distant from humans, past or present? These questions became real to us after Quent, while digging footings for the station's front porch, found an oil lamp that was made of stone. The lamp was in no way elaborate, just a scooped-out hollow in a rounded greywacke stone with a notch in one side to provide a place for the wick. Even so, the undecorated stone was unusual enough to cause Quent to pick it up for closer examination. No doubt this crude object had been a valued furnishing of a former home, providing both heat and light as a twisted grass wick soaked the seal or whale oil from the concave bowl and slowly burned with a flickering flame.

Our isolated location may have been the reason we felt a close connection with those who once lived in the place we now occupied. Not much was known about these former residents. In 1955, the complete island was national forest land; no white person, except perhaps an occasional trapper, had ever occupied the surrounding areas. We would have to literally dig into the past to gain insight into the land's prior occupants.

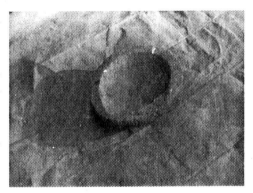

Figure 43. Stone oil lamp found by Quent Edson.

The few land-scars visible from twentieth-century occupation included the occasional tent pegs hidden beneath the moss; standing trees with long, vertical slices removed near the base of the trunk; wounded trees oozing pitch for fire-starting material; and the few decayed log-remains of a tiny cabin. These signs no doubt came from trappers, or from a wandering prospector, fisherman, or clam digger. The vertical slices cut from the trunks of trees (which had nearly died as a result) puzzled us for some time before a fisherman told us the reason. By using the natural angle of the tree where it curves outward from the straight trunk and extended down into the curved roots, the fishermen were able to make strong dory knees (boat ribs). The largest of the cut curves were the "spruce knees" that were fashioned into keels for trading boats or for an occasional schooner. A large, slow-growing spruce was valued because of the natural curve of its base as well as for its close grain that gave it strength.

We desired to go further back, to learn more about the people who had lived here permanently, not the wanderers of the last fifty years. These ancient inhabitants would have been the owners of the stone lamp and the ones who had enjoyed the scenic surroundings we now claimed as ours. Anthropology, which to us had been a drab, uninteresting subject, became alive and meaningful.

General information taught us that the Aleut natives at one time lived in *barabaras*—sod-roofed, semi-dugout houses supported by driftwood. Native fishermen had described the dwellings to us as having had driftwood limbs or poles for the roof that was covered with dry grass and sod. Such a home, half underground, would have been well suited to cold, windy winters. In our mind's eye, we could easily see a family comfortably sitting on skin rugs around the central fire, appreciating the light of a stone lamp. The wind might be strong, but inside their earthen lodge with a semi-tunnel entrance and only a small hole in the roof to release smoke, the storm would have little effect on their comfort and safety. Probably they had been just as protected and warm, if not more so, as my maternal grandparents had been in their Nebraska Sand Hills sod house.

During our trips along the shoreline, we began keeping a lookout for possible sites of ancient or abandoned native villages. At first we had difficulty finding sites because the dense, summer vegetation of grasses, elderberry, salmonberry, and forbs concealed the depressions that indicated the location of *barabaras*. After finding our first site with its rounded, sunken depressions, we knew which specific features to look for and soon found five former villages along ten miles of shoreline. The sites had a number of traits in common besides a few trenches (probably entrance tunnels or passageways between dwellings) and the rounded, pockmarked, contour left from the pit houses. Most of the sites were on a headland location with few surrounding trees, near a stream, and adjacent to clamshell mounds (midden heaps). Vegetation on the sites was similar from site to site, but it differed from other shoreline areas. Almost always, these sunny sites had tall herbaceous plants that the natives call *pushki* but what Bob and I called cow parsnip. *Pushki* thrives in organic soil, and archeological sites are often a natural, rich habitat.

After we had actually located some of the village sites from some prior civilizations, our image of the people grew broader and perhaps more accurate. We gathered a number of interesting facts from the shared characteristics of these former villages. Aleuts' tendency to select a slightly raised location on a headland could have been for protection and for circulating air. The excellent view of surrounding water from a promontory caused us to visualize lookouts placed on continual guard lest an enemy war party be sighted. We could imagine a winter's storm beating against a rocky point while a village remained protected above the reach of the sea. Furthermore, we could picture row upon row of dried fish hanging to cure in the smoke of many small smudge fires, while an offshore breeze swept the resulting pall into the distance. Both the wind and the smoke would have helped discourage the ubiquitous hordes of mosquitoes that we ourselves often battled. Perhaps the lack of trees was a result of midden heaps as generation after generation occupied these same areas. The areas, however, may have been treeless at the outset, chosen for the absence of roots that would hinder the digging of the sunken dwellings, or the areas might have been chosen to take full advantage of sunlight. The nearby stream would have provided fresh water and a supply of salmon in the summer and fall. The nearby beach would yield abundant clams for their staple food, along with other varieties of fish, mussels, and seafowl. No doubt the occasional porpoise, whale, or seal (having first been sighted from the promontory), and even bear added variety to their diet. Seafowl eggs and the many edible summer berries and plants must have also provided a welcome change. A number of the plants—sea lettuce, scurvy grass, and wild celery—we ourselves had picked and enjoyed in salads. All the Pacific Coast tribes frequently ate the umbrella-like scapes and stalks of the *pushki*. Tender stems are good raw, especially in the spring, and larger stalks can be cooked like rhubarb, sometimes mixed with oil. Even the roots can be used, cooked and mashed into a poultice to ease common aches and pains. The abundance of available food at our present time (1950s) indicated to us that the natives likely had fared well, unless a dense population had overtaxed the food resources.

One day when we were especially energetic, Bob and I selected one of the sites to spend an hour or two digging for artifacts.[13] At the site we were at a loss regarding the best location to start digging. Where would the discarded knives, plates, or lamps be tossed? Perhaps at the edge of the house, either outside or inside, we

---

[13] Digging on public lands is no longer permitted, except by native Alaskans and authorized archeologists. State and federal laws such as the National Historic Preservation Act of 1966 have helped to preserve the numerous sites.

decided, so we began to dig a section through what may have been the wall of a dwelling. We felt foolish to be needlessly punishing our muscles when the prospect of finding anything was so low. It was like digging for a phantom treasure chest in a large root forest without the aid of a treasure map. Yet others had found artifacts; so perhaps we would also.

We sifted each shovel of soil through our fingers. Running into clamshell rubble and charred rocks made the digging more enticing since we could surmise the reasons for the burned rubble. Were we digging where clams had been steamed? Were the rocks used in a *banya* fire? We had heard that these steam-bath chambers were still used in places by the natives on the islands. (We jokingly surmised that the steam bath our summer help had built was only following long tradition in the Kitoi Bay area.)

"What kind of bone is this?" I asked Bob as I unearthed a large specimen.

"That looks like a bear femur."

"I found it quite deep. How would they possibly hunt bear back before they had guns or metal implements?"

Bob gave me a lengthy answer. "According to native legends, a wooden pole was the only weapon used. One end of the pole was burned and charred to a point in the fire. After an all-night ceremony asking protection from their gods, a group of men would take their crude spears and go bear hunting. When a bear was found, the group of chanting, yelling men would surround the animal, teasing and confusing it with their abuse. Then when the enraged beast could stand it no longer, he would charge at one of the men. That was when it took real nerve. The charged hunter would quickly brace his spear on the ground, pointing the sharpened end toward the maddened-bear's throat. If all went well, the bear could not stop his rush to avoid the spear so would impale himself on it. The impact usually broke the shaft and sent the daring hunter flying against a tree, but before the bear could slap the protruding end of the spear from his throat, the remaining men would pounce in with their wooden weapons for the kill."

"That's vivid enough to dream about tonight."

Every fifteen or twenty minutes I would find what I thought must be a scraper, or a knife, or yet another stone tool. I could picture fat and flesh being scraped off sealskin, but each time Bob vetoed my judgments.

We continued digging for two full hours before deciding to stop. In the same way that a fisherman decides he must catch one more fish, we decided to scoop one or two more shovels of dirt. Nothing of interest appeared. Our ditch had become three-feet wide, three-feet deep, and eight-feet long.

"Shall we go?" Bob again asked.

"Yes, I may be too stiff to crawl out of bed tomorrow as it is."

But as Bob picked up the shovel and pick, I noticed a different rock barely visible at a bottom corner of our diggings. Scratching the dirt out from around it, I tugged out a flat, thin object.

"I really have found an artifact!" I yelled as I ran toward Bob. "You can't say this isn't. It has carvings on it."

With astonishment he replied, "Yes, definitely. These are petroglyphs!"

By measuring the depth of dark soil that had been on top of the artifact and comparing it with the amount of soil accumulated on top of the volcanic ash layer deposited by Mt. Katmai's eruption in 1912, allowing for compaction, we crudely estimated that the 1½x6½-inch stone with petroglyphic markings had been left there about five hundred years ago.

This find naturally led to various conjectures: Were the carvings a form of writing? Was the object an idol? Was it an endearing love letter? Or was it merely an artistic drawing representing a village hero? Some have suggested such rocks with carvings may have been used for games or perhaps were memorials to commemorate a wedding or a funeral. The carvings on ours made a picturesque design, but we were never able to identify the reason for the particular image.

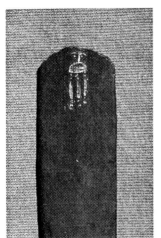

Figure 44. Izhut Bay artifacts.

Several weeks later, on a village site that had been eroded by wave action, we found more artifacts. In the exposed fifteen-foot-high midden heaps, we dug out several knives or scrapers (undoubtedly used to scrape fat and flesh off seal and sea otter skins), a crude grinding stone, and a two-pound stone that likely was either a hammer head, a knocker (for breaking shells or bones), a war-club head, or a net sinker. Clearly, it had been chipped and ground into the desired shape.

One end of the 3x5-inch rock had a perfectly rounded head; the other end was completely flat. The sides were smoothly rounded with two exceptions: one side had a flattened area, perhaps carved to fit a handle; on the opposite side was a groove, likely made to provide a method of tying the stone head onto the handle. Another time we found an Aleut oven or fireplace, which we left intact even though it would soon be sloughed into the ocean by the erosion of winter sea storms.

By this time our curiosity about the Aleut ancestors had sharpened. Later on our one vacation Outside, we hunted for any published material we could find on this intriguing subject. We read about the Aleuts' skill as sailors and their part in the exploration of the new world and settlement in Russian America. Even so, we found that little archeological work had been done on the island at that time. The Smithsonian Institution had sponsored a survey in 1926 under Dr. Aleš Hrdlička. His book (*The Anthropology of Kodiak Island*, Philadelphia: The Wistar Institute of Anatomy and Biology, 1944) provided answers to some of our questions, but for other "answers" we had to continue to rely on our imaginations.

Figure 45. Aleut oven.

Dr. Hrdlička's interpretation of the human past of the Kodiak-Afognak Island group is intriguing. Whether it is completely accurate, we cannot be sure. The first permanent settlers, he feels, probably arrived fifteen to twenty centuries ago by boat from a cultured Asiatic background. These people, whom he called the pre-Koniags,[14] degenerated through isolation and consequential inbreeding, even becoming somewhat cannibalistic. Later, about four hundred years ago, a simpler, less-advanced people known as the Koniags came to the islands and probably annihilated the older inhabitants through warfare. This new group, completely distinct from the pre-Koniags, were neither Indian nor Eskimo but resembled closely the Aleut Indians of the Alaska Peninsula. The Koniags were different in skeletal measurements from the Aleuts. Even so, when

---

[14] Dr. Hrdlička speculates petroglyphs "may well have been of pre-Koniag origin." Yet this does not fit with our soil accumulation estimate where we found the stone artifacts with petroglyphs.

the Russians first came to the islands in the eighteenth century, they called the Koniag natives "Aleuts" because of their close resemblance. Gradually, the Koniags began accepting the name for themselves. Later the name Aleuts was adopted by the Americans and was the favored term for many years.

Digging, reading, and thinking on our new interest in the former inhabitants who must have lived and walked on our same territory stimulated our desire to know more. We began to form mental pictures. If only we could talk to some of the older natives who lived in outlying villages on other Kodiak Archipelago islands or even talk to ones in Afognak Village, the native settlement to which Pete Olsen had attempted to take us, they might contribute oral stories. But our isolation and limited means of transport prevented us from ever even seeing Afognak Village, a string of dwellings facing the sea, on the distant southwestern part of our very own Afognak Island.

A Changing Culture

Present and past Aleut culture continued to interest us. How had this civilization changed over time? Some cultural groups go thousands of years with only gradual changes over the generations. But our reading led us to believe that powerful forces had influenced—almost required—these Alaskan natives to change their shelters, language, clothing, economic system, and perhaps to a lesser degree, their food and values. First had been the adoption of many Russian customs, and then twentieth century schools, religion, government, emigrations and the military build up of WWII brought immense cultural transformations in a relatively short time period.

History of our area was becoming fascinating. Glancing backward helped me understand the present. I again remembered our visit with Pete and Nina Olsen in Kodiak and my surprise when I observed their comfortable home and contemporary lifestyle. During my youth in the Willamette Valley of Oregon, all acquaintances had been people with European heritage. Thus, I immediately noticed the darker skin coloring, the black hair, and slightly different facial features among the Aleuts. I envisioned a cultural gap between Aleut and non-Aleut lifestyles, but I discovered the cultural differences were much fewer than I had expected. The Olsen family appeared to be an example of the effects of rapid change in the Koniag-Aleut culture. Nina Olsen's parents, Afoni and Christina Lukin, had lived in a *barabara*, whereas Nina and Pete lived in a modern home in Kodiak. Why the transformation? What exactly had occurred in our area over the past two hundred years?

It has been reported that when the Russians discovered Kodiak Island in the mid-1700's, they found it thickly populated by the Koniags, a major American tribe. The Koniags were living in small villages throughout the Archipelago, and they were persistent whale hunters. Extended families of fifteen people or more occupied each of their partially dugout dwellings.

As early as 1785, Russian fishermen, fur traders, and trappers built a fortified station on Afognak Island at what was then called Aleut Village, later known as Afognak.[15] During these early years natives were forced to produce food and to hunt sea otters for the Russians. Even after surrendering to the Russian conquest, struggles must have continued to occur between the ideas of the new arrivals and

---

[15] The name of the village was taken from the name of the Island.

the ideas of natives, who would have naturally resisted change. Changes challenge our equilibrium. For the natives, disease, epidemics, and increased alcohol[16] use were deeply damaging; yet the introductions of such items as saws to cut lumber, salt as a preservative, and even buttons on clothing brought progress. Aleut knowledge of the particular conditions and nuances of the area must have been valuable for the Russians. Each would have borrowed knowledge and culture from the other.

In the nineteenth century Russians continued to be drawn to the Afognak Village area and other Alaskan sites—sometimes for exploring—but mainly for fishing and trapping. The large population of sea otter provided pelts to sell on the world market. Fox farming was introduced on some of the islands, and fox pelts soon started to be shipped directly to San Francisco. Afognak Village developed an Aleut section (Aleut Town) and a Russian section (Russian Town), but even so the cultures began to blend. The Russians became more congenial, and the natives gradually accepted the Russian customs and even the Russian language. The two groups exchanged ideas, borrowed, and invented new ways of doing tasks. The men from both sections spent much time away from the settlement fishing, trapping, and cutting wood for fuel. Unfortunately, diseases brought in by the Russians and others continued to reduce the native population.

The Alaskan territory was called Russian America. Even after the United States purchased "Seward's Icebox" in 1867 for two cents per acre, the remote Kodiak Archipelago was only gradually settled by people from the United States. The Americans who did come were adventurers or settlers seeking a new land of opportunity. Some of these opportunities were taken by American companies starting salmon canneries, by individuals building stores, and by ones entering the fur trade.

Heritages in the village of Afognak continued to merge through marriage and mixing of knowledge. Natives born of mixed marriages were known as Creoles. Fishermen from Sweden and Germany came to fish and to trap, and then Chinese and Italians arrived to work in the salmon canneries that began to be established on the Kodiak Island group. Multi-cultural forces created more adjustments and more blending of races.

Since Russians had brought metal tools and whipsaws, small log cabins and lumber-framed buildings soon replaced dugout shelters. Afognak Island continued to have some *barabaras*—especially on trap lines—into the early 1900s. Modifications on the *barabaras* included cut wooden slabs sunk into the ground and inclining upward. These slabs were then covered with sod. However, by the

---

[16] Fermented juices of raspberries had been used even before the coming of the Russians.

early years of the 20th century, most dwellings were log and/or frame buildings. Sitka spruce was plentiful, and the Russian Orthodox Church in the village of Afognak was built with solid spruce walls.

With the Russians had come Christianity. Through the influence of early Russian missionaries and inhabitants, the majority of natives accepted the Russian-Orthodox faith, and it had widespread influence. After the church baptized a native, his/her status changed to a Russian citizen and the person was treated as such. Well known in Nina Olsen's childhood was Father Gerasim Schmaltz, who had come from an area near Moscow, Russia. As the priest of Afognak Village's Russian Orthodox Greek Catholic Church, he taught Orthodox Christianity. Besides its sustaining religious value, this church contributed a social life and a regular rhythm of calendrical days. Of great value to the settlement were the church's records of births, marriages, deaths, and an annual registration of the congregation.

Although quite common, not every person in the little village of Afognak accepted the Russian Orthodox faith. Nina Olsen, who was raised in Afognak, and her husband Pete Olsen were Evangelical Protestants. Likely, the Protestant influence came to the village and other areas through Scandinavian fishermen. In recent history, the Baptist Mission (orphanage and church) founded in 1893 by the American Baptist denomination on nearby Woody Island opposed and discouraged the practice of Russian Orthodoxy. It has been said that the children in the Baptist Orphanage were not allowed to attend Orthodox services. Protestantism was undoubtedly also strengthened by the ministry of Peter Deyneka, Sr., who was born in Russia and was the son of a Russian fisherman. He was a member of the Russian Gospel Association, later changed to the Slavic Gospel Association, which became active in Alaska in the 1930s and worked among the Russian-speaking Aleuts.

The natives of the Russian-Orthodox faith celebrate Russian Christmas. This comes in January instead of December 25. When WWII brought the short-wave radio into common use, the Aleuts adopted this modern electronic invention as a means of promoting their fast-dying native tongue and of celebrating their centuries-old Christmas customs. During their Christmas week, many native village choirs presented short concerts over 2512, the short-wave gossip frequency of the Islands. We enjoyed this novel means of Christmas caroling. One choir boomed forth with its predominance of male voices in a slow, guttural song, probably a hymn, sung in the native language. Groups in the other native settlements, especially the older folk, thrilled at the privilege of hearing their native tongue sung by neighbors. The elders had long been important authority figures, but with the rapidly changing culture and the passing of each elder, this role was fading.

As we listened to the caroling by the villagers at Old Harbor during the 1955 Christmas season, Bob and I were impressed even without understanding the words sung in the native language. We again were drawn into the Christmas spirit even though we had celebrated our Christmas two weeks previously. Each note of the unfamiliar melodies was drawn out, especially the first beat of each measure, and no musical accompaniment was present. The concert numbers continued for about fifteen minutes without a break between verses, perhaps a result of part-singing or rounds—our musical knowledge was too limited for us to know. Even from one song to the next, no break occurred because one group would start the new song while another was still ending the first.

At the end of the Old Harbor concert, a group of young girls sang "Silent Night" in English, followed by the complete group chorusing the greeting, "Merry Christmas!" The listeners from other settlements then began transmitting their thanks and compliments, also in English.

The transmitter operator for the group at Perryville replied to the group at Old Harbor, "We really enjoyed your singing here. That was real good. You have a good choir and it sounds like you have a lot of older voices. We don't have any older folks here; most of us are just young shrimp, and we miss hearing the older people. Could you let a couple of the older ones say a few words to us?"

"Old Harbor back to Perryville: Yes, we have a number of older people who help out with our choir. Here is Mike Pestrikoff. He is seventy or eighty. I'll let him say a few words."

A rather shaky voice then came on the air. "I'm not so young anymore. I'm seventy-one years old. Still I can dance a jig."

"Next we'll let one of the men who is here from Karluk talk to you. He is seventy-two."

"I like to help the church and sing in the choir. I can't read or write. I help the church along by singing. I hope next Christmas will come before I kick the bucket."

Then a group from Alitak gave their choral presentation in the same manner as the Old Harbor group. A fishing vessel, no doubt a stranger to the islands, broke into the singing by attempting to call another boat, but the forceful voices drowned him out.

After twelve minutes of unbroken singing, a young man's voice recited or read in the native tongue and then changed to English and began "Now when Jesus was born in Bethlehem of Judea…"

After hearing the distinctiveness of the native language, Bob and I feared that English words would continue to seep into the annual caroling and would soon steal even the last fragments of this beautiful native tongue. Even Nina Olsen's

Alutiiq[17] speaking ability had not been passed on to her children. The Russian Orthodox priests in her home village of Afognak taught after-school classes in Russian, and Russian or Alutiiq was spoken in the homes. But the Territorial Department of Education that established a school in Afognak in 1886 forbade either of these languages. The teaching was in English. Naturally, children were also taught in the Western educational style instead of the older method of gathering in community houses to listen to the recollections and observations of the elders. Then, it had been the families who educated the children. These oral stories of history and traditional Aleut knowledge told by the adults educated, entertained, and helped to preserve their heritage because children were taught to listen and remember. We wished the cultural traditions of the native residents could be maintained, but at the same time we understood the goal of assimilation.

From Bill Stone, our friend and superintendent of the native Kodiak Orphanage, we had learned more on the present-day Aleuts. Many families were interrelated, but the few full-blooded native relatives of the children in the orphanage had disappeared rapidly during the ten years that the Stones had worked in the orphanage. Bill explained that the natives had intermarried first with the Russians, some with Scandinavians, and now were intermarrying with Americans. Many of the Aleut girls, because the small ratio of women to men in Kodiak gave them a wider choice, chose to marry white men. Many were going to the States as wives of sailors from the nearby Kodiak Naval Station and likely would be accepted without any racial prejudice. But this left the unfortunate native men without potential wives. He concluded, "Before many years, the natives as a group may become indistinct."

Nevertheless, in contrast to Pete Olsen's ease with us, some of the Aleuts who had been hired on the boats bringing construction supplies to Kitoi Bay would not enter the station, presumably because I was a white female. The culture of the indigenous residents seemed to be rapidly changing, but less so in remote settlements. It would be a shame, we felt, to have their language, values, and power vanish in their struggle to keep pace with the extreme changes of modern culture. Change is inevitable, but the last hundred years had caused a cultural collision for this group.

---

[17] It was decades after our years in the region that the word Alutiiq more correctly replaced the word Aleut. Alutiiq refers to both the language and the people. The plural of Alutiiq is Alutiit. Nina Olsen did not remember either Aleut or Alutiiq used to refer to her people when she was a child. They used Sugpiaq, a word meaning "a real person" or the plural, Sugpiat, meaning "real people." Actually, the word Aleut in the Sugcestun language is Alutiiq.

Our front yard beach, as well as other nearby beaches, was cluttered with whalebones. Why were they there? What was their historical significance? How did they connect to the human past of this bay? History is based on correct interpretation, but according to tales that were further supported by the whalebone remains, Kitoi Bay had been an Aleut whale-butchering ground. Besides relying on fish, fowl, and clams, these earlier residents would have hunted bear and whale for food as well as for clothing and tool-making materials.

Kitoi Bay is attached to the larger Izhut Bay, where a one-hundred-fathom (600 ft.), deep trench apparently attracts feeding whales. We would often see whales spouting and breaking the surface in their rolling, circular dives. In fact, the word "*ketoi*" is a corruption of a Russian word for whale. Since no *barabaras* were found near the station area, it could be that the stone lamp dug from under our doorstep had been used to burn sea mammal oil 1000–7000 years previously in a purely ancient civilization, but more likely it was used merely 200–1000 years ago during bustling butchering activities.

As we looked from the station at the twelve-foot jawbones and the twelve-inch-diameter vertebrae cluttering the beach, we could visualize the historic scenes that lay behind them. In our imagination, we saw a lookout standing on the promontory scanning Izhut Bay near the lagoon-entrance village in late May or June. His eyes are peeled not only for marauding enemies but for sea life as well. A flock of circling seagulls warns the watcher to scrutinize the water more closely. A dark shape rises out of the water. A lingering, twenty-foot-high fountain of warm, vaporous breath condenses in the cold morning air before the wind sends it gracefully eastward. The first spout is followed by two, three, four more.

The lookout hurries to inform the villagers, who quickly prepare for a whaling expedition. Six kayak-like skin boats, *bidarki*, loaded with men and equipment leave the lagoon for the deep water at the mouth of Izhut Bay. The leader in each *bidarka* is the harpooner crouched in the bow. He is silently proud of his inherited position and thankful for the charms about his neck, which protect him and give him supernatural power. A heavy, crude harpoon with a long slate point is in his hand ready to be lifted at a moment's notice. At his feet and connected to the harpoon by a rope of braided kelp is an inflated stomach of a seal, a most buoyant float. Several lances lie in the stern, ready for quick use.

Powerful, sure strokes from the kneeling paddlers send the *bidarki* through the choppy bay to the vicinity of the whales.

"There they are," points a harpooner as the great black bulk of a whale exposes first his head, then his back, and finally his giant flukes.

Trying to guess where the whale will surface next, the boat crews fan out, each anxious to have their leader throw the first harpoon into the monster so they might receive the resulting praise and distinction.

A boiling movement of the water is seen, and a giant hulk surfaces twenty feet from one of the *bidarki*, dangerously rocking the craft. Spray from the geyser-like spout drifts into the tense, drawn faces of the crew. They move closer. Knowing a quick slap of a fluke could easily mean death, they position their *bidarki* carefully. But they must move almost within touch of this mammal. With quick reflexes and a tremendous heave, the harpooner hurls his heavy harpoon. Brawn, patience, and years of training reward him: the whale is struck just below the small dorsal fin. Another strong-bodied companion quickly throws the kelp rope and seal float overboard just as sheets of water blur his vision. The whale beats his powerful flukes in the water, nearly swamping the fragile craft.

All becomes still. The sharp eyes of each native scan the water's surface for the telltale float that will appear first, telling where the whale will again surface. After twenty minutes, the float is sighted, but swift paddling by the racing crews does not bring even the nearest *bidarka* within harpooning distance before the monster again dives into the protective waters. Within a few hours three more harpoons are in the hard-to-conquer beast, and one is in deeply enough to cause large red streaks to appear in the green water after each dive.

Late afternoon has arrived; and the whale is tiring. As the animal again surfaces, one *bidarka* paddles close beside it. Nimbly, a bold native jumps onto the giant, glistening back and with all his strength quickly drives his lance deep into the animal. The wounded whale gives a mighty shudder and again submerges leaving a brilliant, deep-red streamer trailing him into the depths. The daring man is left in the foamy water to be pulled out by his companions. Upon the whale's next surfacing for air, the perspiring men use quick footwork to stay on top of the mortally wounded beast and thrust two more lances deep into the body cavity.

Finally just as dusk is settling, five *bidarki* paddle slowly into the sheltered waters of Kitoi Bay with the nearly lifeless carcass in tow. The hunters have not only been successful, but they have conquered the dangerous animal in a third of the usual time. It usually took three or four days for the whale to die of his wounds and float to the surface.

The sixth *bidarka* hurriedly returns to the village to tell of the good fortune. Almost all the villagers drop their other work and are now at the butchering cove. This giant would provide much food as well as needed oil for lamps and cooking. The flickering fires built on the beach encourage the tired, pleased hunters onward.

Now it is nearly midnight (and fortunately high tide) when the carcass is floated onto the beach. Several climb onto the whale to check the markings on the spear points to learn who receives credit for killing the animal. The water recedes; the butchering begins. According to custom, choice pieces go to certain members of the tribe and hunting crew. The cutting and scraping really isn't work because a festive air reigns throughout the long, working night. Foxes, hungry for a scrap, are skulking just back of the firelight, but little will be left other than the flesh surrounding the spear points. This is cut out and thrown away. The fat will be rendered for oil, the skin made into clothes, and linings (from stomach, bladder, and intestines) made into rain gear or used to cover roof-holes to admit light in the sleeping rooms of the dwellings. Even the cords of sinew will be used to make sea nets.

Late the next day butchering is complete and the villagers have returned home laden with meat, oil, and the choice tail vertebrae for chairs or headrests. They even took the disk epiphyses to use for plates. A variety of forest life has descended on the area to pick over the remains: foxes quarrel for scraps; ravens, magpies, and bald eagles soar overhead; a big brown bear picks up a huge bone, lumbering up the beach to chew on it in a more leisurely fashion.

Now in the mid-1950s on our Kitoi Bay beach, the giant ribs and scattered vertebrae stood alone as epitaphs of a former way of life. We had viewed them as junk. Now we saw them as memorials to the ancient Aleut people.

Many times we would sit at our table, gaze across Kitoi Bay to Izhut Bay[18] and see spouts of water vaporizing in the cool air. Or on a crisp, fall morning when traveling by skiff to some distant lakes, a pod of whales would surface around the boat. Seeing their shiny, black backs and their powerful, horizontal flukes made us feel vulnerable. At these times, the seventeenth and eighteenth centuries felt so close—almost close enough to touch. History is real. Cultures are changing. We were participants.

---

[18] Izhut Bay is an indentation of Marmot Bay, a favorite feeding ground of whale.

Figure 46. A whale rib made a good bench.

Transitions

We were now at the close of our first full year on Afognak Island. Autumn was approaching; our Noisy Season would soon become a suppressed murmur and fade into the Silent Season. The summer workers were becoming restless and anxious to leave. "Gotta get my ears lowered," said Gene, referring to a haircut. We would miss Gene's smooth-tongued speech rich in slogans and showy slang.

The one most anxious to leave was Pinkie. Finally, the week he thought would never come arrived. It was Monday, the day before his expected departure. His old outgrown and worn clothing had been burned, and he was completely packed and ready to depart. Late Monday afternoon we heard a roar overhead and in came the plane we had not expected until Tuesday morning. I decided that his sudden departure was probably better than a delayed one. Pinkie had grown very close to Bob and me, and from his quick goodbye I believe we also meant much to him.

Tears pooled in Milt's eyes on his departing, so incongruous with his usual coarse speech and nature. Although we could not envision the thoughts behind those wet eyes, perhaps they contained an appreciation for the interest, friendship, and attention we had given Pinkie.

The next few weeks included a rapid series of good-byes, each difficult to make as we realized that we would never see most of these men again. This crazy-quilt pattern of people was soon going to be torn again into individual blocks. We had shared, laughed, worked together and grown surprisingly close. As we shook hands with each, little did we realize that in a few months Leo would be married; Claude would spend his summer's wages in drunken unconsciousness; and Molly, in addition to his many accomplishments, would soon have another title: mayor of Juneau. Votes for him had been overwhelming. These good-byes were sure signs of the Silent Season's approach. Other signs were the humpies' continued battling upstream to spawn, the jumping of the silver salmon that had entered the bay, the finishing of the hatchery and the large wooden pipeline, and the rushed flying of Kodiak Airways

Figure 47. A humpy swimming upstream to spawn.

as they transported the many cannery workers from the outlying salmon canneries into Kodiak for the first step of their mass exodus to the Outside.

This was the time of year that seagulls blanketed the skies at the mouth of Big Kitoi Creek because the salmon were dying after depositing their eggs. The birds would feast on the spawned-out fish. The seagulls' noisy chatter blared upward to awaken us early in our bedroom on the knoll directly above the creek. Even so, we were thankful they kept down the foul odor that otherwise would have developed from the fish carcasses.

Jack was the very last of the Noisy Season workmen to leave, and since he was sleeping in the bunkhouse that had now been built, we prepared to move into the station for the winter. The upstairs bedroom area had to be cleaned and scrubbed to remove the strong smell of smoke. The one 3x6-foot window was covered with such a thick smoke film that I could not see through it. But a reward of moving included no longer having to make a bed that touched three sides of the room. Besides this, we would have space and warmth in our station loft.

Unfortunately, Jack sprained his back before he was scheduled to leave Kitoi Bay. He and Bob had just finished putting the heavy logs in place for a weir at the mouth of Ruth Lake when it happened. We were concerned about Jack. Also, Bob hated losing his help because another log-and-board weir had to be built at Midarm Lake, some fish remained to be spawned, and the glass-bottomed boat in Kitoi Lake had to be brought down to the bay for winter's use. Bob could not lift the logs for Midarm Lake weir by himself, and even with a block and tackle he could not bring the boat down alone. Jack hated to leave. He had loved his time at Kitoi Bay and was appreciative of everything, especially the food. Being careful not to infringe, he took sponge baths in the bunk house instead of using the station's shower; he washed his clothes on the washboard instead of using the gas washing machine. A former hobo, he never complained and was the best worker of anyone we had at Kitoi Bay. Meal-time entertainment was hearing about Jack's past, including his solitary confinement on a bread and water diet when he had been in the Navy and overindulged in alcohol. He seemed impressed with our lifestyle and would likely have worked without wages just to stay at Kitoi Bay.

Meanwhile, at Bob Hall's Kodiak Airways, Gil Jarvela had fallen off the wing of a Grumman Goose onto a concrete floor. The fall had broken his arm and shattered his wrist. So Bob Hall himself had to do some of the flying. It was he who came out for Jack, and we said goodbye to another superior individual. For his replacement, Bob hired Bill Stone of the Kodiak Orphanage to come for a working vacation. Of course, we invited his wife, Zelma, as well, and this turned out to be the week of the Great Bear Hunt (See Appendix A).

The pilot bringing Bill and Zelma to our station told us that he had seen Jack just a few hours after he was flown into Kodiak. The pilot's words were "He was walking down the street feeling pretty happy." Bob and I were sad that such a capable person was so addicted to liquor. Unfortunately, this problem was widespread in Kodiak.

This autumn transition period between our two drastically different seasons brought an unusual number of guests—three groups—who stopped for brief visits. Even more astonishing than three groups of visitors in such a few weeks was the fact that each group included a woman. During all the time we had lived at our island home we had never before had a female, other than Zelma Stone, step onto Kitoi Bay soil. Having three separate women as guests was most shocking and delightful.

The first was the wife of a fisherman who had hauled winter supplies and maintenance freight from Kodiak to Kitoi Bay. As our husbands and the few remaining summer workers unloaded, she and I chatted. How refreshing it was to have another woman to talk with, even though she was a stranger and it was only for an hour or so.

"I can certainly tell you have just arrived in Alaska," she emphatically stated before she was surprised to learn that I had lived slightly over a year on Afognak Island, "because before many weeks you won't be wearing dresses and those little loafers. The only way to keep your feet warm up here is to wear pacs[19]." She was dressed in a heavy work shirt, mannish trousers, and heavy shoepacs. I thoroughly understood her blunt remark and perhaps was even kindly amused as we humans tend to be when finding one of our weaknesses in another. Of course, she was right. Even in our well-built station, the wintertime floors were always frigid and little warmer in summertime. This sometimes led to drastic measures.

There had been the time I dashed to the door yelling, "Help, my shoes are on fire!" to a construction worker. Claude had run inside, glanced at my shoeless feet, and asked, "'Where are they?" as if he could not see the smoke rolling from the kitchen. When I answered, "In the oven," he made a grab for the oven door and, probably with all types of unspeakable thoughts concerning feminine stupidity, raked out the smoldering shoes.

Gradually I had become accustomed to ice-cold feet, but on days when they became unbearable, I would tug around a hot-water bottle for a foot warmer. If I ever became dissatisfied with being a wilderness wife, I am confident that all I

---

[19] Pacs, shoepacs, or shoepacks are heavy, laced, waterproof boots. They are worn with long wool socks and an inner sole insert.

would need to do is to dress day after day in shirt, trousers, and shoepacs. Bob would immediately take me back to civilization.

Our second autumn guests were Harry and Virginia Readings, a friendly Fresno, California, couple who was big-game hunting for Kodiak brown bear. Their guide, Oscar Nelson, brought them into our bay for a visit one evening, probably as a mutual benefit for both couples. The visit provided much-appreciated guests for us and gave the Readings a change from boat life. Of course it could have been that we, without realizing it, were like a sideshow in a circus. *"Step right up, ladies and gentlemen, step right up folks and see a young couple living in utter isolation. These modern Robinson Crusoes never see a road, a car, or a hamburger stand. Step right up, just twenty-five cents to view this Alaskan attraction!"*

While we visited, I had the rather-natural female intuition that I should offer our shower facilities to Virginia. Surely, since she had been the only lady on a forty-five foot boat for three days, a shower would be greatly appreciated. But how does one tactfully ask a guest, who only twenty minutes previously was a stranger and who is wearing a three-carat diamond, "Would you like to take a shower?" But because of Virginia's outgoing friendliness, I ventured the suggestion while showing her through the station. She accepted.

While Harry rowed Virginia back to the boat for a change of clothing and while she showered, I hurriedly prepared hot strawberry shortcake. Such modern refreshments in isolation surprised them greatly and would have been impossible but for the station's newly acquired kerosene-powered refrigerator with a freezer compartment. But neither the hot shower nor the refreshments lessened Virginia's dismay at isolated living. "I just cannot understand how you can stand it," she emphasized. "Of course my three boys would like living someplace like this, but I'd simply go nuts."

Out third guests were Mr. and Mrs. A. D. Stanger, a lovely couple from Austin, Texas, who were bear hunting with Bill Poland in his double-cabin cruiser. Since they were hunting in the Izhut Bay area, they stopped in twice. On their second visit, both had shot a bear. Mr. Stanger's was a nine-foot-six-inch, older bear that they planned to have live-mounted and placed in one corner of their den. Mrs. Stanger's slightly smaller bear pelt would be made into a rug. Although each of our infrequent visitors had a slightly different opinion of wilderness living, we were unprepared for the Stanger's reaction to our pioneer life. "You have a lovely place to live, a nice, convenient home and beautiful surroundings," stated Mr. Stanger, an architect. "I almost envy you." His attractive wife, Ellagene Stanger, was equally enthusiastic: "You mean you all actually get paid for living out here? You must be having a continuous vacation."

After ending our first year on Afognak, we knew this had been an experience like no other we would ever have. In many ways it almost did seem like a vacation: there was no stress of urgent deadlines; we had the freedom to schedule our days as we wished; and we had many opportunities to absorb the Alaskan panorama. We didn't miss the noisy culture of the States: the ringing of telephones, jangling of coins, or tapping of typewriter keys. But we did have other challenges: exhaustion from physical tasks, the tedium of routine, and the frustration of feeling cut off from the world. Vacations are short and superficial; our experience was real.

By September the 25x85-foot hatchery that was added onto the Kitoi Bay Research Station was nearly finished. The rafters were up and the last of the lumber had finally arrived. The millrun lumber that was used was much poorer than in the States, but Bob did not think the price too steep when compared with other items. Delivered at Kitoi Bay, the cost was $90 to $100 per 1000 board feet.

Figure 48. Construction of hatchery addition expanded Kitoi Bay Research Station.

Figure 49. Artificial spawning.

With the necessities of a nearly completed hatchery[20] and running water, red salmon (sockeye) were collected in the fall and held in a holding pen at Little Kitoi Lake. When mature, they were artificial spawned. The female was split open, and the eggs (roe) spilled into a large pan. Next, the male sockeye sperm (milt) were squeezed into the same pan in order to fertilize the eggs. Within a few hours, eggs not fertilized would turn white and were picked out with a baster-like suction tube. Careful handling of eggs during spawning gave little loss. The fertilized eggs were then put in baskets in the new hatchery troughs to await hatching in the spring. These alevin (newly hatched salmon) would be reared in the hatchery where they would develop into young salmon fry. The fry would be planted in one or more fresh-water lakes—not to grow for sport fishermen but to be used in research studies. The fry would grow into smolts during their year in the lake and then would swim to the ocean. After two or three years in the ocean,

---

[20] By 1956 part of the hatchery was heated but final completion with a fully cemented floor came later.

the fully grown sockeye salmon would return to the same lake. Data collected on several of the nearby lakes and on the sockeye salmon would be tabulated and analyzed. The lakes, many unexplored and unnamed, were truly being used as outdoor laboratories.

Three Years Later

It soon became our third year—and our third Silent Season—at Kitoi Bay on Afognak Island. Much had changed. In fact, the station's brown-and-green exterior and the oil-can mailbox were almost the only reminders that this was the same building we had entered when we first arrived. It remained a serious break of Kitoi Bay etiquette when a newcomer mistook the oil-can mail holder for a common can and picked it up to use for gathering specimens or as an ashtray.

We now took for granted the luxuries of a davenport, chairs, a refrigerator, and running water—all conveniences we had to do without during our first Silent Season. Of course an electric mixer, toaster, electric iron, and reading lamps were still out of our world. But the absence of such "luxuries" gave us a greater appreciation of the simpler things of life and revealed where true values lie.

One material luxury that we truly valued was our Leica 35mm camera, flash attachment, several interchangeable lenses, and tripod. Bob could use the new colored film and have pictures developed as slides. And he could place the camera on the tripod, set certain buttons, and jump back into the field of view for pictures of the two of us.

We shipped two whale vertebrae to my grandfather and great uncle in Oregon. They wanted to use them in landscaping and as conversational pieces. Bob tempered the vertebrae in the hatchery until completely dry and then made two triangular wooden boxes for them. Yet he had to trim the bony processes radiating from the 10x12-inch central portion of each vertebra in order to keep the size small enough for travel by bush-plane and parcel-post. Even after this work, the boxes would not go through the small 19x23-inch door of the Grumman Widgeon, so we had to wait until a time Bill Harvey came with his new Super Cub[21] floatplane. It had a larger door. Shipping was further delayed when the post office in Kodiak would not accept the packages. They had to be shipped by boat freight.

---

[21] During WWII the Piper Cub was used as an air ambulance and as an observation aircraft. After the war Piper enlarged the airframe, added a more powerful engine, and named the plane Super Cub.

Figure 50. Bill Harvey beside his new 1957 Super Cub.

Research studies were being done on Ruth Lake, which now had a weir site. Since rough seas from Easterlies often prevented safe travel to and from this lake, Bob designed a 6x8-foot cabin, cut the lumber to size, hauled the lumber to Ruth Lake, and built a shelter so that overnight camping would be easier. The cabin had a stove, window, table, and two bunks. The finished product was fine except for one problem. The location of the stove and door allowed the bunks only on the six-foot side. But Bob's height is six foot,

Figure 51. Ruth Lake cabin.

two inches. Thus, he could not completely stretch out at night. So Bob cut a hole in the wall and built a little box-like addition just big enough to shelter his feet.

Even in the third year, Bob and I never tired of walking the beaches and making new discoveries about the plentiful sea and shore creatures around us. Deer and squirrel tracks began to appear on our end of the island. We also found that for months we had been walking on the rooftops of some unknown neighbors, octopi. Once we learned to catch and cook them, they became a succulent part of many dinners.

We needed, however, still more refreshing changes from canned meats. Since seals were eating so many salmon and a bounty existed on them, Bob shot a number of seals over the winter. Soon I also had to try. In order not to have the kick of the .30-06, I used the .22 rifle. I planted my feet as firmly as I could in the rocking skiff, but missed several shots as I aimed at a seal head popping up and down in the wavy water. Finally with Bob's help—barking at a nearby seal to keep him curious so his head would remain out of the water—I shot and hit him in the neck. We thought he had sunk, but he rose again, still kicking, so I shot him again in the head. Even though it had taken a while, Bob was surprised that I had been successful. I had never hunted with a gun before; perhaps my college archery class helped my aim. Quickly, he started the motor so we could reach the floating seal before it sank. The ones that sank usually washed to shore by the tides where they made for good bear eating. This time we did reach the seal in time, and I grasped a flipper even before the motor stopped. With the two of us using all our pulling power on the weighty mass, we lugged it over the side and into the skiff. Since it was my first game, we decided to skin and save the hide to be prepared for a small floor rug, a future conversational piece and reminder of our time in Alaska.

Figure 52. Ruth and her seal.

It was with mixed feelings that we neared the end of our three years on Afognak Island. We did make one trip back to our home state of Oregon, spending precious time with family and friends. Although these moments of stateside refinement were thoroughly enjoyed, we did not hesitate to return to our pristine Alaskan surroundings, leaving the busyness, noise, and crowds behind.

No matter how detailed or descriptive words can be, or even how clear or accurate photographs can be, nothing truly captures our Afognak experience. It is like a painting that can be admired by many, but only we—like the artist—can thoroughly appreciate each brush stroke, whether delicate or bold, that comes together in such completeness.

Were there times of discouragement? Of course. Moments of loneliness? Yes. Frustrations, irritations, discomforts? Certainly. Yet, the various challenges we confronted were of real benefit. They caused us to admire and trust each other for inventive solutions. Our dependence on each other increased as our separate, independent capabilities also expanded. We were blessed with a greater discovery of who we were, both separately and together. Being able to share thoughts, feelings, and goals with only our spouse caused us to grow incredibly close. Nowhere else would we have such uncluttered time to focus on each other and our relationship.

The simplicity of our tranquil life was enriching in its own way. Our primitive living conditions made us more capable; the lack of social restrictions made us more accepting; the Noisy Season workers made us more tolerant; the Silent Season solitude made us more appreciative of others.

The entire experience was a building-up process, a recharging of batteries. Yet, as we became filled, we felt the need to give. This need to share with other people was the hardest part of living out of contact with the human race. Continually in our hearts was the hope that we would someday be parents and would give ourselves to our children. Also, we felt a desire to become more cultured, especially through education; we saw surfaces of our lives that still needed smoothing. Because of all this, we would not remain on our snug little island for a lifetime, but would venture back to the more civilized world. As we returned home, perhaps the greatest gains of all were the memories of a land and sea so astonishingly beautiful and serene that our souls expanded in worship to a God who was even greater and more faithful than we had ever known.

Afterword

After leaving Alaska, we moved to Ithaca, New York, where Bob enrolled at Cornell University. On an early morning's walk through the wooded area to campus, I saw an imprint in the fresh snow and actually began saying, "the bears have come out of hibernation" before being shocked back to the realization that it was simply a man's footprint. Another flashback to the isolated years would occur whenever I walked across a street: the strangeness of approaching vehicles made me feel uneasy, even so fearful that I could not walk across a street if there were any cars moving toward me, even a long distance away.

I soon adjusted to stateside life again and even achieved my dream of becoming a mother. Bob continued in graduate school and earned a Ph.D. in Ecology at the University of Michigan, taught at both Utah State University and Colorado State University, and served as Staff Ecologist on the National Water Commission, Washington, D.C. Instead of returning to teaching elementary school, I delighted in using those skills in my role as mother. Yes, we were blessed with two daughters, Jan by adoption and Carol as a complete biological surprise. Later, I returned to school to obtain a M.Ed. in Guidance and Counseling and still later taught at Linn-Benton Community College in Albany, Oregon.

Alaska became the 49th state in 1959. Our own Kitoi Bay Research Station on Afognak Island changed from being a small sockeye salmon research facility to Kitoi Bay Hatchery after being purchased by a group of fishermen. It became the most productive fishery hatchery in Alaska, and for many years it was known for its large, stable supplies of pink salmon.

On Good Friday in 1964, a huge undersea earthquake and ensuing tsunami occurred in this new state, claiming more than a hundred lives and causing severe damage on Kodiak and Afognak Islands. This second-worse earthquake in the 20th century had magnitude reports varying from 8.4 to 9.5 on the Richter scale. The Japanese term "tsunami" (meaning storm waves) was not widely used or understood at the time we lived at Kitoi Bay. Bob, with his geological interests, was well aware that one could occur because we were in a seismically volatile region (shifting of the North American Plate and Juan de Fuca Plate). Thus, Bob had put an emergency cache high on the hill. Our plans were to run up the hill as soon as we felt the earth shake or heard a wall of water rushing inward. We were told that when the 1964 tsunami actually occurred, two Kitoi Bay men, working on the bottom of a boat that they had turned upside down near the beach, suddenly realized that water was up to their knees and rising. Surprisingly, these men heard no warning sound. They survived by flipping the boat over and jumping in; there would not have been time to run up the hill behind the station. The dock and the research station with the connecting hatchery were washed away.

At the time of this disaster, we were living in Colorado where Bob was a professor at Colorado State University. From there, we moved to Virginia and then back to Oregon when Bob had to retire early due to medical reasons. In Oregon, we happened to meet at our church a young man named Peter Olsen. Imagine our surprise when he turned out to be the son of Pete and Nina Olsen, the native fisherman and his wife who had so graciously entertained us in their Kodiak home! A close friendship ensued with Peter, and in later years, we had the privilege of having Peter's mother, Nina, visit us in our Oregon home. She and her husband, Pete, had much positive influence on young people in the Kodiak area, and Nina began teaching classes in several native cultures. She had retained her native language, and it finally became part of the curriculum in Kodiak High School. She was truly an example of one who had adjusted to a changing culture and a shrinking world.

Peter, the son, gave us an up-to-date description of Kodiak and Afognak Islands, including personal descriptions of the devastating tsunami. Fishing vessels were badly damaged. The worst havoc was to the native village of Afognak (the village Pete Olsen had attempted to show us). This village was so destroyed that it was abandoned. The inhabitants chose Settler Cove, off of Kizhuyak Bay on the northern coast of Kodiak Island for their new site, which they named Port Lions. Peter further described shoreline configuration changes. In the Kitoi Bay area our prized Razor Clam Beach had become smooth bedrock. Big Kitoi Creek, where Bob dipped our household water, had become saltwater, and the area between the creek and the small beach where the amphibian planes would taxi in and turn around had been filled and leveled. With the lower land level and no gravel bar in the mouth of Big Kitoi Creek, a dam had to be made at its outlet to raise the water level about two feet for the hatchery water supply.

Many have asked us if we ever returned to Afognak Island. Thirty years after our initial arrival, we did return. In our view, the westward and northward movement of the North American population came as a result of people searching natural resources and lifestyles away from the crowds. Thus, I suddenly realized on our return visit that on Afognak Island, timber was the desired natural resource. Much of the island's land had been transferred to a native regional corporation, Koniag, Inc,[22] which was beginning to harvest the dense stands of Sitka spruce.

---

[22] Alaska Native Claims Settlement Act Corporations

We were disappointed to view the many clear-cuts in the slow-growing spruce forest and to find an extensive logging road system built on much of the island. Notwithstanding, we realized that the area was being replanted and the trees were reseeding themselves naturally.[23]

Memories and emotions quickly surfaced when we retraced our footsteps around Kitoi Bay itself. Although I had tried to prepare myself, I was greatly saddened that our quiet virgin nook had perished. Practically everything was different. A new dock constructed by the Navy mainly for training exercises had replaced the tsunami-destroyed one. Three residences and a large bunk-cook house had been built on higher ground from the bay level. An older residence stood on the point. Of course, Kitoi Bay Research Station with its attached hatchery as a research facility for red salmon had long ago become Kitoi Bay Hatchery. Since the original building had been washed away by the tsunami, a new large hatchery building had been constructed including offices, wet and dry labs, and two well supplied shop and supply rooms. Now, no research was done at Kitoi Bay Hatchery; it was purely a production hatchery. The facility was hatching one hundred million pink eggs annually along with chum, coho, king, steelhead, and Kitoi Lake rainbow.

Quietness had evaporated. Calmness of spirit was absent. In just thirty years, Kitoi Bay had become a man-made world of convenience. The simplicity of our years had been lost. Communication had totally changed. A transmitter was atop Duck Mountain; small portables and CBs gave continuous marine weather forecasts and some were pre-set to UHF, the emergency channel monitored by the Coast Guard, the military, and others. Further cluttering the area were mobile units, TV antennas, and the beginnings of a broken-appliance graveyard.

Likewise, the water was populated with boats, including an indoor-outdoor cabin cruiser owned by the hatchery manager. Several commercial fishing vessels were fishing with their seines. This was allowed because the hatchery people had enough fish captured in the mouth of the creek to provide the millions of pink eggs they would be able to rear. Even with all this activity, most people would still consider Kitoi Bay isolated. But life as we experienced it had vanished. To us, Kitoi Bay was no longer pristine, no longer remote, no longer silent.

To our complete surprise, our little plywood bedroom house had been found floating in the bay several days after the tsunami. It was rescued and put to use as a storage shed on the new dock. Also, two poignant landform features remained and brought tears to my eyes: the view and shoreline of the bay from the hatchery

---

[23] Spruce trees are marching southward about a mile each 100 years. In landing at Kodiak, we were surprised to see Near Island with trees. When we lived on Afognak this same island was bare.

area and the bear trail between our former station area and Little Kitoi Lake. The trail was used less than when we and the Kodiak brownies trod it, but it had the same curves, the same up and down sections, the same views of the bay through the spruce, and the same devil's club clumps as well as deep mossy spots.

At one Afognak Island location that appeared to be an old *barabara* site, Bob and I had a closer reintroduction to the devil's club. Just as we remembered, the plant was still attractive and still evil with its thorns protruding both from the stems and from the top and bottom of its maple-looking leaves. Having thought of these thorns, Bob had traveled prepared by bringing his deerskin gloves.

In 1995, eleven years after our return visit, an Alutiiq Museum and Archeological Repository opened in Kodiak. It came about mainly from the efforts of the Kodiak Area Native Association with help from a number of the ANCSA Corporations[24] in the Koniag Region and from a large grant from the Exxon Valdez Oil Spill Trustee Council. This nonprofit museum preserves many cultural traditions of the Alutiit, whom we had called Aleuts, and helps visitors realize these people's gift to the world.

The children of Pete and Nina Olsen, recognized elders of their native community, now play strong roles in the Kodiak area. Their oldest daughter, Ruth A. Dawson, is on the Board of Directors of the Afognak Native Corporation, Inc.[25] and was one of the principal elders who influenced the building of the Museum along with many other issues pertaining to the native community. The Olsen's son, Peter, was Manager of Land and Natural Resources of the Koniag Corporation and is now a private consultant. Pete and Nina's children are an example of rapid cultural change in that their grandparents, Christina and Afoni Lukin, had lived in a *barabara*.

Another person with a prominent Kodiak role is Steve Harvey, son of Bill Harvey who was one of our favorite bush pilots. Steve and his wife, Mary Ann, run the Harvey Flying Service. Steve flies a Grumman Widgeon plane just as his father and other bush pilots did decades ago. Although Widgeon parts are no longer made, Steve manages to order parts to rebuild portions so his plane stays in excellent condition.

In recent years humans have continued having their impact on the Kodiak Archipelago. Attitudes on wildlife, predators, and newcomers have changed, and the world of convenience has had its influence. Yet, the area continues to influence lives, including our own. Living on the island of Afognak fifty-plus years ago

---

[24] One of several regional corporations that manage community lands. Natives are the shareholders.

[25] A non-profit group that provides social, health, and political-advocacy services to the indigenous people.

left us several legacies, both minor and major. One was a life-long tradition of Bob making pancakes every Saturday morning, his skill learned from Molly back at the station. This tradition has been passed to our son-in-law, Darrell, and on to our grandson, Kyle. On a deeper note, another legacy is that of learning to be content whatever the circumstances and, furthermore, to recognize that the non-material things are the real part of life—faith, family, friends, character, giving. Finally, there has been the legacy of a strong, deep love in my relationship with Bob. His recent death has been my greatest challenge ever, but it pales in contrast to the strength, hope, and assurance I have in God's unfailing love. Truly, our time on Afognak Island granted us enduring gifts and invaluable memories.

Appendix A: Bear Hunt

We decided at some point during the winter that we would really like a bear rug that might eventually adorn the floor or wall of a future home. Also, Bob, as an experienced Oregon blacktail-deer hunter from his teenage years, was rather eager to shoot his first bear—especially the famed Kodiak brown bear, a unique subspecies of the grizzly bear that lives exclusively in the Kodiak Archipelago.

Bob had hired Bill Stone, our friend who was superintendent of Kodiak Baptist Mission (orphanage), to come to the station in order to help build two weirs. He and his wife, Zelma, arrived on a late October mail plane. On Monday near the end of their week's stay, Bob and Bill spotted a bear at the point where they were turning the skiff into Izhut Bay. They returned immediately to the station and said they had decided to go bear hunting. Bob was pleased that Bill had had some experience in bear hunting and skinning. I had dearly wanted to go along, but Bob, citing the danger of the ten-foot-tall Kodiak brownies—the largest bears in the world—and the difficulties that could arise in protecting me and killing a bear, would not let me accompany them.

After some cruising and "glassing" (peering with binoculars) from the skiff, the men soon spotted what was likely a yearling brownie scrounging for food along the small point jutting into the bay and also a large bear, probably the mother. It was the same knoll where they had first sighted a bear. Quietly and quickly, they beached the skiff as far as possible inland on the peninsula. Feeling they had the bears' escape route covered, they began the stalk. Bob and Bill decided to stay close to each other so waded together through the thick, brushy underbrush. The adverse wind was blowing toward the bear. This only complicated the skillful maneuverings required to approach the two brownies. Closer and closer the men stealthily advanced. Knowing the two bear were cornered, they separated enough to keep both sides of the point in view and continued to advance through the spruce trees. Suddenly Bill raised his rifle to his shoulder. This was it at last! **Kapow!!!** And then another thunderous roar vied with the pounding surf in the background as Bill fired again from behind the spruce thicket. "I got them both!" came the excited shout. Immediately, a large brown animal came bounding toward Bob. With his 30-06 rifle in position, Bob fired right into the chest. "I got the big one!" shouted Bob as the bear rolled end over end in a limp heap.

Figure 53. Kodiak brown bear.

Bill had missed both his shots. Then came the waiting for the second bear Bill had missed but to no avail. Closer observation showed the dead bear to be the small one, only eighteen months old. Knowing the danger of killing a cub with the mother around, the men kept keenly alert. A long, careful futile search of the point produced no bear except the one that was dead. The gigantic mother bear had escaped.

Next, the men discussed the mystery of Bill's two missed shots when he was at such short range. They found that the rear sight had fallen from his rifle. In the excitement of the hunt, he had not even noticed. (So much for seasoned veteran hunters!)

The skiff came roaring back into Kitoi Bay much earlier in the day than Zelma and I had expected, and, yes, we could see two men and a big lump of fur in the boat. Now the fun was over and the work began. Ropes were attached to each hind foot and the monster with its thick, coarse fur was hoisted into the air for skinning. They threw each rope over a limb of a spruce tree, and then both Bob and Bill pulled to hoist the 250–300 pound brownie into position. Being a cub, it was only as tall as a man (five foot, nine-inches) and would be the perfect size to fit on a future wall or floor.

Skinning was slow because of the fat layer. The men had to be careful not to cut or even nick the skin, which would reduce the pelt's value. Neither did they want to make any unnecessary cuts of the hair. As they made the ventral incision from the front legs, which were now hanging downward, upward to the tail area, they kept the knife well under the skin, pulling upward, so as not to cut hair. They slit each leg to the paw, carefully staying in the center and keeping the knife under the skin as they worked.

Pulling off the hide was somewhat similar to skinning a deer, but as they pulled and cut between the meat and hide they did so with much more care because the pelt was of more value than the meat. Also, they left the head attached to the skin. A "real" Alaskan souvenir was their prize, so they took it "slow and easy," carefully pulling and cutting the skin away from the fatty, man-like-looking carcass. To Bob's surprise, he could not find a single parasite, whereas he had never skinned an Oregon deer without finding some. Taking time out only to sharpen knives, Bob and Bill took several hours removing the skin. They were thankful that the bear was not any larger than it was.

Finally, they worked on the head, skinning it out entirely with special care of the lips, ears, and other features. They finished the skinning, but the work was far from over. Butchering and fleshing were yet to come.

Bill and Zelma returned via the Tuesday's mail plane to Kodiak, leaving the two of us with the task of saving both the meat by butchering and the skin by fleshing. The butchering part was easy; the fleshing part was grueling. Bob and I had worked together in butchering deer stateside, but fleshing was a new experience. Many, many hours were spent face down, just inches from the thick oily hide, removing the fat from the pelt. With October's shorter daylight hours, much of it was done by dim lantern light. Because great care was taken not to nick the skin as we removed all the flesh, it was extremely tedious. Never had we bothered to save deer hides, but *this* brownie pelt was being prepared for salting and then would be sent to a taxidermist to be made into a rug with a full mounted head. We wanted to do the best job possible. During the hours of wielding my small, narrow-bladed pocketknife, I recalled hearing how pigs were boiled to slip the skin easily from the flesh. Mentioning this to Bob, I mused, "That must be about as easy as pulling off a wet swim suit.... But perhaps some of the fat would still remain on the pigskin.... Surely there must be a quicker way of de-fatting this pelt in front of me."

Crunched over, we continued the monotonous fleshing. We worked on the table, the same table used for eating, studying, and everything else. As the fat resisted separation from the skin, I could readily understand the superior way early squaws had of chewing the bearskin and spitting out the fat before drying or tanning the pelts. But I was not about to try their way. Carefully, half-inch by half-inch, we slipped the sharp knives between fat and skin. Fleshing the head was exceedingly difficult because nicks in the facial features would be difficult to repair. The lips had to be split at the beginning of the inner gum line, turned inside out, and scraped. We turned the ears inside out with cartilage left attached. After all possible fat was removed, we covered the flesh side of the stretched-out skin with pounds of table salt, at least a half-inch coating, and rubbed the salt in. The lips, ears, and nose were further packed tightly with salt. I felt as though I came to know bears from the inside out!

While in Oregon, we had used venison as a main meat source—almost an economic necessity—and enjoyed its tastiness, but deer had not yet been sighted on our part of the Afognak Island. Bob's "getting his bear" substituted for "getting his deer," but would it be good to eat? Others had said that bear meat could be quite good. How would ours taste? Either fortunately or unfortunately, the already below-freezing temperatures enabled us to freeze the meat. Since the cub was just a little over a year old so would have been feeding on mother's milk and tender roots dug from the hillside, we expected the meat to taste good. Yet, it did not. Even so, it provided additional meat for our limited larder so we ate most of it. Instead of using the bear fat, we had ordered suet from Ben Kraft in Kodiak to grind with the bear meat. But neither baby brown bear burgers nor bear steaks were tasty. Various creative ways of cooking it with spices and tomatoes were disappointing. Yet we persevered in eating it. We were carefully saving our money for adopting a child, possibly, or attending graduate school. Although Bob's salary had steadily increased, he had turned down promotions with the Alaska Department of Fisheries since it would mean living in Juneau and traveling frequently. We did not want that kind of life or marriage, one requiring Bob to be gone for days at a time.

Thus, we would leave Alaska and merely file this bear hunt into our memories. Perhaps some day Bob could make up an entertaining tale of "The Great Bear Hunt" to tell his grandchildren.

Appendix B: Menu Planning

After we obtained a kerosene-powered refrigerator, our menus greatly improved. Even so, fruit and vegetables were often canned. Cinnamon rolls and cookies were always homemade. My one cookbook was the First Edition of *Betty Crocker's Picture Cook Book*, 1950. Lots of rich foods such as gravy and pie were served, and I had learned the secret from my mother that most men think a meal is good if it ends with pie. Following are two weeks of my rotating month of planned menus.

Day	Lunch	Dinner
WEEK ONE		
Tue.	Creamed Dried Beef (or Tuna) on Toast Tossed Salad Raspberries	Fried Oysters (or Chicken-Fried Steak) Mashed Potatoes Asparagus Pineapple and Cottage Cheese Salad Toast Apple Pie Alamode
Wed.	Baked Macaroni & Cheese Cabbage Slaw Raisin Bread Applesauce & Cookies	Roast Chicken Dressing Boiled Potatoes Frozen Peas Cranberries Bread Fruit Cocktail & Cookies
Thur.	Leftovers: Chicken & Dressing Fruit Salad Raisin Bread Apple Crisp	Hamburger & Gravy Boiled Potatoes Green Beans Corn Warmed Bread Peach or Pumpkin Pie
Fri.	Homemade Soup Deviled Eggs Celery Pickled Beets Cornbread Chocolate Pudding	Pork Roast & Gravy Baked Potatoes (or Franconia Potatoes) Buttered Corn Frozen Spinach Waldorf Salad Bread Apricots and Cookies

Day	Lunch	Dinner
Sat.	Sausage & Noodle Casserole Tossed Salad Bread Gingerbread with Whipped Cream	Swiss Steak Baked Potatoes Buttered Cabbage Carrot Sticks Bread Pears & Cookies (or Baked Apples)
Sun.	Leftovers: Roast/Steak in Gravy Pear & Grated Cheese Salad Biscuits Custard (or Bread Pudding)	Fried Ham & Gravy Brussels Sprouts (or Green Beans) Boiled Potatoes Grapefruit Jell-O Salad (or Radish Roses & Cauliflower Florets)
Mon.	Soup (left from Friday) or Omelet Carrot & Raisin Salad (or Pineapple & Cottage Cheese Salad) Crackers Cupcakes (or Baked Alaska)	Chicken Pie (or Liver & Onions) Mashed Potatoes Peas Celery Biscuits Jell-O with Whipped Cream

WEEK TWO	
Tue. Scalloped Potatoes & Ham Leftover Vegetables Toast Cupcakes & Boysenberries (or Jell-O with Whipped Cream)	Meat Loaf Baked Potatoes Broccoli Twenty-Four-Hour Salad (or Cheese-Carrot Jell-O Salad) Bread Frozen Peaches
Wed. Lunch Meat & Toasted Cheese Sandwiches (or Tuna-Potato Patties) Hot Tomato Juice Tossed Salad Angel Food Cake (or Upside-Down Cake)	Roasted Beef Heart & Dressing (or Fried Pork Heart & Gravy) Mashed Potatoes (make extra for Thursday's hash) Cranberry Sauce Celery Creamed Cauliflower Bread Cherry or Blueberry Pie
Thur. Corned Beef Hash (or Macaroni-Meat Casserole) Green Jell-O Salad Bread Meringue Shells or Torte	Fried Chicken Gravy Boiled Potatoes Green Lima Beans Carrot Sticks/Pickles Muffins Plums & Cookies (or Bananas in Red JellO)
Fri. Leftovers: Beef Heart, Meat Loaf, etc. (or Macaroni & Tomatoes) Tossed Salad Bread or Toast Cinnamon Rolls & Applesauce	T-bone Steak Green Beans Homemade Rolls Sliced Tomatoes on Lettuce Fruit Cocktail & Cookies

Sat.	Oyster Stew (or Yankee Doodle Macaroni) Peach Half & Grapefruit on Lettuce Toast & Crackers Tapioca Pudding	Rolled Beef Roast (or New England Boiled Dinner with Potatoes, Carrots, Onions & Cabbage) Gravy Boiled Potatoes Glazed Carrots Cabbage Wedges Garlic Bread Chilled Cream Dessert
Sun.	Cold Roast & Cheese Slices (or Dried Beef in Creamed Macaroni) Spanish Rice Pickles Cracked Wheat Bread Peaches & Cookies	Pork Steak or Chops & Gravy Boiled Potatoes Spinach or Summer Squash Celery Bread Berry Pie (or Apple Dumplings)
Mon.	Chicken Noodle Soup Hash-brown Potatoes Creamed Coleslaw with Oranges and Peaches Hot Biscuits Fruit & Cookies	Wieners & Sauerkraut Fried Potatoes Buttered Peas (or Parsnips) Carrot/Pineapple Salad Homemade Loaf Bread Hot Cake with Whipped Cream

Perishables to Include in Grocery Order

Some items such as bread, eggs, potatoes, and milk were always on the weekly grocery list with additional perishable items added depending on my week's menu. Twice a year a fishing vessel brought out non-perishable grocery supplies, which kept the upstairs attic shelves well stocked with canned goods from canned apples to Kilm, which was dried whole milk. In the States we had only used dried skimmed milk and had never seen dried whole milk for sale. After we had refrigeration, frozen vegetables replaced most of the canned ones.

WEEK ONE	
Breakfast sausages	Cabbage
Oysters, fresh or frozen	Carrots
Whole chicken	Cottage cheese
Round steak	Oranges
Pork roast	Apples
Ham slices	Pears
Ground beef	Lettuce
Stew meat (for soup)	Tomatoes
Cranberries	Celery
Tillamook cheese	White bread
Frozen spinach	Raisin bread
Frozen peas	Whipping cream
Frozen strawberries	Table cream
Frozen Brussels sprouts	Crackers
Ice cream	Grapes
WEEK TWO	
Frozen chicken	Carrots
Lunch meat	Parsnips (perhaps)
Beef or pork heart	Frozen peaches
T-bone steaks	Celery
Ground beef	Cabbage
Ground pork	Oranges
Rolled beef roast	Bananas
Pork chops	Pear
Wieners	Lettuce
Frozen green limas (or broccoli)	Tomatoes
	Tillamook cheese
Cauliflower	Ham hocks

Our Attic Larder

Recipes

Following are recipes of several favorite menu items served during our Noisy Season. Two of the recipes, Octopus and Duck Soup, were solely used during the Quiet Season. Additionally, I tucked in a few classic recipes, ones referred to in the book, from both my mother and grandmother.

MOLLY'S PANCAKES (See p.133)

Molly would cook them right on the hot surface of the stove—no skillet—and he did not measure ingredients.

Stir together 1 cup flour, 2 tsp. baking powder, 2 Tbsp. sugar, ¼ tsp. salt. Mix in approximately 1 cup milk, 1 egg yolk, and 2 Tbsp. oil or melted butter—remember that beating toughens pancakes. Gently fold in 1 beaten egg white. Follow directions below for cooking. Serves 2 to 4.

BOB'S POWDERED BUTTERMILK PANCAKES (See p. 185)

Bob later refined Molly's procedure and added some creative variations.

Stir together 2 cups flour, 6 Tbsp. powdered buttermilk, 1½ tsp. soda, 2 to 4 heaping tsp. baking powder, 2 heaping Tbsp. sugar, and ½ tsp. salt.

In a small bowl, beat 2 egg whites until stiff (sometimes Bob added a bit of cream of tartar and a few Tbsp. of sour cream). Set aside.

In another small bowl, lightly beat 2 egg yolks, 2 cups water or milk, and ¼ cup oil (or melted butter). Gently fold this liquid mixture into the dry ingredients, just enough to moisten.

Gently fold in the beaten egg whites; do not over stir.

Have the griddle hot; drop large tablespoonfuls onto griddle, spreading batter a bit with the spoon. Turn cakes with a light flip as soon as they are puffed and full of bubbles but before the bubbles start to break.

Serve immediately on a warm plate with butter and warmed syrup. Serves 4 or 5.

Variations: One of the following may be added: 1/2 cup oats; 1 cup blueberries; 1 cup chopped apples; 1/2 cup raisins; 1/2 cup nuts; 1/4 cup oat bran with a bit more water.

BOB'S FRESH BUTTERMILK PANCAKES

These pancakes are my favorites. Use the above Powdered Buttermilk recipe with these changes: Omit the powdered buttermilk. Instead of using the water or milk, use approximately 3 cups of fresh buttermilk. The amount of liquid depends on how thin or thick you desire the pancakes.

IRENE ANDERSON'S LAVENDER SOAP (See p. 50)

1½ pints cold water
1 pound can lye (caustic soda)
1½ Tbsp. borax
½ cup ammonia
5½ pounds fat, melted but not hot
1 Tbsp. oil of lavender

Put the water into a wooden pail. (*This is used because lye corrodes metal.*) Add lye and stir with a wooden spoon or paddle until it is completely dissolved. Add borax and ammonia.

Slowly stir the melted fat into this mixture and continue stirring until it is the thickness of honey. If small amounts are made, vigorous beating will make a more compact, even-grained soap. Add the oil of lavender. Pour into molds. The best molds are shallow wooden or paper boxes lined with waxed, paraffined, or oiled paper. When the molds are filled, cover with a cloth to prevent the loss of heat. Let stand two or three days. Remove from molds and cut into cakes with a wire or strong string.

THE PINKIE-PUNCHED CHOCOLATE ROLL

One afternoon Pinkie shuffled discontentedly into the kitchen and began pummeling what to him probably looked like a small roll of laundry sprinkled and waiting to be ironed. It happened to be the dinner dessert, a delicate sponge roll that I had just baked and then rolled in a sugar-coated dish towel so it would retain a rolled shape when unrolled and filled with whipped cream for the dinner dessert.

"What's this?" Pinkie asked as he socked away.

"I'll uncover it so you can see," I calmly replied, actually more amused by my anticipation of his reaction than provoked by the ruined dessert.

Both the chocolate sponge roll and Pinkie lost their puff. Pinkie's eyes widened and his freckles stood out more noticeably than ever on his whitened face as he gazed at the flattened, indefinable mass. He realized it was food but did not know what type or the reason it had been rolled in cloth. "Yikes! What did I do? Gee, I'm sorry. What is it?"

My explanation of the purpose of the roll made him even more remorseful since he realized the tasty goodness of anything containing whipped cream. The fact that I did not scold him and did not mention the incident to the others probably made Pinkie more apologetic about his misdeed than he would have been otherwise. During dinner, the tall tales continued to lace the conversation, but Pinkie did not look too perky. Dishes clattered. The men chatted. Pinkie sat subdued. The men did not notice his quiet manner or his occasional downcast eyes, but it was easy for me to discern his thoughts as we ate the evening dessert of canned apricots.

The next morning he said, "Ruth, that was awfully nice of you not to mention what I did to our dessert last night. What are you going to do, make another one?"

After my affirmative reply, Pinkie ventured the question, "What are you going to do with the one I punched flat?"

Before replying, I hesitated and pondered whether it would be a reward for misconduct to give him permission to eat the remainder or whether it would be a bite-by-bite reminder of his unthinking conduct. After evaluating the price of many expensive eggs being wasted if the sponge roll were thrown away, I told him he could eat it. This he did, piece by piece with mouse-like nibbles!

Recipe: ½ cup sifted cake flour
½ tsp. baking powder
¼ tsp. salt
2 squares unsweetened chocolate
4 eggs
2/3 cup sifted sugar
1 tsp. vanilla
2 more Tbsp. sugar
¼ tsp. baking soda
3 Tbsp. cold water
Powdered sugar
1 cup heavy cream
¼ tsp. almond extract

Grease a jellyroll pan and line with waxed paper. Heat oven to 375 degrees.

Sift flour, baking powder, and salt onto piece of waxed paper. Melt chocolate in a small saucepan over hot water. Meanwhile, break 4 room-temperature eggs into large bowl. Beat eggs with the sifted sugar until very thick and light (*with an electric mixer if available*). Fold flour mixture and vanilla into egg mixture.

To the melted chocolate, add the additional sugar plus the soda and cold water, stirring until thick and light. Quickly fold this chocolate mixture evenly into batter. Pour batter into the prepared jelly roll pan. Bake 15 to 20 minutes or just until cake springs back when touched in center with a finger.

Spread a clean towel on the counter and sift over it a <u>thick</u> layer of powdered sugar. When cake is done, loosen edges with spatula and turn onto the sugared cloth. Carefully peel off paper and with very sharp knife trim edges of cake to make rolling easier. Cool for 5 minutes and then roll up the cake. First, fold hem of towel over edge of cake and then gently roll towel in it. (*This prevents cake sticking.*) Gently lift roll onto wire cake rack to finish cooling (*at least an hour*). Just before serving, carefully unroll cake and quickly spread 1 cup heavy cream, whipped and flavored with ¼ tsp. almond extract and perhaps a teaspoon or two sugar, within 1 inch of each edge. Roll up the cake using towel as pusher. (*In modern homes with a refrigerator, the roll can be prepared and refrigerated 2 to 3 hours before slicing and serving.*)

MARR'S SCOTTISH SUET PUDDING (See p. 54)

1 lb. suet, cut finely (not ground)
1 lb. currents
2 lbs. raisins
1 piece orange peel
2 pieces lemon peel
1 tsp. each–nutmeg, allspice, cloves, cinnamon
1 cup sour milk (1 tsp. soda in milk)
4 eggs, beaten
2½ cups flour
1 cup white sugar
1 cup mild molasses or brown sugar

Mix all together thoroughly. Wet a flour sack in boiling water. Spread sack out smoothly on table or board. Sift a smooth sprinkle of flour over center and rub out smoothly with hands. This is to seal pudding. Pour pudding on this. Pat and shape into a smooth ball. Gather up edges and tie with a strong cord, leaving loose for pudding to rise. Drop in kettle of boiling water with something in the bottom to prevent sticking. (*Grandma always used her water-bath canner with its wooden rack in the bottom.*) Cover and boil 5 hours, adding more boiling water if necessary. (Note: This pudding is actually submersed in water, not steamed.)

Dip for the Scottish Suet Pudding: Mix one cup sugar with 2 Tbsp. flour (or 1 Tbsp. cornstarch) and a pinch of salt. Gradually add one or two cups boiling water. Cook on low heat until clear and thick. Flavor with brandy. (*Although not on Grandma's recipe, I usually add 2 Tbsp. butter.*)

GRANDMA MARY MARR'S CHRISTMAS SALAD
(1940's simple one; see p. 54)

Grind 1 pound cranberries. Over the berries put 2 cups sugar and let stand two hours. Add 1 cup finely chopped apples and ½ cup finally chopped celery.

More modern versions of this add red grapes, walnut or pecans, and whipped cream.

GRANDMA MARR'S CRANBERRY COCKTAIL (See page 54)

Boil 1 cup cranberries in 3 cups water till they burst. Strain; bring juice to boiling point. Add ¾ cup sugar; boil two minutes. Chill and serve ice cold over equal parts diced pineapple and bananas (1 cup diced pineapple and 2 bananas). (*In Grandma's time cranberry juice could not be purchased.*)

PINKIE'S COCONUT-CREAM PIE

To fulfill a promise to Pinkie, I made a coconut-cream pie for him to eat all by himself. His eyes widened with delightful anticipation.

"You may eat it whenever you wish," I told him. "If you'd like to have it for dessert this noon, you may, or if you'd rather eat it when the men aren't around, that is fine, also."

"I don't want you to think I don't appreciate it, but I'd rather eat it now so the men won't see me."

He had no sooner picked up a fork—and stuffed what for an average person would have been four large bites into his mouth—than in walked Bob.

"Say, how do you rate around here? I never get a whole pie to eat by myself."

"You won't tell anyone, will you, Bob?" Pinkie asked hesitantly, not certain whether Bob would or wouldn't.

"Well, I'll tell you what. For a nice big piece I might forget I even saw you in here."

"I guess I'll have to give you a little piece. Those fellows would never stop teasing me if they knew."

Crust: Prepare and bake a single 9-inch pie shell ahead of time. Mix 1 cup flour and ¼ tsp. salt. Add 6½ Tbsp. of chilled shortening. With a pastry blender or two knives, cut in half the shortening, until the mixture is like tiny grains of rice. Cut in the remainder coarsely until the size of giant peas.

Sprinkle about 3 to 4 Tbsp. icy-cold water, one tablespoon at a time, into the mixture, tossing lightly with a fork until all particles are moistened. Gather the dough into a moist (not wet) ball with fingers. Chill in refrigerator three to twenty hours. Remove it an hour before rolling.

Filling: In a medium pan, mix 2/3 cup sugar, 2½ Tbsp. cornstarch, 1 Tbsp. flour, and ½ tsp. salt. Gradually stir in 3 cups milk and cook, stirring constantly, on medium heat until mixture thickens. Boil one minute. Remove from heat.

Beat 3 egg yolks slightly; then slowly stir in a few spoonfuls of the hot mixture. When yolks have been warmed, pour them into the hot mixture. Cook until thickened, stirring constantly.

Remove from heat and blend in 1 Tbsp. butter and a scant 2 tsp. vanilla. Fold in about 3/4 cup shredded coconut. Cool, and then pour filling into pastry shell. Cover the pie with whipped cream. Sprinkle with a bit of toasted coconut.

ALASKAN CHICKEN AND NOODLES

This was my quick, emergency recipe that I would sometimes serve over mashed potatoes or biscuits for an unexpected meal.

Heat liquid from a 3 lb.–4oz. canned whole chicken, adding about ¼ cup minced onion and celery leaves. (Meanwhile pick chicken off bones and put in serving dish. To this add a 5 oz. jar of boned chicken.)

When liquid reaches boiling, add about 2 oz. raw noodles. Season as needed with salt, pepper, thyme, and chicken bouillon cube. When noodles have cooked, add thickening made from a paste of canned milk and flour. Lastly, add chicken and heat.

ALEUT DUCK SOUP

Duck soup was a favorite Aleut dish that we often prepared. We did not make the mistake of cooking tough loons. Gadwalls were easily obtained and good. But of the many ducks we cooked, ptarmigan was the most delicious. Ptarmigan live on top of the mountains and turn white in winter. Ours came from Will Troyer who worked with Fish & Wildlife in Kodiak and who had been a classmate of Bob's at Oregon State College. He stopped by in his chartered boat, Swallow, *when making some game counts on Afognak Island.*

Cut one 3-pound duck into four pieces. Parboil it 2 minutes. Drain and wash. Place in kettle. Cover with cold salted water. Add ½ sliced medium onion, 2 stalks of celery, and 1 clove of garlic, cut in half. Bring to boil; then simmer for 2 hours, adding more water when necessary.

Remove duck and strain broth. There should be about 4 quarts of broth. Cut the duck meat from the bones, chop, and add to broth. Also add the juice of ½ lemon. Add ½ cup chopped celery; 1/3 cup green pepper, cut in strips; and 1 small carrot, sliced thinly. Season with pepper and boil 15 minutes. Stir in ½ cup uncooked rice; cover and cook 5 minutes. Remove from heat but keep covered. The rice will steam-cook and be light and delicate in ½ hour. Re-heat when ready to serve.

OCTOPUS

At low tide, often with the aid of moonlight and a lantern, we enjoyed wading in the shallow Kitoi Bay waters investigating sea life. Even in this reduced light, the sea anemones were as colorful as parrots. They would flop over as the water receded, relaxing in limp napkin-folds until the waters again enveloped them, and stimulated by the plankton-filled sea, they would elegantly unfold their bright, lacy "leaves" to feed. The starfish, sea brittles, sculpins, and the tiny clusters of zooplankton in the water attracted our interest as well as the blennies, limpets, and snails hiding under the rocks. It was during one of these seashore investigations that we found octopus dens. The entranceways were so small that it seemed impossible for an octopus to squirm through. A big four-foot octopus can wiggle in an extremely tiny hole under a rock, and the den is recognizable only by the gravelly fragments the octopus has scooped out from under the rock in preparing his home. We wanted to taste this delicacy even though it looked ugly and grotesque.

Soon we came up with the following recipe:
1. Lift the rock roof off the den and scoop the octopus into a bucket.
2. Remove the animal from the bucket. This task is not simple because with its dozens of tiny suction cups the octopus holds tightly to the bucket. With four hands, get the eight sticky tentacles all free at one time.

3. Remove the eight tentacles from the body.
4. Flail the tentacles for tenderness by repeatedly striking each tentacle over a plank.
5. Soak the tentacles in saltwater.
6. Wash the curly, button-covered legs well.
7. Open windows before the next step.
8. Put the meat into heavily salted, boiling water. As the cooking process begins, the water will turn beet-juice red. Boil for 20 minutes.
9. Drain the cooked meat.
10. From each tentacle, peel and scrape off the outside skin, which includes the suction cups. This is tedious.
11. Cut the long ropes of meat into small cross sections. This delicately flavored, white meat can then be used in tossed salads, cocktails, or tomato-octopus soup.

Index

A

Afognak Island 1, 3, 7–9, 21, 38, 76, 77, 81, 107, 127, 153, 158, 159, 161–163, 173, 180–184, 190, 200
Afognak Native Corporation 184
Afognak Village 8, 76, 77, 112, 159, 161, 162, 182
Airplane 3, 12, 27–29, 63, 69, 70, 72, 75, 76, 80–85, 105, 113, 115–117, 177, 182, 187, 189
    Amphibian 3, 80, 182
    Constellation 6
    DC-3 7, 20, 91
    Grumman Goose 10, 172
    Grumman Widgeon 5, 7, 27, 29, 30, 55, 56, 103, 104, 115, 177, 184
    Piper Cub 29, 70, 177
    Super Cub 177
Alaska vii, 1–4, 11, 12, 33, 43, 53, 77, 81, 82, 105, 106, 108, 109, 119, 126, 127, 134, 135, 144, 150, 155, 159, 161–163, 173, 179–182, 189–191
Alaska Communications System 47
Alaska Department of Fisheries 5–7, 11, 18, 98, 106, 112, 128, 135, 190
Alaska Peninsula 31, 80–82, 88, 159
Alaska Steamship 57
Alaskan Territory 1, 2, 71, 81, 94, 105, 112, 162

Albany, Oregon 181
Albrecht, Ray 27, 76, 82, 85
Aleut 8, 42, 76, 105, 106, 108, 113, 130, 154, 155, 158, 159, 161–163, 165, 166, 168, 184, 199
Aleutian Chain 31, 91
Alitak 164
Alsea River 5
Alutiiq 165
    Sugpiaq 165
American Baptist Church 105, 109, 163
American Legion 105
Anchorage 6, 7, 20, 110
ANCSA Corporations 184
Anderson, Clarence L. 6, 12, 18
Anderson, Irene v, 1, 3, 33, 50, 191, 195
Anderson, Loyd L. 3, 73, 74
Anthropology 154
Appendicitis 69, 71, 76
Archaeology 155
Archeological Repository 184
Archie (Last name unknown) 135
Army 5, 58
Artifact 108, 155–157
Asphyxiation 76, 78

B

B & B (Beer & Booze) 111
Bald eagle 21, 127, 168

Barabara 154, 161, 162
Barkley, Paul W. vii
Basketball 48
Bathhouse. *See* Steam bath
Beachcombing 28, 145
Bear. *See* Kodiak brown bear
Bear hunting 106, 187
Bearskin 108, 189
Beaver 21
Belleau, Tom 27
Belmont 111
Benson, Benny 105
Bidarka 166, 167
Big Kitoi Creek 11, 13, 16, 31, 35, 121, 126, 149, 150, 172, 182
Big Kitoi Lake 55–57, 70, 120, 149
BIOLA 47
Blenny 200
Brittle star 28
Bush pilot 46, 70, 76, 82, 85

C

California 5, 174
Cape Chiniak 106
Castles, Harry & Gwen 59
Chanham, Ben 27
Chignik 31, 32, 80–84
Chiniak Bay 106
Chinook. *See* Salmon, Chinook
Chitons 144
Christianity 163
Christmas 53, 59–61, 163, 164
Chum. *See* Salmon, Chum
Church 3, 4, 103, 105, 107, 163, 164, 182

Clam 28, 29, 49, 92, 144, 154–156, 166
   Alaska surf 93, 144
   Bent nose 144
   Butter 28, 144
   Cockle 144
   Gaper 93, 144
   Littleneck 28, 144
   Razor 28, 92–94, 144
   Red neck 144
   Soft shell 144
Clamshell 119, 144, 154
Claude (Last name unknown) 10–12, 119, 133, 138, 171
Coho. *See* Salmon, Coho
Colorado State University 181, 182
Cormorant 37
Cornell University 181
Corvallis, Oregon 8, 104
Crab 28, 29, 97
   Dungeness 98
   King 97–99
Crab fishing 81, 97
Cratty, Al 27, 29, 56, 82
Creoles 162

D

Daly, Vince 10
Dawson, Ruth A. 113, 114, 184
Deer 21, 127, 189, 190
Devil's club 10, 70, 123, 184
Deyneka, Peter 163
Dolly Varden 143, 149
Dons, USF 48
Duck Mountain 8, 94, 183

E

Ed (Last name unknown) 119, 122, 125, 131, 133, 141, 181
Edson, Quent 10, 12, 103, 120, 123, 124, 131, 136, 146, 147, 153
Eisenhower, Dwight D. 132
Elderberry 127, 154
Elk 21
Erickson, Henry 31
Eskimo 159
Evangelical Protestants 163
Expansion 31, 57
Exxon Valdez Oil Spill Trustee Council 184

F

Fields, Leslie Leland vii
Fishery biologist 6, 7, 10, 11, 17, 19, 106, 119, 120, 130, 134, 135, 138, 143, 200
Flounder 99
Forest Grove, Oregon 3, 53
Fox 21–24, 28, 44, 49–52, 58, 62, 70–72, 91, 95–98, 162
Fox fight 22
Fox sparrow 70
Freeman
    Eugene 53
    Marjorie 3, 53
Frog 87, 150

G

Gadwall 199
Galbreath, Jan vii, 181
Gaper clam 144
Gene (Last name unknown) 119, 125, 133, 146, 150, 171
Geriene, Verlyn 27
Gill, Slats 48
Gill, the engineer (Last name unknown) 135
Goldeneye 99
Great Depression 3
Gruening
    Clark 126
    Ernest 126
Grumman Widgeon. *See* Airplane, Grumman

H

Hall, Bob 27, 103, 105, 113, 172
Halligan, Reggie 48
Hare, snowshoe 21, 24, 28, 29, 36, 91
Harlequin 99
Harpoon 166, 167
Harvey
    Bill 27, 31, 55, 82, 85, 177, 184
    Mary Ann 184
    Steve 184
Harvey Flying Service 184
Hatchery 9, 17, 69, 72, 76, 120, 121, 128, 136, 147, 171, 175–177, 181–183
Headache 69, 76, 107
Herring salteries 88
Holmes, Dr. 100, 101
Homer, Alaska 7
Hook Bay 84
Hrdlička, Aleš 158
Humpy. *See* Salmon, Humpy

I

Indians 105, 158
Ithaca, New York 181
Izhut Bay 8, 36, 41, 144, 157, 166, 168, 174, 187

J

Jack (Last name unknown) 119, 138, 172, 173
Japanese Current 33
Jarvela, Gil 27, 63, 82, 115–117, 172
Jennifer Lake vii
John (Last name unknown) 119, 138
Johnson
    Milt 119, 121–123, 133
    Pinkie 119, 121–127, 130–134, 146, 149–151, 171, 195, 196, 198
Johnson, Dr. A. Holmes 69, 76
Jones, K.C. 48
Juan de Fuca Plate 181
Juneau 6, 18, 119, 122, 126, 132, 135, 171, 190
Juno 99

K

Karluk 27, 83, 164
Katelnikoff, Tim 85
Kenai 7
Kitoi Bay vii, 3, 8, 9, 11, 12, 19, 27, 29, 32, 36, 42, 45, 59, 60, 71–73, 75, 104, 107, 109, 110, 119, 132, 135, 144, 165–168, 172, 173, 175, 177, 181–183, 188, 200
Kitoi Bay Hatchery 10, 181, 183
Kitoi Bay Research Station 6, 9, 10, 13, 16, 17, 19, 31, 60, 87, 94, 107, 117, 139, 175, 181–183
Kodiak 3, 7, 8, 11, 17, 18, 20, 29, 47, 48, 54, 57, 69, 72, 81–84, 97, 103–112, 114, 115, 119, 127, 131, 134, 139, 161, 165, 172, 173, 177, 182–184, 189, 190, 200
Kodiak Airways 5, 12, 27, 29, 55, 57, 69, 70, 75, 80–85, 103, 113, 114, 171, 172
Kodiak Archipelago 1, 8, 79, 82, 159, 161, 162, 184, 187
Kodiak Area Native Association 184
Kodiak Baptist Mission 108, 163, 187
Kodiak Baptist Orphanage 108, 163, 165, 172, 187
Kodiak brown bear 13, 15, 16, 21, 44, 108, 121, 127, 128, 146–148, 155, 168, 174, 181, 184, 187, 188
Kodiak Hospital 31, 76, 85, 110
Kodiak Island 3, 81, 82, 104, 106, 115, 127, 161, 162, 181, 182
Kodiak Naval Station 105, 106, 110, 161, 165
Koniag 158, 159, 161, 182, 184
Kraft, Ben 17, 190

L

Lawless, E.J. 27
Lazy Bay 27, 82–84
Limpet 143, 200
Linn-Benton Community College 181
Little Kitoi Lake 15, 34, 122, 123, 127, 149
Loon 19, 21, 37, 128, 199
Lowden, Alice Vincent 4

Lukin, Afoni 161, 184
Lukin, Christina 161, 184

M

Magpie 168
Mallard 54
Marbled murrelet 99
Marmot Bay 77, 168
Marr v, 3, 4, 154, 197
    Ernest 53
    Mary 3, 31, 53, 197, 198
    Myrtle 53
    William 31, 53
McAllister, Hiram 97
McIntosh, Donna Anderson 3, 79
McRae, Alex 7
McRae, Margaret 7
McSpadden, Molly 119, 121, 131–133, 136, 138, 141, 145, 146, 148, 171, 185, 194
Merganser 37
Midarm Island 141, 142
Midarm Lake 76, 172
Middle Bay 107
Monkey flower 145
Monmouth, Oregon 5
Montana State University 119
Montgomery Ward 31, 48, 101
Mosquito 149, 155
Mount Fairweather 7
Mouse 20, 21,
Moynihan, Debbie Reddington 58
Mt. Katmai 88, 157
Museum, Alutiiq 184
Muskrat 21
Mussel 143, 155

N

Navy 5, 109, 172, 183
NCAA basketball 48
Near Island 107, 115, 183
Nebraska Sand Hills 154
Nedrow, Anne Ruth 79
Nelson, Oscar 174
Nina 25
North American Plate 181

O

O. Kraft & Son 112
Octopus 74, 179, 200, 201
Old Harbor 27, 164
Old squaw duck 37
Olsen
    Christine 114, 115
    Kathleen 114
    Lydia 114
    Mark 114
    Nina 25, 76, 77, 113, 114, 161, 163–165, 182, 184
    Pete 25, 26, 76, 77, 112–115, 159, 161, 163, 165, 182, 184
    Peter 163, 182, 184
    Ruth 114, 115, 184
Oregon 1, 3–6, 8, 13, 28, 36, 53, 59, 92, 98, 104, 117, 161, 180–182, 187, 189, 190, 200
Oregon State College 5, 8, 48, 69, 200
Orphanage 105, 108, 109, 163, 172, 187
Orthodox 163
Otter 21, 49, 68, 161, 162

P

Pacific Northern Airline 20, 91, 99
Pancakes 132, 133, 194, 195
Parker, Robert 6, 8, 11, 12, 15, 120
Parks No. 6 25
Paul's Lake 98
Perenosa Bay 98
Periwinkle 143
Perryville 83, 164
Pestrikoff, Mike 164
Petroglyphs 157, 158
Pinkie. *See* Johnson, Pinkie
Pipeline 120, 121, 136, 171
Piper Cub 29, 70, 177
Plankton 30, 200
Point Banks 113
Poland, Bill 174
Polar Bear Café 106, 112
Porpoise 155
Port Bailey 8, 9
Port Heiden 82, 83
Port Lions 182
Port Wakefield 98
Port Williams 113
Portland, Oregon 6
Pre-Koniag 158
Protestant 163
Ptarmigan 199
Puffin 21, 141, 142
Pushki 155

R

Rabbit. *See* Hare
Radio. *See* Short-wave radio
Rainbow trout 4, 149, 183
Raven 124, 125, 168
Razor clam 144, 182
Razor Clam Beach 90, 93, 182
Readings, Harry & Virginia 174
Red salmon. *See* Salmon, Sockeye
Reddington
    Dan 58
    Mae Vincent 4
Redds 35
Reliance 80, 83, 84
Richter scale 181
Rifle 16, 36, 95, 123, 125, 136, 146, 179, 187, 188
Robins, Rob 48
Rockaway, Oregon 92
Root Lake 30
Russell, Bill 48
Russia 71, 163
Russian 105, 158, 159, 161–163
Russian Gospel Association 163
Russian Orthodox Greek Catholic Church 163
    Russian Christmas 163
Ruth Lake 76, 143, 144, 172, 178

S

Salmon 1, 11, 15, 17, 69, 107, 124, 127, 129, 155, 162, 172, 179, 181, 183
    Alevin 176
    Chinook (king) 129, 183
    Chum (dog) 129, 183
    Coho (silver) 11, 35, 124, 129, 171, 183
    Fry 143, 176

Humpy (pink) 35, 129, 149, 171, 181
Smolt 123, 124, 127, 176
Sockeye (red) 1, 11, 35, 99, 121, 124, 129, 143, 176, 181
Steelhead 183
Salmonberry 10, 76, 123, 154
Sand dollar 144
Sand Point 83
Sauna 129, 130
Scallop 144
Scaup 37, 99
Schmaltz, Father Gerasim 163
Schooner 154
Scoter 36
Sculpin 200
Sea anemone 28, 200
Sea brittle 200
Sea lion 37, 38, 127
Sea urchin 144
Seagull 68, 104, 142, 143, 166, 172
Seal 21, 37, 94, 98, 153, 155, 166, 167, 179
Sears Roebuck 101
Seattle, Washington 31, 32, 110, 114
Seavers, Andrea vii
Sellers, Charlie & Thelma 53
Settler Cove 182
Seward 31, 57, 105
Shecam wood 42
Shoepacs 173
Short-wave radio 1, 17, 29, 47, 48, 65, 66, 68–71, 73, 77, 79, 80, 82, 83, 85, 134, 163
Shorty (Last name unknown) 119, 136, 137
Shotgun 36
Shrimp 97, 164
Shuyak Island 113
Siwash line 38
Slavic Gospel Association 163
Smithsonian Institution 158
Snail 200
Snake 150
Snowshoes 90–92
Soap, homemade 50, 195
Sockeye. *See* Salmon, Sockeye
Spawning 17, 35, 171, 172, 176
Spruce 2, 10, 42, 43, 59, 70, 75, 106, 108, 154, 163, 182, 183, 187, 188
Spruce knees 154
Squaw 189
Squirrel 21, 127, 178
St. Elias Range 7
St. Laurent, Yves 18
Stafford, Albert & Wilma 53
Stanger, A. D. & Ellagene 174
Starfish 60, 200
Steam bath 128, 130, 156
Steinmetz, Jerry & Marge 6
Stevens, Reed & Ri 106
Stickleback 143
Stimpson, Miss 126
Stone 108, 109
    Bill 107–109, 172, 173, 187, 188
    Nelda Jane 108
    Zelanna 108
    Zelma 107, 109, 172, 173, 187–189
Sugcestun 165
Super Cub 177

Surf Lake 33, 35, 39, 41
Swallow 200

T

Teegarden
    Carol vii, 181
    Darrell vii
    Kyle 185
Territorial Dept. of Education 165
Thanksgiving 85
The Mailboat Monitor 31
The Portland Oregonian 46
The Sue 98
Thompsen, Leo 11, 119, 132, 133, 136, 171
Tide 1, 28, 38, 60, 70, 119, 121, 125, 126, 145, 168, 179, 200
Timber 182
Titration 44
Top shell 144
Tracks 16, 38, 68, 90, 92, 122, 178
Trapper 87, 88, 153, 154, 161
Tribe 155, 161, 168
Trout
    Cutthroat 4
    Rainbow 4, 149, 183
Troyer, Will 199
Tsunami 181, 182

U

U.S. Navy 5, 109, 172
Uganik 83, 107
United States 12, 33, 71, 81, 135, 162
University of Michigan 181
Utah State University 181

V

Vertebra, whale 166, 168, 169, 177
Vincent
    Dave 4, 5, 58, 79
    Eva 5, 69
    Veneta 79
    Walt 4
    Walter 5, 79
Violets 145
Von (Last name unknown) 119, 138

W

Washington, D.C. 18, 181
Water sampling 36, 40, 44
Weasel 20, 21, 91
Weir 15, 17, 123–125, 127, 172, 178, 187
Whale 155, 161, 166–169, 177
Whalebone 166, 169, 177
Whelks 143
Whiteman, Tex 48
Widgeon. *See* Grumman Widgeon
Wildflowers 145
Willamette Valley 1, 161
Women's Bay 107
Woody Island 109, 163
World War II 3, 5, 6, 42, 69, 95, 161, 163, 177

Z

Zooplankton 200

978-0-595-37256-0
0-595-37256-2

Printed in the United States
49180LVS00004B/1-39